I have known Shan Watters for close to thirty years and through this time she has thoughtfully expressed *Holy Mother's* grace through her visual and written art. *Holy Mother's* dance is a creative dance in which we all participate, and Shan's words carry readers on the waves of grace. Coming to know the innate wisdom consciousness of the *Divine Mother*, the reader will discover a guide for both individual and collective wholeness. We are the dreamers, dreaming the dream. All together dancing to the *Divine Mother's* drumbeat.

— The Venerable Dhyani Ywahoo
Spiritual Teacher and Author,
Voices of Our Ancestors
Learning Cherokee Ways

I have known Shan Watters more than twenty-five years. She is a full blown mystic and a spiritual adept. She has immediate access to higher beings and energies from very lofty dimensions. I have personally witnessed this. She has spent this lifetime dedicated to her spiritual practice and meditation. In her new book, *Mothering the Divine*, Shan shares her journey and invites you on your own journey. She gives you the tools, the attunements, the insights and the lunar timetable to empower that journey. A valuable work both for the spiritual neophyte and the adept.

— Drew Lawrence
Vedic Astrological Consultant
Author and Lecturer'

Mothering the Divine is the perfect message at the ideal time. For those that are seeking to birth their Divine Self, Shan Watters' beautiful book is the guide we have been waiting for. Mothering the *Divine* is an oasis of inspiration and insight from the heart of the *Divine Mother*. Guiding us through the journey with the thirteen moons it shines as a beacon of Love for those who have been searching, whether they knew it or not.

— Rev. Jennifer Hadley
Creator and Spiritual Director,
The Power of Love Ministry

Spiritual teachers preach that in the face of our planetary crisis we need to find our way back to the *Divine Feminine*. Fortunately, in *Mothering the Divine*, we have been given the road map. Shan Watters' wise and generous book provides a graceful initiation into the divine feminine, one that will serve to change your life, certainly, but perhaps also the world.

— Mary Reynolds Thompson, CAPF, CPCC
Author,
Reclaiming the Wild Soul
Embrace Your Inner Wild

Mothering The Divine

Birthing, Nurturing and Celebrating
Your Divine Self

Shan Watters

To learn more about *The Divine Mother*, please visit:
www.motheringthedivinewisdom.com

This book is dedicated to everyone
who has ever had a mother.

Table of Contents

Acknowledgments

THIS BOOK IS THE FRUIT OF THIRTY YEARS of dedicated spiritual practice to connect more deeply with the divine in my life. My intention to write it was embedded with the wish that my experiences and insights would help others to do the same.

First, I bow with deep gratitude to the wisdom of all my teachers in this lifetime and especially to my root Lama, His Eminence Chagdud Tulku Rinpoche, and the light of my heart, the Venerable Dhyani Ywahoo. I have been abundantly blessed to have been embraced in their wisdom presence and compassionate hearts and without their generous guidance would most certainly have gotten confused and lost my way. They inspire me to keep going, and their wisdom blessings continually unfold truth and beauty.

The most vital support in writing this book has been from my husband, George, and the midwife of this project, Emily Corey, writing coach and editor extraordinaire from *Write On the Wind*. Emily's constant support, full of love, and dynamic interchange made all the difference in this work coming to fruition after ten years of on again, off again struggles and attempts.

I also would like to thank Mary Thompson Reynolds, from *Write The Damn Book*, for her invaluable support, creativity, clarity, and feedback. Many others encouraged and supported me including my beautiful daughters, Jenny Masa and Jessamyn Davis, and my lifetime good friend and brother, Graeme Marsh. I am thankful for my dear friend Jennifer Hadley's constant faith in this project and willingness to discuss any aspect in detail over the years with enthusiasm and vigor. Additionally, my spiritual family and sangha has been ever there for me as a reflection and source of wisdom and love.

And, I am grateful to my own *Mother* for being such a strong teacher for me in this lifetime.

Most of all I am grateful for the *Divine Mother* who holds the space of unconditional love for us all and shows us how to birth joy and nurture love throughout all our experience. May *Her* wisdom continue to unfold in each of us and may *Her* voice be heard more clearly for all to benefit from.

Divine Mother Blessing

Holy Mother of Grace,
Your blessings are revealed in every face,
Every word arises from the spaciousness of your womb.

May all recall and trace their roots to the heart of wisdom,
not separate from Holy Mother's grace.

The Venerable Dhyani Ywahoo

HYMN TO THE DIVINE MOTHER

Ma Amba Lalith Devi Parashakti Sundari,
The Divine Mother is everywhere,.

Namastasyai Namastasyai Namastasyai Namo Namah,
She is in everything.

Ma Amba Lalitha Devi Mahamay Mangale,
She is the Divine Essence that lives within all beings.

Namastasyai Namastasyai Namastasyai Namo Namah,
Her domain is the field of life,
for She gives to all beings the sustenance that is needed for life.

Ma Amba Lalitha Devi Mahakali Bhairavi,
Her beauty lives in the natural world,
and spans the universes in all their splendor.

Namastasyai Namastasyai Namastasyai Namo Namah,
She has been called by many names,
for all traditions recognize Her.

Ma Amba Lalitha Devi Mahalakshmi Vaishnavi,
Into each consciousness, the knowledge is given of the sacredness of life.
This sacredness IS the Mother.

Namastasyai Namastasyai Namastasyai Namo Namah,

She is the holy generator of the physical world,
joined to the heart and soul of every living thing.

Ma Amba Lalitha Devi Ma Sarasvati Brahmi,
All of the Earth is one with Her.

Namastasyai Namastasyai Namastasyai Namo Namah,
All beings of the Earth owe their life to Her,
for she is the Mother of all,
The One who bestows all gifts of life.

Ma Amba Lalith Devi Durga Devi Shankari,
Her gifts come to the deserving and to the non-deserving alike,
for the sun does not choose upon whom to shine.

Namastasyai Namastasyai Namastasyai Namo Namah,
She is the source of divine blessing,
the part of the Oneness that bestows the graces that fill life.

Ma Amba Lalitha Devi Uma Parvati Shive,
We have not seen Her because Her being is cloaked in silence.

Namastasyai Namastasyai Namastasyai Namo Namah,
She emerges now as part of the Oneness where
She has always resided, blessing all, giving to all.

Ma Amba Lalith Devi Ma Bhavani Ambike,
All who bow before Her are sustained by the life within them.

Namastasyai Namastasyai Namastasyai Namo Namah,
All who honor Her are sustained by life's gifts,
both within themselves and beyond.

Ma Amba Lalitha Devi Annapurna Lakshmi Ma,

The purpose of existence is to join with Life
that lives in all dimensions and all realms of being.

Namastasyai Namastasyai Namastasyai Namo Namah
It is the Mother that creates this evolving, this unfolding journey.

Ma Amba Lalitha Devi Kamal Katyayani
For She is the fabric of Time itself, the means by which all things grow.

Namastasyai Namastasyai Namastasyai Namo Namah,
She is the template for life that exists within Her.

Ma Amba Lalitha Devi Tvam Brahmani Gayatri
She is the substance and form of all that shall ever come to be.

Namastasyai Namastasyai Namastasyai Namo Namah,
May all be blessed by the blessings of the Divine Oneness.

108 SACRED NAMES OF MOTHER DIVINE
Craig Pruess and Ananda; Heaven on Earth Music, LTD.

Introduction

The Divine Mother's Wisdom Cycle

*Y*OU ARE ABOUT TO EMBARK UPON A SACRED, transcendent journey to meet the *Divine Mother* and to be blessed with *Her Wisdom*. This book is an invitation into *Her* many aspects that are emerging once again in our collective mindscape. It is both a journey and a loving celebration of both the *Divine Mother* and *Her Wisdom Cycle*. This conversation is a pathway to expansion into a delightful realm that when willingly entered into, becomes living wisdom within you. *Mothering the Divine* is a journey of discovering, birthing and nurturing your own *Divine* nature, which is supported by all of creation.

Ready for renewal and restoration, this vital facet of the *Sacred Feminine*, which has been hidden away in our culture, is ready to take center stage once again. *She* is ready to bring each of us to the awareness of how precious and glorious life is, and to help save us from the negative forces that fail to honor or nurture life.

The *Sacred Mother* has been forgotten in too many aspects of our lives. Submerged by a patriarchal mindset that has dominated for centuries, our innate *Mothering* qualities have become a shadowed afterthought, a subcategory in our self-descriptions as modern men and women.

Many spiritual masters, in many cultures, have given directions about how to survive and master the energies of transformation needed in these perilous times. His Holiness the Dalai Lama, Paramahansa Yogananda, Guru Padmasambhava, Khandro Yeshe Tsogyal, Sri Anandamayi Ma, Swami Sivananda Saraswati, His Holiness Dudjom Rinpoche, Sathya Sai Baba, Krishnamurti, Mahatma Gandhi, Dr. Martin Luther King Jr., Mother Teresa, Mata Amritanandamayi, Thich Nhat Hanh, Pope Francis, His Holiness Dilgo Khyentse Rinpoche, and countless others, have given pure and reliable teachings on how we can evolve and ascend during this challenging but also opportune time in our history. Interestingly, in all these masters' teachings is the calling forth and heralded revival of the *Sacred Mother*–the *Divine Feminine*.

Mothering, in all its various permutations, is one of my life's karmic themes. Perhaps this is because my own mother abandoned me emotionally after my father died; perhaps it is that a failed marriage and a cancer diagnosis separated me from my daughters off and on when they were young; and perhaps, as it is with so many women, it's because I have yearned all my life to meet with the feminine face of compassion, nurturing, and love. Whatever the roots of this desire, I only know that my story has unfolded just the way it should. While my path has been rocky—full of twists, turns, and detours—every minute of my confusion, grief, love, and stumbling has been worth it. It led me to experience a deeply intimate relationship with the many facets of *Mothering*. Ultimately, it has led me to meet the *Divine Mother* face to face.

Whatever your story or your struggles, my hope is that this book can be a pathway for you to connect with the *Divine Mother* in service of your own life and dreams. Once I came to know the *Divine Mothe*r, I realized *She* is a pure spiritual facet of our true nature. Every human being, male or female, can embrace *Her*. When we do, we expand our tools for living spiritually and foster a deeply effulgent joy in being alive.

The spiritual journey you are about to undertake will teach you how to reawaken and learn to utilize various innate aspects of the *Divine Mothe*r's wisdom to expand your conscious awareness and enrich your life. What exactly do I mean by the *Divine Mothe*r, and what is the process of *Mothering the Divine* you are embarking upon?

Simply put, the *Divine Mother* is both the feminine face of *God* and the force of creativity that brings forth and nurtures new life. *She* is the pulsating frequency of energy that gives life, enhances life, and sustains life. *She* lives in virtually every physical form of creation from the human body to limitless universes. *She* has many aspects and appears in human consciousness as the *Divine Mother Goddesses* that we witness in various cultures, worldwide. Everyone has these *Mother Goddesses* within them. When you recognize the truth of this, it is an incredibly expansive, illuminating, and powerful experience. You will meet many *Mother Goddesses* during your journey who represent different aspects of the *Divine Mother*. You will learn how they are alive inside of you as real, living, spiritual energies that you can draw upon and expand within.

If the *Divine Mother* is the feminine face of *God*, then *Mothering the Divine* is the spiritual excavation of *Her Divine* essence within us. *Mothering the Divine* is about tuning into the *Divine Mother* in a deeply transformative way. It will ideally bring forth times of contemplation, observation, and subtle activism and will also cause you to shift some core beliefs and rethink some old attitudes. *Mothering the Divine* is a pathway of connection that is deeper than anything you have yet encountered. As you take this journey, you will experience an intensely felt sense of your interconnection with all other beings, helping you to unfold the realization of oneness within and instill a deep sense of love for life itself.

Coming to know the innate wisdom consciousness of the *Divine Mother*, you will discover a reliable guide for both individual and collective wholeness. You will tap into a view of the world as a co-creative, life-supporting partnership with the *Divine* and begin to see life as a self-actualized exploration. In the process, you will participate in the *Divine Mother Wisdom Cycle* of creation; fertilization, gestation, ripening birth, nurturing, living, and death/change. Together we will explore the thirteen *Moons* that embody this wisdom cycle.

The wisdom of the *Moon Mother* is something you can attune to and reflect upon throughout this journey. In indigenous cultures, the *Moon Mother* has a new name every month with new aspects that are reflected in the world. Each chapter of this book will introduce you to the corresponding month's *Moon Wisdom*. Tracking your inner world of dreams, feelings, and intuition alongside the waxing and waning of the *Moon* cycles is powerful medicine. Since early times the *Moon Mother* has been a symbol of the *Great Goddess*. As you listen and breathe with *Her* heartbeat, you will come into the heart of the *Divine Mother*. *She* has much to teach through *Her* traditions and ways.

The cycle of birth and death, after all is a multidimensional

Mothering wisdom that permeates your entire being. Its spiraling *Divine* force is a cycle that evolves in your inner world. When you attune to this cycle, which is embedded in your inner world, you discover a vibrant consciousness that eventually allows you to navigate and understand the outer world more richly. When the two unite, it brings great joy, wholeness, connection, and happiness. It is also a powerfully consistent, reliable, and ever-revealing mystery that nurtures you throughout the various stages of your life.

The willingness to turn your attention inward is a primary requirement in your journey towards *Mothering the Divine*. To begin, you must be willing to see and accept everything within yourself. It is no easy task and I understand why most do not wish to engage in it consciously and intimately. Yet, here is the rub. Turning our attention inward leads to richness beyond imagining. Our innate nature, our inner life, can be cultivated and treasured as much as our outer life. The inner journey is not to be entered into lightly however, as many myths clearly illustrate. The classic journey of the hero or heroine in mythic tales, is laden with pitfalls and difficulties, so why do we ever begin?

For me there was no other choice. Sometimes being brought to our knees is the only way spirit can get our attention. When I was thirty-eight years old, I found myself on my knees, begging the universe to help me find my teacher. My own journey had come to a crossroads and going back to my old ways was no longer an option. I begged, pleaded, and offered up my soul because that was the only thing I had left to offer. My journey with the *Divine Mother* truly began in that moment when I surrendered myself to *Her*. I had been on the run from childhood pain for a long time; it was time for a change.

The wisdom of the *Divine Mother* came alive in my consciousness when I began to meditate regularly. *She* did not come instantly, but as a result of doing consistent, daily Tara practices, which are Tibetan Buddhist Tantric practices. Slowly, *She* began to take up residence in the deepest part of me.

Over the years, the *Divine Mother* unveiled *Her* wisdom to me like an unfurling scroll. I committed to a three-year retreat cycle in my home and spent hours every day in meditation practice.

Gradually, a clear insight emerged of the *Divine Mother's* spiraling activity in all phenomena. I experienced *Her* in every relationship, thought, emotion, and action. At first, I was bereft and stunned that I had so rudely ignored *Her* presence in the past. But I also began to understand that my ignorance stemmed from the dictates of my culture, which supported progress and success, no matter what. I wasn't taught to honor life and that which sustains it. I didn't know how to acknowledge and appreciate *Her* presence, which is in virtually every aspect of life.

In time, I came to understand that when we honor life, we honor the *Divine Mother* both within and without. Fortunately, *She* is unconditionally loving. *She* let me know how to forgive myself and to simply get on with it.

Today, *She* is making *Herself* known and is emerging from the veils that have shrouded *Her* for so many centuries. It is *Her* time now, and that is why *She* has called forth this book. The inspiration to write *Mothering the Divine* rose up from this understanding and it is heartening to intuit and to see so many others awakening to this wisdom.

If you have picked up this book, then the *Divine Mother* is calling to you, too. *She* is whispering in your heart-mind to see *Her*, feel *Her*, and live with *Her* aliveness. *Her Wisdom Cycle* is so innate and present we do not always consciously experience it as a formal spiritual path. *She* is hidden in plain sight. In Western culture we rarely think to use *Her Wisdom Cycle* as a pathway that can direct our lives. Our culture, driven by accomplishment and dominance, is deeply at odds with the energy and wisdom of cultures that still honor and revere the life-enhancing activity of the *Great Mother*. Gloriously complex and layered, the spiritual traditions of India are a wonderful example of a deeply embedded understanding of the importance of the *Divine Mother* and *Her* role in creating and nurturing life. Native American traditions also embrace both the *Mother* and *Father* aspects of the *Divine* with ceremony and prayer traditions that honor *Mother Earth* and all *Her* creatures. Their understanding is that without *Her*, there is no life at all. I share that belief.

May your journey towards *Mothering the Divine* be deep, stalwart, and filled with grace and joy. May it truly benefit every living soul.

An Outlaw On The Run

Chapter 1

An Outlaw On The Run

She became an outlaw on the run,
Reaching for stars and looking for fun,
Hair streaming outward, bleached to the sun,
She loosened restraints for any old bum,

She partied 'till morning to jazz way cool,
And swallowing pills like nobody's fool,
She ran from this and faster to that,
'Till nothing held long except for the fact,

That Her fun didn't last with Her home nowhere,
Her children crying, Her soul threadbare,
Frantically searching around She found a key,
An air-tight solution that just might be,

That being an outlaw wasn't Her game,
Or covering Her tracks or even Her name,
Or dyeing Her hair and liking cheap praise,
Might be titillating, but still an empty malaise,

So, when the old women whispered, honey, there ain't no hell,
Worse than living a story that's not yours to tell,
She ran to Her hideout and trashed Her disguise,
And became very still, to learn from the wise,

She now lives happily dancing thru every day,
Her true nature the only tune pressed to play,
SHE is the mystery, a universal koan,
without Her, no life could ever be known.

Shan Watters

*O*N THE DAY I LEFT HOME AT AGE SEVENTEEN, I became a runner. All I had was my backpack, a few clothes, and a twenty-dollar bill I had taken from my Mom's purse. I wanted to travel light. I ran from a life I did not want and an emotionally and psychologically abusive childhood. My upbringing, full of neglect, fear, anxiety, and pain was counterpoint to the nurturing, loving, compassionate world I longed to know, embrace, and live in. I wasn't sure how to get to a world like that, but I knew I had to try. I ran towards it as fast as I could possibly go.

The rich tunes of the 1960s were my accompaniment, spurring me on and keeping the pace lively. I became an outlaw as I was underage and had many youthful companions. Theoretically, after I left, I went to college, but mostly I went to concerts, dropped acid, and hung out at love-ins, totally enthralled with the fresh, vibrant culture of hippy love. The music was incredible at that time. Every week an original sound emerged from the heart of the *Muses*, and we celebrated it in our braids, tie-dyed velvet, and bare feet. I went into the underground of the SDS to rant against the Vietnam War and embraced radical politics. How I stayed in college was a miracle in itself, until I fell in love with an actor à la concert producer. We got married and ran off to Europe to leave American culture behind forever. It didn't last and we ended up back in the States. My husband decided to go to law school to become one of *Ralph Nader's Raiders*. I waitressed and put him through law school. The minute he graduated, I became pregnant. It was the happiest day of my life. I had always wanted to become a *Mother*. I felt like it was part of my destiny. To this day, my two daughters are still the greatest love story of my life.

Right on the dot of seven years, our marriage went haywire and I began running again. I left our home in the Sierras and moved to Los Angeles to immerse myself in the art world. I worked three jobs to sustain my daughters and myself. I was totally on my own with no support from my ex, my family, or anyone. The strains were palpable. I barely slept and began to have intense pain in my back, abdomen, and uterus. There were days when I was so tired I couldn't clean the house, read to the girls, or fix them a nutritious meal. I started to feel lousy all the time, barely able to go to work and make ends meet. I finally went to a doctor and was diagnosed with cancer.

I knew I couldn't heal and get back on my feet with things they way they were. I vacillated for weeks, going back and forth until I finally broke down and asked the girls' dad to take care of them for a few months while I took care of my cancer. This arrangement would last for longer than I initially anticipated until it evolved into a joint custody agreement.

Confronted by the periodic loss of my precious daughters, I began running in earnest towards anything that would take away the pain, fear, and terror that I had just made a huge mistake; that my body was run down and I was in trouble; or, more importantly, that I had freak'n cancer and might not beat it. I ran through bad relationships and anything else I could use to distract myself. At first I showed up for my cancer treatments, but then I ran even from those when the doctor who was treating me sexually molested me in his examining room. After that, I tried substances, which didn't help at all, but I did begin to understand the lure of drug addiction. Freaked out and scared to death, I ran to whatever might work to keep me from feeling anything.

Nothing really worked until I found work. Work became my solace. I opened my first fine art gallery and a year later, my second one. I was on my way, but I worked like a fiend. I worked fifteen hours a day, went home and dropped into oblivion, and started again fresh a few hours later. By then I was thirty-five.

After the horrible experience with my doctor, I began to retreat in a new way, hiding deeply within myself. I found myself going further and further inside and adapting myself to be successful on the outside. I began to wear men's clothing. I had all male business partners in my galleries and adapted their ways of doing business and followed their leads. They all thought I was pretty cool, so I kept myself hidden and grooved their world. It really wasn't that difficult. It was like acting. It was acting. I owned and ran two very successful fine art galleries in a very competitive market in Los Angeles and learned how to compete and make money from them. It was the perfect American dream, except for the part of finding happiness.

Polished and successful as I looked on the outside, inside I was completely disconnected and lost. A spiral of fear, separation, and intense anxiety threatened to pull me under. I was "successful" but not happy. I was pretty but not radiant. I was cool but totally alienated. I was never alone, but always lonely. I was fragile but not soft. I was high but not aware. I was a thoroughly modern woman. I was a mother but not really a *Mother*.

Looking back, I realize now that the thread that ran through my entire life was around *Mothering* and my own *Mothering* history. My relationship with my own mother was extremely difficult, both emotionally and physically, and I was treating myself the same way that she had treated me. I had wanted to be a *Mother* all my life, but the model for healthy *Mother*ing never presented itself and I was unavailable in many ways to my own children.

At the time all of this was not obvious because I was too immersed in my process to see it. I was a good *Mother* when I was one, but I didn't do it all of the time. I did not realize how important the innate nurturing, life-sustaining energy of a *Mother* was. I was a part-time *Mother* and my girls were suffering because of it. I was suffering because of it as well. Though I was unaware of it at the time, I was not honoring and actualizing my innate *Mothering* wisdom of loving kindness, nurturing, creativity, and compassion that was inside of me. The *Divine Mother* too often retreated into the shadows when other more seemingly important things took precedent such as health, career, success, and finances. The voice of my culture was too strong in my head and my *Mothering* legacy was a deep, dark, and frightening shadow I had run from for most of my life. I pushed *Mothering* from the forefront because it was associated with the pain of my childhood. My karma was ripening and accelerating beyond my control. Life had become unmanageable and I became desperate.

I became conscious of a sense of alienation and lack of spirit in my life. I longed to feel the happiness and joy inside me when my children and I were together playing and having fun at the beach.

To have the complete joy creating a painting gave me. I realized that the simpler things in life were more satisfying and I wondered why. Success in business was just not what I thought it would be. Making lots of money didn't feed my inner needs. This pushed at me until I began to look for some answers. I didn't realize it at the time, but the *Divine Mother* was gently whispering to me in the form of questions that began to arise in my heart.

What is the *Mother* essence? How do you learn to *Mother*? We learn from our own *Mothers* and beyond that, where is the model? Where is the inspiration? Where is the power? Where and what is the bigger picture of *Her*? Where is *She*, anyhow? Was *She* ever there? Where did the *Divine Mother* disappear to anyway? These were the questions that began to fill my being. Then I realized *She* had become invisible, and not just to me. *She* was invisible in our culture. How did *She* get so buried?

I began to search for *Her* and what *She* had to offer. My inner quest had begun to seek the loving and nurturing part of myself that must be *Her*. I began to pray and go to the Self-Realization Fellowship Center in Malibu, California. There I found a sense of peace and joy in the beautiful lake shrine hidden from the busy world of Los Angeles. I began to meditate and read mystical books. I began to wonder about *Mothering* and why it was such a powerful force inside of me, why it mattered so much. I tried to comprehend my situation. Immersed as I was in a male dominated culture, I realized the answers were going to require my time and effort. I pulled out all my old books on feminism from college and looked around for more. I spent my days off at the Bodhi Tree Bookstore in Hollywood, a favorite haunt for spiritual seekers. There was a multitude of material written by male teachers and adepts, but very little by or about women mystics.

At the same time, I found myself becoming aware of footsteps; their sounds, rhythms, shapes and indentations in the sand at the beach. They began to show up in my sketches and dreams. Since I had a lifelong interest in mythology, I began to do research on their deeper meaning. The *Divine Mother* introduced me to *Atalanta*, the ancient Greek *Goddess* of Running. As it turns out, *She* let me know that running is not always a negative activity. As *Atalanta* clearly demonstrates, there can be positive aspects to running including when you are running towards something beautiful.

I learned that *Atalanta's* physical body is something to behold. It adheres to the classical ancient Greek's love of beauty and perfected form. *She* embodies grace and ease. I was all for that! While especially lithe, *Her* strong and elongated limbs are well toned and the envy of all the *Gods*. *She* is often depicted running with a great deer who symbolizes the *Great Mystery of the Goddess*, and who also represents *Her* simultaneously. This exhibits *Her* ability to take you deeply into the mystery of the cosmos instantly, without having to go through a long drawn out ordeal to get there, which is what most traditions indicate. Spiritual aspirants often have to spend their whole lifetime journeying towards understanding spiritual truths. It is a great thing to then meet *Atalanta*, as *She* has the capacity to help you travel in the cosmos instantaneously. In delight, I dove into the cosmic waves and became immersed completely.

Atalanta was the first *Goddess* to guide me towards the *Divine Mother*. *She* can be yours, too, if you are ready to stop running away and start running towards something. Right here, right now, you make the vow to slow down, to begin your transformation where it needs to begin. This requires a change in your viewpoint and a great deal of courage. Ignoring and running from the part of you that is the *Divine Feminine*, whether you are male or female, is a powerful enculturation. Suspending your everyday way of doing things for a moment may feel awkward, strange, or strangely corny! In order to shift your point of view, you may need, as I did, to make a big adjustment in your energy and your perspective. How can we bring this about? Does *Atalanta's* story hold even more wisdom for us?

When *She* was born, *Atalanta* tells us, *She* was left on a mountaintop to die because *Her* father wanted a son, not a daughter. This is the way I felt as a child, that part of me was left to die. *Atalanta* survived and was raised by bears and hunters and wow, could *She* run. But *She* always ran with purpose, never away. And *She* could hunt. As you begin your journey towards *Mothering the Divine* you too are a huntress in search of wisdom. *Atalanta* is right there to help you. No matter how lost you feel or how intense your running away may be, *She* says the truth is, you are still on a journey to meet the *Divine* within you. If you can just entertain the possibility that there is a way out of the confusion, fear, and isolation, then more will be revealed to you.

Atalanta is your reliable model and guide for becoming a Huntress of the *Great Divine Mother Wisdom Cycle*, especially in *Her* form as a deer. Get ready for a wild adventure. Take a breath and welcome yourself home from the long run, as a longing calls you to your essence to live in the arms of the *Divine Mother* who loves and cares for you unconditionally. Where is *She*? How do you find *Her*? Ask *Atalanta* to help you transform your running away to running towards *Her*.

The revered Chinese philosopher, Confucius said, "No matter where you go, there you are." Here you are; all of your history, memories, judgments, hopes, fears and dreams; you in your totality. In moving towards *Atalanta*, take a moment to contemplate the possibility of there being a new way to be–a different way to navigate this worldly plane. You might feel afraid to take a risk, so just relax a bit. Breathe in and out, look to something outside yourself that brings you a little peace such as music, a soft pillow, or a walk by the sea. Now that you are more relaxed, take a gentle look at what is going on inside of you. What parts of you see running away as a strategy to keep you safe? What are you running from? Allow the answers to rise, calling on the strength of *Atalanta* to be with you on your questing journey. Does running really keep you safe or is it just an adrenalin reaction? Right now you are resting, no matter what, and you are still safe. Let yourself just be, and consider making the commitment to release running away as a strategy.

Just for now, so you can remain calm while you quit running, slow down and sit still for a moment. Remember, even inside of stillness there is movement. It is just a different kind than you are used to. Sitting still is wisdom in itself and ironically, running towards something demands of us an inner stillness. When you sit still you can begin to examine things more closely and see behind the surface to what the truth really is. So many times what we run from is our own feelings, our perceptions, and ourselves. Now it is time to stop and rest. Baby steps.

The Moon Mother; The Goddess Luna

It is exciting that outside in the heavens, right now at this very moment in time, there is a living, visible example of the *Divine Mother*; the *Great Queen of the Night, Luna* the *Moon Mother*. The *Moon Mother* has many names around the world including *Luna, Diana, Artemis*, and *Selene*. *Luna* is a great being that has circled planet Earth for millions and millions of years. Every atom, every being on Earth is affected by *Her* gravitational pull. It is here, with *Luna*, that you meet the *Divine Mother* that lives within you. Whatever *Luna's* form is in this moment, just take note of it. This particular form might hold a special message for you right now. By form, I am talking about *Her* shape, *Her* size, *Her* luminescence, and *Her* place in *Her* twenty-eight day cycle.

In ancient times, people were more connected to the rhythms of the natural world than we are today. Reawakening and vivifying this connection is important for each human being. The *Moon Mother* demonstrates and re-awakens the ancient way of determining space and time in the physical world.

Luna has both a monthly and yearly cycle. The *New Moon* begins *Her* journey every month in darkness and cycles through all of *Her* phases until *She* reaches *Her* fullest aspect. *She* shines *Her* bright, *Full Moon* light into that very darkness every twenty-eight days. This monthly cycle has been celebrated in many cultures and harnessed as a way to ritualistically understand and celebrate nature.

Moon Mother Attunements

To lead a balanced, harmonious existence, it is beneficial to become one with the cyclic rhythms in your body. When you learn the signals, and adapt to them, you can ride the waves of energy with grace and ease. Everything in the physical world is made up of vibration, light, sound, and rhythm. Everything is in perpetual motion and constantly changing. This is true of all forms and all life. This is the eternal pulse; this passing in and out of being that connects you to everything. The *Moon Mother* attunements will help you to explore your own inner world in its relationship to your own inner rhythms, emotions, and thoughts so you can then begin to attune yourself to the natural world through the *Moon Mother's* influence, which is the initial phase of your journey into the *Divine Mother* within.

The *Goddess Luna* has a yearly thirteen-month cycle and all lunar calendars depict a thirteen-month year. In this book, I will guide you through all thirteen cycles. Although traditionally, each *Moon Mother* would be met in the corresponding month of the year (the first being January, etc.) it is beneficial to meet *Her* where and whenever you begin. Women innately carry *Her* cycle within their bodies. Men do as well, although more subtly. These cycles represent the Moon time. Many natural phenomena are related to the Moon time, from the ebb and flow of the ocean tides, the weather, plant growth, animal habits, menstrual cycles, and pregnancy. Because of the power of the *Moon Mother's* energy on this planet, many rituals and celebrations have been created to celebrate *Her*. In this work of discovering The *Great Mothering Wisdom Cycle, She* is the first *Divine Mother* you are meeting. In indigenous cultures, the *Moon Mother* has a new name every month. Each chapter of this book introduces the corresponding month's Moon wisdom and indigenous name. As you are breathing in and out, relaxing and resting, please take a moment to reflect upon the power of the *Moon Mother.*

Fire, having become speech, entered into the mouth.
Wind, having become the breath, entered into the nostrils.
The sun, having become vision, entered into the eyes.
The four quarters, having become hearing, entered into the ears.
The moon, having become the mind, entered into the heart.

The Upanishads

Invite *Her* into your heart and ask that *Her* wisdom unfold naturally throughout your journey. *She* is with you every step of the way and you can embrace *Her* as a reliable source of wisdom.

Moon Mother Goddess Luna

Attunement 1

SNOW MOON

FIRST MONTH OF THE LUNAR CALENDAR

*I*N THIS FIRST CYCLE OF THE YEAR, THE *Goddess Luna* is traditionally called the *Snow Moon*, because of *Her* connection to winter. You are in the beginning, or winter, of your journey. Up in the sky, the *Snow Moon* embraces you in *Her* light. Picture yourself being bathed in the luminosity of the *Snow Moon* in a completely pure landscape of white, glistening ice crystals. It is a time of newness, a beginning, and one that is completely perfect. And so are you, just as you are.

Imagine being enveloped in this landscape. Let it fill your entire being with its clear, gentle light so you can see what is truly going on inside yourself, no matter where you are on your path. This light is like the clear light of a quartz crystal and it sings to you of your heroic journey into yourself.

For the twenty-eight day *Snow Moon* cycle, you will want to procure a clear quartz crystal. A clear quartz crystal is a great tool to work with. With this quartz crystal you will begin building a *Moon Mother* mandala, or sacred design, which will be a focusing tool on your journey.

Take a large piece of blank paper. Draw a large circle and place your crystal in the center as a symbol of the *Snow Mother*. Next, section off the circle into four equal parts, each part symbolizes a week. Place pictures or drawings in the section of the *Snow Mother* just as *She* appears in the sky. There is no right way or wrong way to do this. It is up to you and perfect in however you choose to create your *Moon Mother* mandala over the next twenty-eight days. *Her* form changes a little everyday from the *New Moon* to the *Full Moon*.

You can place notes or drawings next to the *Moon* image you display in the circle, for future reference of your observations, thoughts and musings. You can continue this process for as many months as you like tuning into the *Moon Mother*.

HOME FUN

- Observing the *Snow Moon's* journey for twenty-eight days will help you to go deeper into *Her* wisdom.

- Begin wherever you are in the cycle. Don't wait for the first of the year or the first day of the month. Just mark on the mandala where you being your cycle.

- Watch *Her* increasing and decreasing throughout the cycle.

- What do you notice within yourself during these phases?

- Are there times your emotional body is stronger than others?

- Are there times your intuition is stronger than others?

- Are there times your dreams are clearer/stronger than others?

- Does the energy shift for you during this cycle?

- What are the energy shifts you sense during this cycle?

Being Hid

Chapter 2

BEING HID

My internal forbids,
got mean old skids.

That my blues tried to kid,
when they thought I was hid.

Till my getup and go's,
poking at the nowhere in no's.

saw these sore spots,
were just not so hot.

So cruising from my exile in,
a new kind of style.

I discarded my blah's,
and embraced my hurrah's.

So now you go and retrieve,
your own make-believe.

Put your forbids in their skids,
and your no's gotta go.

When yourself you can kid,
that it's good being hid.

Shan Watters

WHEN I FINALLY DECIDED TO STOP RUNNING, the next phase on my journey was to locate my hideout. All outlaws have hideouts. Hideouts are full of your internal forbids and soul skid marks. It is where the big "No" lives inside of you. Sometimes it is hard to give up those hard-earned skid marks when you have made them your badges of honor. After a while, they become who you are and how you identify yourself. Most people have a bit of the outlaw in them, in the sense that they are fugitives from their own awareness.

Hideouts come in many guises. They can be thoughts, obsessions, fears, emotions, rebellions, denials, roles, attitudes, angst, or stuff we just like including alcohol, drugs, food, or entertainment. Hideouts can be our religious or political dogma.

Hideouts are where we lose sight of the *Divine Mother's* goodness and light and believe the shadow world is more powerful. Hideouts are where you go into denial to hide from what is going on in order to keep your awareness safely shrouded in the dark. Hideouts are where you do not see clearly and openly. Hideouts are closed, isolated, and soul suppressing. Some hideouts look beautiful but they still conceal and cover up your light. Concealing is the nature of hideouts. They are meant to hide you and for a while they make you feel safe. That is their inherent paradox. At first you feel like your hideout is a loving place to be but ultimately you discover it is an unreliable illusion that separates you from the *Divine.*

When you walk in the world as an outlaw, you don't ever really belong anywhere and cannot be authentic to your own Being. Outlaws are always on the fringe, on the run, hiding and taking from others. Sometimes glamorous, sometimes rebellious, sometimes sad, outlaws become legends but as one, you never really know who you are because you are too busy covering your tracks. Your legends become full of your deeds but your essence remains concealed. For example, codependency is a great hideout. You can look to others for your identity, never looking within to see what is there. It seems like a great hideout but it makes demands that rob many of their birthright. Competition is another hideout because it keeps you from connecting to people on a heart basis.

All people have places inside themselves where they hideout, and I imagine you can think of a few places right now where you tend to go underground, or to become the outlaw, forever on the run. I sought my hideout because I feared there was no safe place anywhere. That is why I found my hideout so irresistible. I thought it would keep me safe. But my life had become a living nightmare. A toxic relationship caused me to break down and I realized that there was no safety to be had.

Into my heart during this crisis, came some immense and loving force. I found myself on my knees, begging for help and solace. Everything in me wanted out of this suffering. I wanted to let in the light. This was when the whispering of the *Divine Mother* began to be palpable. *She* said that is was time to quit hiding and running and to begin walking in the world in a new way. It was time to trust *Her* because *She* was me.

Now is the time to take the blinders off. You can do this right in the middle of your hideout and begin to immediately transform it into a place in you of knowing and wisdom. It just requires your willingness to quit hiding, and to consciously choose the way you are going to live, think, and feel every day. It is time to turn and face the mirror of self. It is time to integrate the Sun and the *Moon* and to live by a different Light. It is time to come to the centering point of your spiraling, cosmic dance in tune with the *Divine Mother's* blessing. It is time to awaken to the realization that you are not a spectator or outlaw. You are not a shadow. You are a *Luminous Being*, a beloved child of the *Divine Mother*.

When you are able to do this, the paradox of the shadow reveals itself as an ally and a deep resource of potentiality where things can sprout and begin to grow. Just as the lotus begins its life in the mud, it is right here that is the perfect place to be, in your own mud puddle. A friend of mine uses the term, starry puddle and I love that. The stars in the puddle are the dancing lights of the *Divine Mother's* blessing, guiding you to a new way of being.

I have a dear friend who always hid out from her own sensitivity. It had become her own darkness, her shadow, and a living storm inside her. She covered it in weight and staying separate from others. She was afraid of intimacy and terrified of her feelings. When she broke through this by accepting herself and nurturing herself in healthy ways, her sensitivities became the way she learned to navigate authentically in the world. She effectively turned her hideout into a sanctuary. She allowed her sensitivities to go full cycle into the *Full Moon* light. She no longer fears them but embraces them and her life is changing dramatically in the process. It is joyful to witness. It helps to realize that if you are not being yourself, who is? No one can be you but you. Self-acceptance is a gigantic step in the attainment of the *Great Divine Mothering Wisdom Cycle*.

While I was working on self-acceptance in my own life, one day a miracle happened. I had been on my knees praying for my teacher to appear and three days later, *She* did. *Her* powerful spiritual strength and presence stopped me in my tracks and my need to hide evaporated as I instantly felt a heightened sense of well- being and welcome.

We first met, propitiously, when my fine art gallery was planning a benefit called Caring for Babies with AIDS. A colleague was hosting a meeting to discuss the details of the benefit in her home. At the same time, upstairs, there was another meeting going on of an esteemed group of Native American Elders who were on their way to the Vatican to ask for the sacred medicine bundles to be returned to the Native peoples. As I headed to the ladies room, I literally ran right into a woman from this meeting upstairs.

As *She* took hold of my hands to steady me, time stopped. I looked deeply into *Her* eyes. I literally saw galaxies upon galaxies of swirling light. A spark of spiritual fire was ignited in me in the moment *She* touched me and something inside of me began to quicken. Tears came to my eyes as a deep remembrance stirred in my heart and my awareness shifted into a grace-filled state of all-encompassing joy through the blessing of *Her* radiant presence.

Her eyes held the mystery, *Her* laugh a secret memory, and

Her smile a welcoming I had never felt before. I knew *She* was the *Divine Mother* incarnate the minute *She* appeared. *She* seemed to abide in a field of serenity and beauty. *She* embodied what I had been reaching for in my heart for so long. I was utterly grateful and energized all at the same time. I felt as if my sense of separation from self had melted away in that instant.

She kindly offered to come speak to and sit with us, in our meeting, and gave us a blessing for working with the babies so ill with AIDS. During *Her* time with us, I knew *She* was my teacher. There was no striving or intellectual discourse; it was the deep, deep knowing that was the adornment of *Her* blessing. There was a tremendous kindness and great warmth in *Her* presence and an ever-alert and attentive concern for others.

I knew my life had forever changed by this meeting. I felt at peace, as if the world was right, finally. My knowingness became a palpable force within me that I could accept without measure. I felt *She* was speaking in a symbolic language that I wanted to learn and understand. There was a sense of freshness and magic in the air that beckoned from dimensions I could not yet perceive but wanted to.

My formal study and exploration of consciousness began in earnest that day. I had asked and the Universe answered me. My heart began to open and speak to me so that what had been hidden and shrouded in fear, anxiety and angst began to come into the light. I experienced the sensation of unconditional loving acceptance. The brightness of *Her* light was what I had been seeking. *Her* sweet effervescent presence enfolded me in ways I had never experienced before, emanating as the perfume of spiritual peace and love.

The woman I ran into was the Venerable Dhyani Ywahoo, the twenty-seventh generation holder of the ancestral Ywahoo lineage in the Tsalagi/Cherokee tradition and a well-respected teacher of Vajrayana in the Drikung Kagyu and Nyingma traditions of Tibetan Buddhism. In that moment, I surrendered completely. I suddenly knew life was going to be different through *Her* grace and blessing. I decided right then and there to quit hiding and to change my ways. *Her* goodness opened my heart. It was through *Her* magnificent presence and blessing that I was able to make this internal shift within. This kind of miracle happens when you are in the enlightened presence of very holy people. The light within is able to emerge and bloom with new possibilities, which comes from the spacious awareness of the great being you are merging with. The more you merge, the stronger it becomes. It was then I realized that being in the presence of holy beings was paramount for my spiritual awareness to grow.

I was done with the old habits and needed help finding a new way. It was really, really hard, and then, suddenly it wasn't. Within a year of inviting *Her* in, my life was one hundred eighty degrees different. One day, a wonderful man walked into my gallery and bought some artwork from me. The minute I met him I knew we would get married. And we did. My younger daughter came back to live with us, full time. It was a miracle. I was happy and jumped into being a full time *Mother* with great zeal and joy. Later, my older daughter came to live with us as well. It was wondrously magical.

Years later, what I have come to realize is that I did not really know then that I mattered, that my being was enough. This is true for many people. I did not understand then the powerful force of nature that a *Mother* is and her innate bond to her children, creation, and the relations *She Mother*s. In essence, I did not understand *Mothering*. I did not know the *Divine Mother* exists in every human being and that *Her* presence is a magnificently powerful source of wisdom you can rely on. *She* had been buried so deeply within I no longer knew where to find *Her*. Unknowingly, this was my karmic path, to deepen my spiritual growth through my *Mothering* lens.

I learned how to welcome in the *Divine Mother* in a way that was totally new, present, and life affirming. I learned that beauty shines in the muddy soil as well as the flowering sky. I felt for the first time I was talking to and meeting myself honestly. I was finally home. *She* who had been hiding in plain sight was finally awakening in my heart. It was time for me to look at all my own hideouts and transform them into a place of forgiveness and sanctuary.

Transforming your hideout to a place of sanctuary is a

sacred process. The word sanctuary is derived from the Latin word sanctuarium, which means a container for something holy. A sanctuary is a place of refuge, a place where hiding can change from running away from the world to a time-out or renewal. It is a safe container for this part of your journey and can continue to support you throughout the rest of your life as new hideouts are revealed.

Sanctuaries are places of peace, contemplation, and inspiration. They are places where all of the internal voices you are becoming familiar with can become one, clear voice that sings of your luminous radiance. A sanctuary is a place of holy energy that speaks of you as *Divine*, as someone even you can fully accept and love, storms and all. It is where you can feel your heartbeat and the heartbeat of the *Divine Mother* singing in concert together.

Your hideout can begin right now to be a place of sanctuary simply by you deciding it will be just that and letting in a little more light every day. Prayer and meditation are very helpful for this because they help you relax into becoming more open through calming the constant chatter in your mind. Taking quiet time for yourself to contemplate your internal landscape is essential at this point.

How wonderful you have this opportunity. It is one of the most precious gifts of being a human being, having this capacity for self-evolvement. It is your choice to transform. When you take this step in your journey, you begin to build confidence in your own ability to evolve spiritually. A *Spiritual Seeker of* the *Divine Mother* and the outlaw share a similar desire for peace and security. But the spiritual pilgrim is moving consciously towards the Light while the outlaw is moving consciously or unconsciously towards the shadow world. And so we are at a choice point.

Having this choice is something I have become particularly grateful for. It has led me to the realization that I do not want to waste one moment of my life. When someone sings with his or her sacred voice, the entire world is a better place and shines a bit brighter. Instead of hiding out, you are birthed into the star-studded blanket of the cosmos where your heart-mind resides in its innate luminosity and you realize your immensity. This requires your clear intention to shine and not hide, to put your feet on this path every day, and travel within the *Divine Mother's* astounding blessings. It sounds so simple but it requires commitment to let your own hidden magic emerge. Let it quit hiding from you, from others, and from the world. Your magic light is needed now more than ever. We need it to survive, grow and prosper. We need it to live.

There is magic hidden in everything. Hidden magic is the great un-manifest potential carried in the *Divine Mother's* sacred womb. In a tiny seed is hidden a tree, or a flower, or a piece of fruit full of more seeds. In a raindrop is hidden a ferocious storm. In a newborn child is hidden a president, an artist, a musical genius, a great adept, or a *Mother*. Hidden within you is a being of great light, awareness, and wisdom, and right now is the time to set your intention to find *Her*.

STORM MOON MOTHER

At this point of the journey, you are in the second cycle or month of your *Moon* time, known as the *Storm Moon Mother*. The hardships of a deep winter can be challenging and as changing our habits often is as well. Consider the twenty-eight day cycle of the *Moon Mother*. *She* begins in the darkness of the hidden *New Moon* and cycles around, in twenty-eight days, to the *Full Moon*, which illumines the *New Moon* darkness fully. Now is the time to allow the storms to arise and see them as cyclical, temporary, and part of the life-enhancing cycle of the *Mothering Wisdom*. These storms allow you to see where you are stuck and that growth can arise through letting in a little more light every day; just like the *Moon* does.

It is important here to remember the *Moon* time is a cycle; one that begins in the dark of the *New Moon* and adds a little more light each day until the *Moon* is completely full. This cycle is very beneficial to tune into during your journey because you can take an issue or worn out negative habit and place it in the *Moon* cycle at the time of the *New Moon*, and by adding a little light every day, begin to transform it. By the time the *Full Moon* arrives, you can see it in its entirety and transmute it to a higher form of consciousness. The *Storm Moon Mother* is all about passages and gentle transformations and is a reliable source of light wisdom.

What are the storms within you right now? How strong are these storms? Have they been raging for long or are they fairly new? Do you know their source? It is time to begin another new cycle, this time starting with the *New Moon*, when the night sky is dark, for in the deep, dark stillness much can be revealed.

Once you become quiet, an ancient voice can be heard. *She* is calling you. It is a voice of peaceful authority that already knows you, that has been with you for your entire existence. This sacred voice can be heard in the deep recesses of your being as it speaks to your intuition, subconscious mind, and your own hidden magic.

Slowing down and becoming aware of the breath are great tools for being able to hear this ancient voice. Take a moment right now to light a candle to sanctify your space (if possible) and breathe slowly, just observing what is going on in your mind. Simple breathing and slowing down is great. Let your mind relax. Observe your thoughts, but just let them be. You cannot do anything wrong; it is exactly perfect whatever your mind is doing right now. Visualize your hideout as a transformed and sacred safe sanctuary that will nurture your growth and understanding.

At this point in your journey you begin to feel like someone is reaching out to you, but you can't quite hear or see *Her*. *She* is that part of you that is silent, but wishes to be known. It is a silent calling from the great Void, beckoning you to keep going, and it is your soul's invitation.

You are sending a voice to me, sending a voice to me,
From where the sun goes down,
Talking to me as she comes.
From the place where the sun goes down,
Our Grandmother is seen,
Our Grandmother's voice is calling to me,

That Winged One there where the Giant lives,
Is sending a voice to me. She is calling me,
Our Grandmother is calling me!

Oglala Sioux Song

In this beautiful song, the *Grandmother's* call is your soul's voice. When you feel your soul calling you can hear it through the ear of your heart. It is a silent calling, but it is immense. To hear it is an act of love for yourself, as well as an act of gratitude for the preciousness of this life you have been given.

AMOUNET, THE ANCIENT EGYPTIAN MOTHER GODDESS: THE HIDDEN ONE

There is an ancient *Mother Goddess* who can assist you in hearing your soul voice clearly. *She* is the voice of an ancient aspect of our collective consciousness known as the Egyptian *Mother Goddess Amounet. She* appears now from *Her* mysterious hidden realms of the Great Void. *She* is the primeval Egyptian *Goddess of Air and Hidden Forces.*

She is the *Goddess of the Invisible. Her* name means *The Hidden One* and you already know *Her. Her*s is the voice that called to you in your hideout in the first place. Why? Because *She* knew you needed a place to hide for a while until you were ready to hear *Her.* Her voice is that same voice as your intuition, your inner knowing, your soul's calling. *Amounet* represents the inner soul calling, the place within that is purely *Divine.*

Amounet is most often depicted with outstretched wings. *Her* head is shown as either a hawk or a snake (cobra) depending upon *Her* role. The hawk represents the freedom aspect of the mind apparent in the invisible. The snake symbolizes the power in the Otherworld, the invisible realms of the *Great Mystery* from whence *She* comes. *Her*s is the gift for those initiates who are ready to venture into the hidden mysteries of the subtle realms and *She* shows you their wisdom and magic through *Her* immense presence. The snake also represents the power of the subconscious mind, which is usually hidden, but is the source of thought. This is part of *Her* hidden, or silent aspect. In ancient Egyptian culture, the snake is associated with conscious dreaming. The columns in ancient Egyptian dreaming temples were inscribed with snake images and snakes roamed freely inside the temples because the subconscious mind is so alive and free in the dream time.

Amounet's symbology with the snake's head is also associated with the *Underworld*, the place of *Earth's Mysteries*. *Amounet* is the part of you that you hear calling you to step into the light to experience the light that you truly are in human form. *She* is the soul's voice that is ready to transform your hideout into a *Divine Sanctuary* where you can hear safely and deeply what is going on within yourself; where you shimmer with light and goodness. *She* is the voice of the *Divine Mother* you are seeking, and that is seeking you. *Amounet* is so powerful *She* was evoked during the ancient Egyptians Pharaoh's ascension ceremonies as the hidden aspect of the *Divine Mother* in all.

Invoking this mysterious aspect of the *Divine Mother* and asking *Her* for a blessing, is timely for this part of your journey because *She* will assist you in hearing your soul's voice more clearly. *She* is very ancient and very wise and holds the magic of creation in *Her* being. *She* is one who helps the sun rise every morning. Let's go stand in *Her* sunlight as the new day arrives. Can you feel a glimmering in your heart? This glimmer is a new day for you as well as a new way. Bask in *Her* light as you emerge from your hideout into the new morning sunrise. Welcome in all the hidden wisdom emerging within your being. You have quit running and hiding out and are listening to your soul's call for your emergence into the light. Yippee!!!!

Let the light of the sunrise inculcate your being until you begin to remember, "Ah, yes, this, too, is who I am." Congratulations. You have stepped out of your habitual way of being and have become a spiritual seeker. The world is now forever changed and you are ready for something entirely new to be revealed.

In the golden lid of sunrise,
Is hidden the face of Truth,
Uncover it O Sustainer!
Let the Seeker behold it

The Rig Veda

Moon Mother Goddess Luna

Attunement 2

STORM MOON

Second Month of the Lunar Calendar

*I*N THIS CYCLE IT IS MOST BENEFICIAL TO begin in the *New Moon* time, where the hidden one, *Amounet*, can assist you in sensing the storms within that need attending. *She* is a reliable aspect of the *Divine Mother* who is here to help you gently uncover whatever is hidden.

HOME FUN

❧ Add another circle to your *Moon Mother Attunement* mandala, outside of the first one, starting to build the concentric circles of the *Moon Mother* cycle. In this circle you will note the issues and the growth of understanding you have about the things you are working on.

✤ Are there any storms or conflicts within you that need immediate attention? Please note these in your journal so you can settle into working with your consciousness.

✤ If not, then take some time to tune into yourself. What is the leading edge of your awareness you would like to work with now? Is there something that has been hidden that you can now sense would like to come out into the light? For example, you might have discovered an old resentment or conflict that still needs healing hidden deep in your heart. Or perhaps a dream or creative project you have forgotten is waiting for you to remember and bring it out of hiding.

✤ Place them in the circle next to the *New Moon* image by writing them on paper and use images to represent the hidden parts emerging.

✤ Every day spend some time adding a little more light to this awareness and seeing what it reveals. Sit with the *Storm Moon Mother* in the evening and make a prayer that She will help to gently reveal Her wisdom to you at this time.

✤ Make notes next to the *Moon* phase images every day, and see what is revealed. For example, as the moonlight increases each day maybe your awareness of a particular spiritual principle such as gratitude or forgiveness is becoming brighter and stronger. During the *Full Moon*, invite this awareness to become part of your being, strong, clear, full, and solid.

The Spiritual Doorway: The Threshold

Chapter 3

The Threshold

Breath on the mirror,
Stray threads from a skirt,
Tie worlds together, reaching across time.

A gentle heart caressed by heaven's light,
slowly opens Doorways in your mind.

Shan Watters

*T*HIS JOURNEY YOU HAVE EMBARKED UPON IS A metaphysical one, full of mystery and magic. Before you can fully enter the journey, however, you will need to cross a threshold. This threshold is a spiritual threshold, a mystical point where things transform. It is here that your heart and soul begin to sing together. This threshold is where your ordinary life is stilled and there is a welcomed interruption. It becomes the mystical place where you are in two worlds at once until you fully step through it and on to the path you have chosen. The threshold is a place of choice and initiation.

Move slowly now because this threshold is all about change. You sense the interior landscape opening up to a larger vista, a wide-open space filled with bird song during today's sunrise. The birds you hear are crows, because in this third *Moon* cycle, called the *Crow Moon*, crows are welcoming in the change of seasons and the beginning of springtime. This third month being March, is one of great changes when winter whispers of spring. This is the perfect analogy for this stage of your journey. The glimmering of a spring-like day coming to life is happening within you at this very moment, but very subtly. How perfect to be here and accompanied by the *Moon Mother* and *Amounet*! Take a moment to bask in the transcendent light of the new day, making ready to be on your way. A vibrant golden rose light illuminates the pathway ahead as you stand at the threshold.

Taking one half step you can ease your way through the threshold opening. Stand with your legs apart, in the yoga standing mountain pose. One foot is still inside your sanctuary and one foot is over the threshold. Gather your strength. Feel your feet anchored to the Earth, your body strong and full of clarity. Feel the loving embrace of the *Divine Mother* in the beautiful rose-hued sunrise and take a step onto your new path.

Since you have transformed your hidout into a place of sanctuary, it is always there when you need to return for rest and recuperation. The soft light of candle flames, the smell of smudge and incense, and the soft sounds of chanting envelope you with comfort as you stand in the doorway to this next part of your journey. Now that you have stepped out, you realize the doorway to the *Divine* within you is open and you have been initiated into the world as a spiritual pilgrim.

While addressing spiritual pilgrimage, *Saint Francis of Assisi* said, "That what you are looking for is what is looking for you." Your looking is always waiting and always open to you, because it is you. It is the symbolic threshold to your interior realms of you looking for yourself. Your awareness travels with you to discover the mystery of the *Divine Mother* and how to *Mother* your own holiness. As you make your way to the *Divine Mother* within, *She* is also making *Her* way towards you. It is a spiritual truth that by setting your intention to meet and reveal *Her* within yourself, you have begun *Her* movement towards you. Take a moment to see if you can trust this. As you cross over the threshold you face an invisible landscape. Into what new frontier will this journey take you? How do you find the courage to face the unknown?

The invisible, the unknown, is a way of describing change arising. Change is immutable. It is a fact of life, but the perception and movement of the change is up to you. In a sense, every day when you open your eyes in the morning you are facing the unknown even if your life has regularity to it. Every day new circumstances, conversations, phenomena, and events are experienced. Most likely you do not consider this as you make your way through your day. Every moment is an opportunity to experience the unknown. It is an opportunity to create in each moment the life you intend to have.

As you cross this threshold you confront the sentinels guarding it. The sentinels are the gatekeepers or guardians you have placed there to protect you from change; they are the voices, attitudes, or fears that have kept you hiding and running from yourself. These sentinels are ultimately just the ignorance of separation from the *Divine*, but they have many voices and many faces. The good news is that because they are a part of you, there is nothing to be afraid of. They are something you can transform or cosmically update. Take a moment to self-reflect on those aspects that have kept you from stepping onto your path and let them go with love. Their attraction is strong and their reasoning and habitual patterns are fierce. Just relax and begin to look at them with love and see what happens to them.

The gatekeepers here at the threshold are not always easy to pass by. But if you are crystal clear with your intention, they will let you pass. The motivating force here must be more than curiosity. It must be a genuine desire to learn about yourself and to step into the archetypal role of the hero on a spiritual quest, as you become a holy pilgrim seeking sacredness with truthful purpose.

A ritual of writing down the habits that have held you back and thanking them for doing their job is a good way to begin to transform them. Burn what you've written and offer the smoke and ashes as an offering to bring benefit for everyone's transformation. You are physically releasing the energy with the intention of benefiting all. Energy is never lost, but it can be transformed. When you let the old form go, it makes space for something new to arise. The release of an old form also allows you to relax more deeply into your own natural awareness.

You contain many energy fields particular to you, so it is good to check in with them at this juncture in order to become more attuned to yourself as you move forward. Your physical, emotional, mental, astral, and etheric energies combine in your auric field and each have their own vibration and response to other energies. Classically, a field is an area in which a force exerts an influence at every point. Like all energetic forms, a field involves a vibration of energy and can carry information. These fields are both within and outside of your body and they communicate at differing vibratory rates with each other. All responses in the physical, emotional, mental, astral, and etheric vibrations begin in your mind. When you change the way your mind works, you change your experience in all of these fields. You change your vibratory structure. You also learn to meet other energy fields in a new way. There are all kinds of other energy fields as all living beings have their own energy field. This includes all the nature kingdoms, the sky, the earth, the elements, animals, and so on.

How are your energy fields responding to this threshold experience? What is going on within you right now? It is important to look and see how things are, for it is the next step of working with your mind.

There are many energy therapies that can assist you at this point, to help you sensitize and familiarize yourself to your energy fields. Some of these are acupressure, biofeedback, breath work, craniosacral therapy, energy medicine, essential oils, Feng Shui, flower essence healing, gemstone therapy, Hakomi, Iridology matrix work, Naturopathic medicine, Pranic healing, spiritual healing, Tai Chi, Yoga, and meditation. Whatever form you choose to work with will likely be appropriate for the energetic space you are in at the present. Like energy attracts like, so follow your intuition if it directs you to a specific way of tuning in and working with your subtle energetic bodies. My favorite is meditation, which I have increased over the years to now doing every morning for several hours. The first part of my meditation practice I ground myself into my body to be able to hear and feel myself more deeply. Then I proceed with my practices, including silent meditation, spaciousness meditation and then formal ritualistic Tantric practices. But it took a long time to get to this point and as my love of the *Divine* increased, so did my sacred commitment.

There are so many distractions in modern life and rituals can support shifting awareness from the exterior to the interior. Rituals can also set your mind on the right track, a way to repeatedly reprogram the way your thoughts travel. Rituals are a way to mark the vibrating threshold of the numinous realms where the interior journey of self-exploration unfolds. In ancient times, ritual was embedded in the fabric of tribal and nomadic societies, where interior and exterior were one consciousness because of their deep appreciation for all of life. Today, global consciousness is shifting perceptions and to get centered and focused in this way takes on new meaning and challenge.

Rituals are specific. They are as elaborate as traditional nine-day tantric rites or as simple as a family dinner prayer. Engaging in ritual is a way to make meaning in a particular and measured way.

Rituals are symbolic and are another way to signal the sacred and say, "Hey, we are aware we are joining you right now." Rituals are formalized ways to give appreciation, to make apology, to bring things into balance, to be present at a threshold, and to help you to walk onto your path consistently. Rituals are a way to reprogram your mind, habits, and heart. It is important to create rituals that are personal and specific to your particular lifestyle and belief system.

You may feel a little vulnerable at this point in your journey. Walking out of your old habits and enclosed hideout can feel a little uncomfortable. It can feel as if you are hanging over a huge precipice in a wide-open canyon. You think, "Yikes, this is really not fun, not safe; I want to go back inside my hideout!" But wait; there is a tool to help you! It is beneficial at this point to learn to access the breath as an ally. It is a magnificently simple tool to assist you on your journey and also a very reliable one you can tune into throughout your day.

The breath is a reminder of your connection to *Mother Earth* and *Her* wind element. Realizing you are a part of something larger than yourself imbues each breath with the sacred. Aligning your breath with the winds of *Mother Earth* connects you to a mighty force of holy, teeming life of which you are an integral part. You are part of the wind's journey through forests, across mountains, in the sky, and across the plains. You matter! As you breathe, so does *Mother Earth*.

In *Her* sacred sites it is said the breath of great beings of wisdom still reside for you to enjoy and access through your own breath. When you breathe consciously, you are welcoming in the magic of where you are through their wisdom presence. In this open doorway where you are standing, breathe the gorgeous light of the sunrise into your heart and know all is well. Face the sun and welcome the day of a new beginning in your life. Be at peace, be at home, be in your breath and the world will become a place of enchantment, your senses a cosmos.

You are standing at a spiritual portal where the doorway faces both inward and outward at the same time. This threshold is where you interrupt your daily life to move into an invisible realm of connection, on pure faith that it will sustain you. How do you do that?

CARDEA: THE ROMAN GODDESS OF THE THRESHOLD

It is time to call on another aspect of the *Divine Mother* to assist you. The Roman *Goddess Cardea* is a protector *Goddess of the Threshold*. *She* is immensely strong and *Her* strength helps to hold the threshold open and clear. *She* is known for having the capacity for holding open more than one doorway into the unknown or from one realm to another. For example, *She* is a doorkeeper of the earth realms as well as the heavenly ones. *Her* spiritual strength is known to be immense and immeasurable.

Her name means "hinge" and encompasses the wider symbolism of the pole or axis around which the earth spins, holding the doorways open to both the North and South directions. *She* is therefore, a *Goddess* helping to actualize the change that comes forth from the centering energy force, or the center of your world and consciousness. As a protector *Goddess, She* will assist you at this juncture by keeping the threshold clear, open, and available to you whenever you need a respite. *She* will help you stay in your invisible center throughout your journey.

Your invisible center is where? What do you imagine it is? It is the deepest, innermost region of your heart where your soul lives.

It is vital to learn to form a pure intention that issues from this invisible center both for the journey and how you will deal with what you meet along the way. Now is where you form your pure intention to keep going and to look deeply inward no matter what is discovered, no matter what is in the way of meeting the *Divine Mother* fully. This can appear as an attitude, anxiety, belief, emotion, habit, fear, or simple unawareness. You know those times when you would rather eat chocolate and fall asleep than be aware. It is important and necessary for you to set your intention and claim it every day in order to remain aware and awake and willing to keep going, no matter what. It is here you choose to welcome back the parts of yourself needed to be able to find freedom. In Tibetan Buddhism they call the hidden forces that inhibit your awareness the "*Maras*," who are the actual enemies of your awareness. Setting a clear and pure intention sends the message to the *Maras* to forget it; they can't stop you. You are on your way because your intention points you in the right direction. Your intention might be to keep a pure heart on this journey to meet the *Divine Mother*. Whatever your intention is, it will become infallible as you focus on it and stick to it. You can call on the colossal strength of *Cardea* to assist you every step of the way.

Establishing pure intention is the way to have the universe work with you. It is a spiritual law that if your intention is clear and pure, you have nothing to worry about and you will accomplish anything you set out to accomplish. Intention, or motivation, is how the universe expresses itself as you. If you consider the infinite powers that reside in the universe, is it not wise to harness them? What could you accomplish if you did? Why not use all the holiness available to you in this vast cosmos, which is the very womb of the *Divine Mother*.

Intention is the seed or the birthing of the *Divine* spark in any action or thought. It is your signal fire to the angels that says, "OK, I want to go here and need some help! Help me out please!" The most incredible thing is they will. The clearer the asking, the more they will assist you. If you plant the seed to hide, you will be in the dark. If you plant the seed, intentionally, to cause a ruckus, you will find some trouble. If you plant the seed to be pure, clear, and awake, you will accomplish that.

I learned about the power of intention from His Eminence Chagdud Tulku Rinpoche, a very accomplished Tibetan meditation master and my precious root Lama. (One's root lama is the original teacher who shows to you the true nature of your mind). He taught that having pure motivation in forming intention is the key to living a spiritual life. If your motive is pure, the result will be as well. If your motive is mixed, so will the results be mixed. Rinpoche explained that forming your intention is like planting a tree. If you plant an apple seed, you will not get an orange tree or a rose bush; you obviously will get an apple tree.

Ask yourself, what is your intention planting? The subtle marker of your intention gets you through the threshold in a very specific way. Intention is the flag you wave to the cosmos announcing the way you are going to go. "Hey, over here I am deciding to stop my old way of doing things and look for a better way, a more enlightened approach, a new beginning." Flags are symbols and the symbol is what your mind creates to steer you in a particular direction at this juncture. You put your foot on this path daily and breathe in the loving breath of the *Divine Mother* with the clear intention of seeking *Her* deeply within.

For me, I knew I needed help and asked for it. I had no idea where the journey was going to take me when I called out to *Her*. I had become a spiritual pilgrim intentionally but with no clear goal in sight, except for the desire to not suffer or be the cause of other's unhappiness anymore. In that moment, my seeking began as I crossed the threshold of change, intentionally. Setting your intention is the seeded beginning of accomplishing your pilgrimage. In the words of the beautiful *Saint Clare of Assisi,*

"What you hold, may you always hold,
What you do, may you do and never abandon,
But with swift pace, light step, unswerving feet,
May you go securely, joyfully and swiftly, intently,
On the path of prudent happiness back to your holier self."

Intention makes you aware of where you are going from the get-go. Without it, it is like getting in the car with no destination in mind. Many people live this way all of their lives but you don't have to because you have the good fortune to know about intention. Without this knowledge you increase your suffering immensely.

We are all attached to ways of thinking and being and to our own suffering. "My suffering, is so important, it is what I endured, tolerated, and abided and it is so different from others suffering." And yet is this really true? I know that I was so identified with my suffering that I did not want to let go of it. This is very common. When we identify with our suffering it becomes a truth for us. But while everyone suffers, no one in their right mind wants to.

Be willing to expand your own story. Your intention can lead you to a new future, a way of experience that is beyond what you dream is possible right now. It is vital to spend time contemplating prior to stepping through the threshold.

How do you do this? How do you know your intention is strong, clear, and pure? The late motivational speaker, Wayne Dyer, wrote a book called the *Power of Intention*. His philosophy is pure and simple. "The law of attraction is this: You don't attract what you want. You attract what you are." If you want love in your life, you have to be loving. It is really that simple. The more loving you are, the more love you will have in your life. Since this is a new time for you, we will call upon a powerful and universally recognized aspect of the *Divine Mother* to assist you in forming your pure intention.

LADY VENUS: GODDESS OF LOVE AND BEAUTY

When you gaze up into the night sky, just a little way from the *Moon*, there is a bright looking orb that looks like a radiating star but is in fact the planet *Venus*. *Lady Venus* is the ancient Roman *Goddess of Love and Beauty*, and is also the same being of the ancient Greek pantheon, *Aphrodite*. *Lady Venus*, in even more ancient times, was the *Great Mother Goddess of Lemuria*.

The *Great Planetary Goddess, Lady Venus*, is a radiant light and as you slow down and gaze upon *Her*, your meandering pathway is flooded with a rose colored light tinged with a luminous golden glowing pulse that is the inner quality of *Lady Venus'* expression. A sublime softness envelops you–a feeling of warmth, beauty, and love. This is the radiant *Lady Venus'* incalculable blessing. *Her* love is the foundational energy for forming a strong intention and *Her* soul beauty is the foundational energy to make it clear and pristinely pure.

The hardened planes and sharp angles of your fear and strident pushing at yourself are being smoothed as you bask in this gloriously transcendent light. This transcendent light helps you to expand in your heart where your pure intention lives. Immerse yourself in *Her* blessing. It welcomes you to another way of being with yourself so just enjoy and relax into it.

Wondrously, a less traveled pathway begins to emerge that

is the most beautiful landscape you can imagine and it is inculcated with *Her* quality. Everything is glowing with *Her* light and beauty that emerges from *Lady Venus* in a never-ending flow. This transcends mere physical beauty, as it is a palpable force you can experience. It is *Her* powerful energetic that imprints the physical world with the exquisiteness of flowers, rapturous sunsets, the loveliness of green hills in springtime. Who doesn't want to be in this field of loving energy? It is your true essence and will help you to relax into it, where your pure intention can flower.

Begin to forge a trail within the loving embrace of *Lady Venus* until you have a loving view of yourself in this gorgeous place. The *Goddess Venus* is often depicted standing in an oyster shell, and this represents *Her* as the very pearl of heaven. *She* inspires poetry, art, dance, and all expressions of *Divine* perfection. The pearl is additionally a symbol of the *Divine Feminine*, which *She* so beautifully embodies in all *Her* glory. *Her* visage is incredibly gorgeous and welcoming to you. *She* invites you into the most beautiful aspects of yourself so that you can truly love yourself and express that love clearly in your actions. Contemplate your intention from this place through the lens of self-love.

Self-love is the most important love you can cultivate because it is the foundation for all other loving we do. It is the pearl in your own oyster shell. Self-love is beautiful. This quality of love is a very high vibration that is the basis of all healing. Unconditional self-love is boundless and unchanging.

Her heart is wide open with a flowing love mirroring the wisdom of grace for all that you are, have been, and will be. *She* radiates this for all beings and, specifically for you. What does it mean to unconditionally love yourself? Unconditional self-love means you bow deeply in total acceptance of who you are and throw in compassion and appreciation for yourself as well. Self-love is a wisdom recipe. You will know that if you have suffered from self-loathing. This is what running and hiding from yourself looks like: denial, the numb zone. You just cannot accept who you really are. Why not? Why can't you?

Most everyone grew up with conditional love. This is not to blame your parents. It is to recognize, honestly, the limited scope of their loving capacity. Most of the time the limitations or conditions placed on you through your relationship with your parents set the foundation for your own loving competence. It is a good thing to reflect upon this and be honest about it. Once you have done this, then take a look at how you feel about your relationship with *Spirit*. Did you project these same conditions on the love that *Spirit* has for you and the love you have for *Spirit*? Most likely you did, as most of us do. As a matter of fact, I would venture to say 99.99 percent of us do.

If you look a little deeper you will find that these two loves–of *Spirit* for you and you for *Spirit*–intertwine with your patterns and capacity for loving. Unless you have already done a lot of work on your ability to love, it is time to take a look. Otherwise you may go through life caught in a family dynamic, not of your creating but of your inheritance. You may have strived your entire life to fulfill this inheritance without realizing that it was not something you chose. Let's change that. Let's look and change your perspective. If you want a new experience, you have to change your mind as well, as all emotion, behavior, and action is a result of what is in your mind.

Since *Lady Venus* is the *Goddess of Love and Beauty*, let's begin with ever-flowing beauty. Ever-flowing beauty is a reliable doorway into pure, unconditional love. This doorway of ever-flowing beauty is about your soul's beauty. This kind of beauty is one of the soul's inner garments, where the heart opens, endlessly, without measure. Pure intention is your ever-flowing soul beauty. Soul beauty is a vibration, an energy that speaks beyond the physical world to you. It carries the energy of peace, harmony, and oneness. It is the pure, simple light that resides between your awareness and your surrender.

> *It visits with inconstant glance,*
> *Each human heart and countenance,*
> *Like hues and harmonies of evening,*
> *Like clouds in starlight widely spread,*
> *Like memory of music fled,*

Like aught that for its grace may be,
Dear, and yet dearer for its mystery,
Spirit of Beauty, that dost consecrate,
With thine own hues all thou dost shine upon,
Of human thought or form—where art thou gone?

Percy Bysshe Shelley

There is so much in our modern culture that is not beautiful. There is so much more that does not contain any soul beauty. It is really a human crisis. When I was in graduate school working on my Masters in Painting, students were literally encouraged to not make "beautiful" art. Depicting harshness and negativity over beauty was the dictate of the day. It was cool to be sophisticated and critical of anything beautiful. It was so weird I eventually left the program because I could not be myself. Beauty is what revives your soul, what inspires you in challenging times, and what marks the way to deep loving of your human experience. Beauty is a doorway to love. Beauty is the doorway into your pure intention.

The Irish writer, John O'Donohue, writes about beauty as the invisible embrace. "The Beautiful stirs passion and urgency in us and calls us forth from aloneness into the warmth and wonder of some eternal embrace. It unites us again with the neglected and forgotten grandeur of life; for in some instinctive way we know that beauty is no stranger. We respond with delight to the call of beauty because in an instant it can awaken under the layers of the heart some forgotten brightness."

Beauty is your soul's truth and *Lady Venus* is the *Goddess of Love and Beauty* in all its fullness. *She* is the aspect or expression of the *Divine Mother* that always respects and reflects beauty. Invite Beauty in and let *Her* surprise you. As you do, Beauty opens the door to your heart and love expands the doorway to infinity. Love is who you are, once you strip away all the layers. Love is the energy of the heart, it is the energy of the universe, and love is what fills empty space. Love and beauty are the language of your heart. Love is you as pure beauty. Love is your pure intention to be all that you can be.

Love is your pure intention to be pure *Spirit*. It is you basking in the energy of real self-love.

"You, yourself, as much as anybody in the entire Universe, deserve your love and affection."

The Buddha

An important, and core teaching in the Dharma is self-love. It is taught that you have to love yourself to be able to love others. It seems so simple, but it is key to your generating unconditional love and the accomplishment of self-realization. The search is internal, not external. It is within you that you have the possibility of finding true happiness and joy in living. Why would you run from that? Simply because you might not believe you are lovable.

Remember the soft, gentle rose light of loving energy *Lady Venus* surrounded you with? All *She* really does is tap into your own light, your own loving nature. This loving energy is your soul talking to your subconscious mind, helping to re-shape and re-parent it.

Offer a prayer of appreciation and love to your child self and your adult self. Offer a prayer of appreciation and love to *Lady Venus* for *Her* unconditional, loving *Divine* energy. Loving yourself is a practice, one that you can embark on every day, beginning right now if that is your intention.

Loving yourself means you become fully conscious of the shadow voices within and learn to distinguish them in terms of tone and volume. The ones that barely whisper are the ones to really pay attention to for they are much more subtle and cunning, and when unlocked may offer the most profound wisdom. To be able to decipher the hidden, whispered meanings of the voices within the voice takes mindfulness, willingness, and quiet time. It is very helpful to journal about your internal voices. Bring them in, give them a quiet party, and hear what they have to say. For example, maybe you are one of many modern women who have a constant inner dialogue of disliking their bodies. The *Divine Mother* gifted us our bodies!

This voice and others have been talking to you for a long time, and it may be a strong, habitual pattern to ignore the voices. Be tender with them so they can emerge safely. If you don't become familiar with your inner voices, you will not be able to help them grow and transform to become the expression of the music of the heart. In order to do this, we need a little help. These habits are ingrained. So let's go outside for a moment here to see your *Moon Mother* in *Her* third cycle as the *Crow Moon Mother*.

THE CROW MOON MOTHER

The *Crow Moon* marks the time of change from deep winter to the first whisper of spring, which is the beginning of transformation in the natural world. I think of this *Moon* turning as profound because crows are known to be the messengers of the *Dakinis*, who are known as the *SkyDancers* and hold all the treasures of all spiritual wisdom and are a very powerful aspect of the *Divine Mother*. The *Crow Moon Mother* evokes the wisdom of the *Dakinis* and their vast potential and untamed female freedom. A *Dakini* knows no limitation. *She* is wild, fearless, and completely pure in *Her* intent. *Her* immense power has the capacity to release blockages in your energy field and can transform hidden patterns so that your mind opens. The *Dakini* is the destroyer of illusion. When you intentionally walk through the threshold, it is the perfect time for the *Dakini* to appear. *She* is beckoned by the *Crow Moon* to assist you to make space within yourself by removing all the worn out old habits that no longer serve you. Something new can finally happen then. *She* will be your transformational coach and ally because *She* has already liberated everything that stands in the way of complete freedom and knows how to assist you in doing the same.

As a mysterious *SkyDancing Goddess*, in Tibetan Buddhism the *Dakini* appears in various tantric practices as both peaceful and wrathful. During this part of your journey, you will call upon *Her* powers of transformation. *She* tames the *Maras* by transforming the poisons of addiction, self-hate, delusion, aggression, greed, hate, and jealousy into the medicines of self-love, generosity, clarity, spontaneous accomplishment, and wisdom presence. *She* embodies female wisdom in a powerful, fiery, and magical display. *She* is the perfect guide on this part of your journey and teams up with *Lady Venus* to enact out the transformation and transmutation of everything you wish to convert into the loving, kind, and spacious being that you truly are.

The *Dakinis'* power is one of fierce compassion for the suffering of others, especially when you forget to be loving. Be you as love. The force of this power is unfathomable, mighty, and immense, and it is your gift from the *Divine Mother, Cardea, Lady Venus*, and the *Crow Moon Mother* and beyond that, it is the gift of yourself to yourself.

This time, at the threshold, is a time of endings and beginnings. It is a significant time of change to step consciously onto the spiritual path. It is a time to make certain you are supported in as many ways as you need to stay clear and focused on your intention. Are you clear? Take your time until you are. Let your intention guide you deeply into yourself as you make your way into the realm of the *Divine Mother*.

At this time, your intention is a longing. Soon it will become a spiritual force in your life as you finally attain its full unfolding and flowering. For now, it is enough to cross into the invisible realm through the threshold with the clear and heartfelt intention of becoming a spiritual pilgrim seeking the *Divine Mother*. It is enough to follow your longing for beauty and love with prayerful intent. Your intention is the end of a golden string that will lead you straight into the *Divine Mother's* realm.

I give you the end of a golden string,
Only wind it into a ball,
It will lead you in at heaven's gate,
Built in Jerusalem's wall.

Unknown

Moon Mother Goddess Luna

Attunement 3

CROW MOON

THIRD MONTH OF THE LUNAR CALENDAR

*I*N THIS NEXT TWENTY-EIGHT DAY CYCLE, beginning in the *New Moon*, work with forming your intention. Remember your intention points the way on your path; maybe you want to come out of hiding at this point, maybe you want to start down this path towards the *Divine Mother*. Whatever you decide it is, experience it with each new phase within the *Crow Moon Mother's* cycle.

HOME FUN

🌿 Begin a journal to track your intention on a daily basis and note how you are doing with it, with no judgment. Just notice it. Is it changing or remaining the same?

❧ Ask yourself, does your intention feel pure?

❧ Work with it during this entire twenty-eight day cycle and then during the Full Moon, place your intention in the northern quadrant of the center of your mandala image.

❧ As any hindrance arises related to running, hiding, or anything else that might prevent you from continuing on your path, call upon the Dakinis' transformative energy to help you move beyond the obstacles that stand in your way and help you to stay on your path.

❧ Note the obstacle and how you work with it.

❧ Work deeply on forming your intention

❧ Journal the qualities you feel are needed for this transformational work.

❧ For example, write a love letter to yourself for this effort with the help of Lady Venus keeping in mind you are the most beautiful of all creations.

❧ Begin to work also on the simultaneous intention to love yourself more every day. See how it evolves, transforms, and deepens. Make notes.

❧ Once you have done this see if you are moved to refine your intention. For example, it might open you up to a deep realization of some aspect of self-love that you have not previously been cognizant of. Or it might mean a new way of being in a particular relationship that is more loving towards you. It might mean taking more time for loving self-care. It might be a change in your daily routine. Whatever it is, focus on the loving expansion that happens within you.

Soul Fertilization:

Mystical Union

Chapter 4

PSALM 109.3

"I saw a form like a lovely maiden, her face glowing
with such radiance that I could not long look at her.
Her garment was whiter than snow and more
shining than stars, and her shoes were made
of the purest gold. In her right hand she held the sun
and the moon, which she tenderly embraced.
On her breast was an ivory tablet and on it the form
of a man, the color of sapphire blue. All creation called
this maiden "Lady." And she spoke to the form that appeared
on her breast these words:
"I bore you from the womb before the morning star."

Hildegard of Bingen's Vision

*Y*OU HAVE STEPPED ACROSS THE THRESHOLD into a wide-open space. As you move into it, you begin to expand your understanding that you are much more than your self-perception. You are part of something vastly miraculous and eternal. This realization creates a deep longing for union. You long to meet *Her*. This longing combined with your pure intention invokes the *Divine Mother's* presence and your soul's fertilization of *Her* mysteries. The *Divine Mother's* energy is your very soul's expression. It is the energy that creates universes, that breathes the world, and is the light-woven invisible fabric of mystical connection to all that is.

A mystical experience, or soul fertilization, is an intuitive understanding and realization that is intense, integrating, self-authenticating, and liberating because it goes beyond self. How can your experience be both self-authenticating and go beyond self? Seemingly another paradox! Yet, it is this harnessing of dualistic energies that catapults you into another level of awareness. The resulting pressure between two seemingly polarized concepts creates a potent force rather like when you stretch a rubber band and then release it. When you are able to experience this tension, this electrical *Mystical Union* between two opposites reveals to you your own self-realization. This cosmic force is a kind of creative tension between awareness and complete abandonment of one's self, which allows you to become pregnant with the *Divine* as your own soul force. Awareness and abandonment of one's self seem to be opposing energies, but it is their marriage that opens the *Divine* within. It is the energy of the *Divine Mother* moving within you. It is a *Mystical Union.*

Mystical Union is the experience or state of the soul where you receive fully the present moment with completely open and alive awareness. You inhabit purity and *Oneness* simultaneously. *Mystical Union* is your consciousness directed by the *Divine Mother* inherently within you. Extraordinary changes occur when the *Divine Mother* is accepted and revealed in you consciously. You begin to feel *Her* expression in your body, mind, heart, and in your breath. *Her* energy begins to move through you as a gentle caress and you begin to feel the glimmering of *Divinity*.

Everything in the phenomenal world comes from the *Divine Mother*. When you receive *Her* into your consciousness and your heart, you enter the vast expansiveness where your own higher self lives, your angel consciousness, your inner *Goddess*. *Mystical Union* sets you free and onto the path of a true mystic. You begin to live in the conscious awareness that your soul's expression is the *Divine Mother*.

Now it is time to meet up with *Her*, to transform your longing into a perfect *Union*. Remember, the way to start is by again forming a clear intention to do so. Once that is established, you will find the pathway in front of you begins to change. Suddenly, you find the wide, easy trail ascending and you make your way up and up until finally, you reach a high ridge where you teeter on the edge of an enormous valley filled with a thick, dark, pungent forest. What is this place, this forested valley?

Fairduddin Attar, one of the most ancient poets of Persia and one of Rumi's teachers, says there are seven of these valleys in spiritual development:

- The first is the *Valley of the Quest*

- The second is the *Valley of the Qualities of the Heart*

- The third is the *Valley of Knowledge*, which Illuminates

- The fourth is the *Valley of Non-Attachment*

- The fifth is the *Valley of Unity*

- The sixth is the *Valley of Amazement*

- The seventh is the *Valley of the Realization of God*

Which forest valley is in front of you in this moment? Each valley's energy builds upon the other, and for most, the Valley of the Quest is where they land initially so let us begin there. In this Quest, you establish your intention that you are a spiritual seeker longing to reconnect consciously with the *Divine Mother*. Imagine that the forest valley ahead of you represents anything that has kept you from the *Divine* truth within which is the innate *Divine Mothering* wisdom that is such a part of you. It is everything that makes you mad, sad, or envious; whatever is not in harmony. It is whatever makes you feel separate. It is whatever makes you feel alone or abandoned.

In your separation and aloneness, the forest darkness can appear and feel like a shroud. Whatever is in there is part of your *Divine* nature waiting for discovery and liberation, but it doesn't feel that way. It just feels scary. Really, all it is, is just energy you have neglected and let fester in separation. It is often the voice of self-doubt, self-criticism, fear, or not belonging. It is what makes you human. It is the un-manifested love of your *Divine Mother* wisdom waiting for revelation, waiting for transformation through *Mystical Union*.

There is only one pathway into the dark valley before you and the *Moon Mother Goddess Luna* lights your way down a narrow, meandering, steep, and rocky path. Remember your pure intention and with bold steps, hold it dear to your heart. Your heart's intention is the key to unlocking the profound mystery in the middle of the looming, dark forest. Your heart's longing is also calling forth a presence, way on the other side of the valley, up on the opposite ridge.

As you travel down deeper into the forest valley, take a moment to look up at the ridge on the distant horizon where you sense *Her* making *Her* way towards you. For this to happen, a transformation must occur. The transformation is engendered through your willingness, longing, and sacred intent to receive *Her* wisdom into your being. Remember, your pure intention is calling *Her* forth.

This *Being* is surrounded by a haloed radiance so bright you cannot see *Her* face. There is an experience now occurring that is beyond verbal and intellectual comprehension; a glimpse of another existence beyond your ordinary reality and it calls forth your own purity and childlike wonder. Yet, it also feels familiar, as if it is a dormant part of you wanting to wake up.

Taking a deep breath, you slowly make your way into the darkening wall of trees, where winds are accented by animal sounds, high and low. The ground is uneven grassland and new scents assault your senses. This place feels like a secret, filled with mysteries. There is running water, a stream perhaps, off to the left of the pathway.

Suddenly, you arrive at a place so void of light and so dense you cannot seem to find your way. Trepidation grabs hold of you in the dark. Senses acute, suddenly a bone-jarring fear grabs you to become fully present and aware. Your mind plays tricks and asks, "What if there is no safe place here?" Then increases to, "What if there is no safe place anywhere?" The ego keeps whispering to you, "Be afraid, be afraid."

Everything falls away in a moment like this. You have to become fully present. Through the trees you see a lightening flash of gold and faint music begins to fill the glade, slowly increasing in volume. Smoky, sacred incense fills the air; bells jingle, and light sparkles from glittering jeweled necklaces. The air is perfumed with sweet flower song. You catch glimpses of a radiant sphere transforming and flowing into myriad forms right before your eyes. Bracelets, earrings, cymbals, bells, painted banners, and elegant parasols are all part of *Her* magical display.

A charged expectancy imbues the flower-strewn pathway ahead, giving you courage to move gently forward. Now you see a headdress made from the gold mines of the Nile and endless yards of rich purple, gold embroidered clothing slowly morphing into a rich saffron robe from India folded over sienna painted hands and feet. Slowly, wondrously, it transforms into a startlingly white beaded deerskin dress as braided locks of long dark hair gently rise in the wind. *Her* beautiful brown skin takes on a blue hue and *Her* clothing becomes ornately strung silk with bone ornaments, delicately carved like a mantle of lace. *Her* eyes gaze at you with such love and remain the same in each of these manifestations as *She* continues to reveal *Her* wonder to you in many forms. Now *She* is adorned with rich rose silk and leis of flowers drape *Her* shoulders and a limitless orb of light surrounds *Her*. Chiming bells strung with precious rubies, sapphires, and diamonds circle *Her* ankles, *Her* feet mark the ground with a steady stream of sacred blessing symbols. *She* is an ever-changing, transformative vision playing over and over in your mind and you realize you have seen *Her* in many manifestations in your own life. *She* is everything you have read or imagined or longed for, the *Divine Mother*. *Her* countenance is pure light; *Her* smile is welcoming, warm, and full of such a deep and abiding love for you. Celestial music floats through the forest as the drum's staccato rhythms punctuate the gongs, rattling gourds, laughing flutes, horns, and violins that celebrate *Her*.

Humbled by this magnificent beauty, hands over your heart, you bow. *She* smiles. Your heart opens. You offer a prayer. You are ready, open, and willing to receive *Her* blessing. The time is now. Your prayer evokes a beautiful stream of light from *Her* heart to yours and a spark ignites within you, a blessing from the *Divine Mother Goddess Shakti Kundalini*. This sacred red fire, as a tiny seed form whispers the wisdom, "Ahhhh, maybe I am *Divine* too."

The perfect teacher of sacred union, the *Divine Mother Goddess Shakti Kundalini,* is from India and is embodied in that holy land. The name *Shakti* means power or empowerment. *Shakti* is the primordial cosmic energy and represents the dynamic forces that are thought to move through the entire universe in the Hindu tradition. *Shakti* is the very personification of the *Divine Feminine* creative power, sometimes referred to as The *Great Mother* or the *Divine Mother*. *She* is responsible for all of creation, and as such, is also its agent for change. *Shakti* is cosmic existence as well as liberation, the cosmic fire. *She* is known in many forms including *Devi, Mahadevi, Parvati, Lakshmi, Chamundi, Lalita, Radha, Sati, Kali,* or *Durga*. *Her* manifestations are diverse and unlimited. Ultimately, *She* is the power, force, and feminine energy that represent the fundamental creative instinct underlying the cosmos and is the energizing force of all *Divinity*, of every being, and every thing. *Shakti* is the term used to describe the operating power of the cosmos, from the smallest atom to the grandest galaxy. *Shakti's* fire is the kundalini energy of awakened wisdom.

Divine Feminine Yoga is an ancient tradition. Tantric doctrine stipulates that mortal women are "life-itself" and *Goddess-like* because they embody the principle of *Shakti*. The sages hold women in great esteem and call them *Shaktis*. To ill treat a *Shakti* (a woman), is a crime. The Tantric synonym for woman was *Shaktiman*, which means "*Mind of Shakti*" or "*Possessor of Shakti*." In the Hindu tradition, the great *Goddess Shakti* is the eternal and supreme power, variously described as manifest energy; the substance of everything and all pervading.

She is the creative principle of *Divine* ecstasy.

She is the *Divine* spark inculcated in everything.

She is the one that shines.

Call on *Her* when you need help, when you aspire to commune, when you choose more light, when you wish to transform something, when you aspire to make offerings, and when you long for *Mystical Union*. *Mystical Union* is *Her* nature and will unfold in your consciousness as your realization expands to understand *She* has always been with you for *She* is the hidden ecstasy in every moment. *Shakti* is the *Divine Mother's* energy manifested in the physical world.

In this moment of *Mystical Union*, your everyday nature of being transforms to your original state of pure, natural connection and golden-white light. It becomes an ecstatic moment of pure joy and remembrance and the true state of your being. In this *Mystical Union* you are given a taste of it once again. Revel in it, see it, and feel it all deeply with every sense perception gifted to you by the *Divine Mother*. Bring this illuminating experience into your heart so you can touch it softly with deep reverence whenever you need to immerse yourself in *Her* blessing. Let the *Divine* spark within you begin to grow and come alive in all your cells. Breathe into it and feel the bliss of ecstatic awareness open. Delight in the *Mother's* flaming world and all experience as *Her* numinous expression, and in every vibrating being as an expression of *Her* light.

Divine ecstasy is ever-present at the core of every sense

experience, mind-state, and emotion, yet the human heart has lost its capacity to fully surrender to the bliss that is its birthright. For this *Divine* ecstasy to be experienced, a journey of transformation must be undertaken. Tantric scholar, Miranda Shaw, says that Tantric Buddhism, or Vajrayana the Diamond Way, was founded on the principle that ecstasy is the essence of the world. In Vajrayana Buddhist practice this is known as the Deity and is profoundly freeing when practiced purely.

When you form a pure intention and possess the courage and fortitude to do so, you call forth this transformative moment on your journey. You were unaware that the radiant *Being* you saw up on the opposite ridge had been making *Her* way to you the second you formed the sacred intention to meet *Her*. The magical truth is that *She* will always meet you right there even in the thickest, darkest, scariest part of your forest, whenever you call for *Her*. *She* was been waiting for your call and will always meet you if you make the effort. *She* has real power and can turn your fear into a celebration of life. That is *Her* promise. *She* has never not been there; you have just forgotten *Her* for a time. If you do not call *Her*, *She* remains an invisible force, enfolded in the great mystery, waiting for you and in the deepest, darkest places where *Her* light shines the strongest and is clearly evident. This *Divine Being*, the *Divine Mother*, is a part of every kind of imaginable phenomena, so *She* is also a part of everything you experience. The key is to see *Her* light shining through it all and to experience *Her* light as a sustaining presence of love, creativity, nurturing, and wisdom. *She* is always holding you and you can never wander from *Her* heart, for you are part of *Her*.

Receive this sacred ignition from *Shakti's* holy fire. Let yourself become pregnant with a *Divine Life*. The seed formed within you will grow and mature through the stages of pregnancy and growth to maturity and service if you tend to it. It will lead you to the ecstasy of your own true nature. You will become a transcendent *Divine Feminine Yogini*, a mystic, an ecstatic.

Mystics are those who so hunger for the *Divine* their life pursues only this. Their dedication is complete and irrevocable. The *Buddha* was like that. He left his kingdom, his comforts, his family, and his friends and went and sat in the forest until he found wisdom. They say he lived as an ascetic for years, surviving on one grain of rice a day until he realized this was not his true path. He then relaxed and became pregnant with the *Divine* and attained full enlightenment.

Mystical Union is when you open to the *Divine* fully, but you don't have to do it like the *Buddha* did. The completeness of the opening is in your heart, not the amount of time you invest. One does not need to leave their friends and family in such a radical way to connect with the *Divine* deeply.

The truth is, your life is filled with *Mystical Union* all the time, whether you recognize it or not. You don't have to become an ascetic in the forest like the *Buddha*; you can be a clerk at the grocery store. *Mystical Union* is not what you do; it is how you choose to live that matters. *Mystical Union* is not about a role you play, it is about the quality of your beingness.

Mystical Union is the deep and reverent surrender to the *Divine* that allows the higher forces and vibrations to lead you. *Mystical Union* is a kind of *Divine Alchemy* that happens every time you transcend a negative point of view, and transmute an obstacle in your life. *Divine Alchemy* is when you love unconditionally. In all these instances, you are unifying with the sacred where the *Divine* fertilizes your awareness to create a new life and a new way of being in your heart-mind. Each breath becomes a star spiral, each heartbeat a galactic pulse.

Mystical Union happens every time you turn anything towards its own innate goodness. Beauty is the key to the magic of *Mystical Union*. When you walk in beauty in the world with goodness, love, kindness, joy, and mindfulness, true magic happens with all the phenomena that greet you on your walk, every day. Staying present with it is the way to deepen each experience and unravel its deeper song.

Welcome the *Divine* into every moment of your life, every thought, and every emotion and to allow its beauty to enfold you and unfold within you. The enfolding is the loving protection of the

Divine Mother and the unfolding is *Her* nurturing. *She* protects, loves, and nurtures you every step on the way. *She* is the *Divine Mother* after all! Bowing and recognizing your moment-to-moment alchemical union with *Her* is indeed profoundly illuminating. *She* is the love-light in all physical phenomena.

The *Divine Mother's* embodiment of ecstasy and joy is *Her* sacred presence that imbues all of physical phenomena with holy purpose. The wonderful philosopher, Mirabai Starr, says it beautifully when she writes,

> " *I am not the only one to notice that the Divine Feminine,*
> *the Divine Mother, has been buried alive for millennia.*
> *But her potency is undiminished and now seems to be*
> *her time to rise from the shadows and radiate into every*
> *arena of the human experience. Not as the alternative to the*
> *masculine model of holiness, but as an equal expression of*
> *the ineffable, formless Absolute as it pours into form.*
> *The Divine Feminine feels to me to be all about embodiment...*
> *and it is the felt experience of the sacred in nature,*
> *in relationships and community, in work for peace and justice,*
> *in the arts. Rather than striving for the vertical ascension up*
> *and out of the world, the Divine Feminine celebrates the*
> *body, interdependence with all beings.*"

You can call on *Her* through many forms. One very reliable way to evoke the *Divine Mother* is through sacred sound known as mantras. Chanting mantra is a sacred technology that has been utilized for thousands of years. There are many, many classifications of *Shakti* power and thus many *Shakti* mantras. A great source for these is entitled *Shakti Mantras*, a wonderful work by Thomas Ashley-Farrand, a Vedic Priest, who has worked with these sacred forms for decades.

Another way to call on *Her* is through devotional music or prayer, such as the *Mother Goddess Devi Prayer* printed at the beginning of this book. It is one of my favorites. Keep opening your heart and *She* will become a daily presence and companion in your life in a very conscious way. *Mystical Union* is cultivated by chanting mantra, listening to sacred music, prayer, mediation, communing with nature, yoga, tantra, contemplating the great sacred rays, and regular, daily spiritual practice. All of these methods are very helpful in shifting your perception to allow this sacred union to happen. The greatest portal to this *Mystical Union* is your own heart.

Surrendering to this process forges your spiritual mastery. This surrendering is a soul initiation of cleansing, healing, trust, and faith. When you surrender, your ego gradually transforms back into your original consciousness of *Divine* nature, which is your true self, the original spark of *Shakti's* fire.

How do you do this? *Mystical Union* is a spiraling relationship that grows and expands with your willingness, effort, and opening. The lotus flower is a perfect symbol of this *Mystical Union* as every day it rises and opens when the sunrise lights the sky and gently closes and sinks into the deep watery world at night when the sun sets. It demonstrates the three principles of willingness, effort, and openness, which is what cultivates the *Mystical Union* each moment, each day. Like any relationship, the more effort put into it, the deeper it can go.

Choose a *Divine Life*. I offer the promise you will be joyful and happy you did. Here you are, on the path, with all these exquisite manifestations of the *Divine Mother* circling and supporting you, revealing yourself to you. *Mystical Union* with *Her* constitutes a deep awareness of the *Divine Presence* and *Shakti* has the ability to destroy any negativity or force that brings you out of balance with the *Divine* within you. Whenever you feel anything but love, joy, and ecstasy, you are separate from *Her* in your mind. This is key to remember at this point because it is a constant reminder to focus on love and joy. It is the compass for measuring your consciousness and the truth is you are never separate from *Her*. Your emotions are a compass with which you can navigate your consciousness, helping you to recall that you are never truly separate from *Her*.

It is sobering to realize how disconnected we feel most of

the time. Every day the practice is to return to *Her* loving embrace, to keep welcoming *Her* into your heart. And you don't have to do it perfectly. The *Great Mother Goddess Shakti Kundalini* is already within you. As your creation mentor *She* can recreate your mind when an obstacle arises and change the way you are thinking about a situation or experience. Dive deep and go for another interpretation. If you need some assistance, call on *Her*. *She* is the one who gave you the holy breath of *Spirit* and holds the memory for you of loving breath. In this place breathe *Her* in lovingly, acknowledging and surrendering to *Her* holy embrace. In that union, you give up your aloneness and isolation. *She* holds you in *Her* arms, and nurtures you, *Her Divine Child* with joy, love, and understanding as you have been and always will be. You were created as an expression of *Her* love. At this point of *Mystical Union* you feel the sweet gentle caress of *Oneness* as your heart merges with *Hers* and you feel *Her* within your physical and subtle bodies.

THE PINK MOON

The *Pink Moon* is all about love. It appears at this time as life within begins to awaken from a deep winter where your spiritual life is awakening with the love of the *Divine Mother's* presence. The glimmering white, translucent moonlight mixes with *Shakti's* powerful fiery force and pink light is formed to bathe the Earth with a gentle, restorative love that urges new life from its winter slumber. Pink light holds the vibration of love and can be used to magnetize and transform anything into its loving nature. The slumber transforms to a new cycle of awakening in the *Moon Mother's* light of love for all.

Under the rose-colored light of the *Pink Moon* all the manifestations of the *Divine Mother* begin to unify as creation in every form, as the pulsing life force increases. Can you feel *Her* pulsing in your body? This sensation, this felt sense of pulsing, is the normal activity of the *Shakti* according to Sally Klempton, a revered Hindu Yogini and teacher. *She* says it is the *Goddess* living as your energy body. The more you become attuned with your energy body and the more you acknowledge your energy as *Her*, the more *She* will begin to make love to you from the inside. The *Goddess* will dance within you, shifting your awareness as *She* starts to show *Herself* to you. Through *Mystical Union, She* is beginning to reveal *Herself* to you right now.

She is renewal, passion, light, and warmth. *She* is the heart of the *Sacred Feminine* fully ripened. Can you feel *Her* in your body? Can you feel Her in your heart? *She* is the breath, the blood, and the giver of your life force. *She* is your goodness and your loving nature, *She* is the gentle summer breeze caressing you. *She* is the high point in every cycle in nature. *She* is your fear, anger, and angst. *She* is every emotion, every thought, every breath. *She* manifests individually, uniquely. *She* knows all about you, loves every part of you, and will never depart if you remember *Her,* honor *Her,* and keep *Her* in your pantheon. *She* is your vulnerability. *She* is your love.

She calls for your wholeness. Every part of you reveals itself to *Her. She* asks nothing more than that. *She* is full of energy, life, and love. *She* calls to all men, women, and children. *She* holds all beings in *Her* heart, the earth, the cosmos, and the great emptiness of eternity.

Her symbol is the circle. *She* is a master of rhythms. *She* sings into being cyclic forms, the vesica pisces, the intersection between two circles. *She* defies gravity and is gravity. *She* is the keeper of universal laws and demands nothing. *She* is here especially for you. All you have to do is open up the secret places in your heart and lead *Her* to your innermost sanctuary, to the accompanying fusion of love, acceptance, and glory, where *She* will take you deeper still. *She* is you in an immeasurable state of grace and immensity, beyond comprehension. *She* is diversity. *She* is beauty. *She* is the tiniest flower, the simplest wave, the furthest star, the angriest rebel, and the lowest realm.

She melts the sounds of the tremendous past. *She* is a revolution. *She* is freedom. *She* welcomes you home. Welcome *Her. She* is the blessing in many cultures and religions and is called many names. *She* is:

Sarasvati

Throma

Tara

Yeshe Tsogyal

Mother Mary

Aditi

Lakshmi

Durga

Mary Magdalene

Kwan Yin

Amaterasu

Uni

Aphrodite

Freja

Mene

Tarrit

Nut

Gaia

Hera

Demeter

Juno

Eir Audhumla

Diana

Venus

Frig Inanna

Tara

Mader-Akka

Mokosh

Epona

Margawse

Aponibolinayen

Atanea

Wahini-Hai

Nokomis

Yolkai

Sena

Changing Woman

Sophia

Nana Buluk

Nzambi

Imberombera

Buffalo Woman

Spider Woman

Shechinah

Brigid

Pachamama

Julunggul

Danae

Isis	Bhuvaneshwari
Dennitsa	Diana
Ma	Red Tara
Lama	Kupala
Padmadakini	Mawu
Nuwa	Venus
Derceto	Cardea
Ninhursag	Jai Ma
Persephone	Mama
Hecate	Ishtar
Medusa	Danu
Nestia	Devi
Athena	Mother Earth
Baba Yaga	Mati Syra Zemlya
Nathor	Cybelle
Maat	Demeter
Devayani	Virgin Mary
Dhyani	Kali
Shakti Kundalini	Atalanta
Babd	White Tara

She is the diamond heart of God that reflects the ripest, most effulgent form of the Sacred Feminine. Welcome Her.

She lives within you.

Moon Mother Goddess Luna

Attunement 4

PINK MOON

FOURTH MONTH OF THE LUNAR CALENDAR

BEGIN THIS TWENTY-EIGHT DAY PINK MOON cycle by reviewing your entire last cycle, especially in regards to self-love and what issues came up for you. Since you are in a *New Moon* time, begin to determine what attitudes and habits need to transform for you to love yourself more deeply, especially in regards to the work you have done over the last three months. Then contemplate what has kept you separate from *Mystical Union*. What still keeps you separate today? Note these tendencies in your journal for the transformation process. For example, doubt is a big obstacle to connection. You might have this appear, as a way for your ego to keep you separate from the *Divine*. The ego has a huge investment in separation to keep control of your world. It is very beneficial to examine this closely when you have doubt arising.

Home Fun

❧ You are going to infuse your mandala with the soft, pink light of the *Pink Moon Mother*.

❧ You can accomplish this imaginatively by sending out rays of pink light to your mandala.

❧ To anchor in this pink light vibration of love, add some rose quartz stones. You can add four small pieces in the cardinal directions or if you have the means, buy twenty-eight stones to represent each day of this cycle.

❧ Make a series of twenty-eight small pink hearts.

❧ On each heart, write an affirmation symbolizing that day's meditation.

❧ Place these hearts on the outside circle of your mandala, forming an outer ring of twenty-eight pink hearts.

❧ Each day, meditate upon loving yourself more. Ask the vibration of the pink ray to melt away any resistance or obstacles that may arise.

Please visit: www.motheringthedivinewisdom.com
to listen to a free guided Mystical Union meditation.

Gestation

Chapter 5

Spiritual Essence is neither celestial nor infernal,
but an aerial, pure and precious body in the middle between
the highest and lowest, the choicest and noblest thing under heaven.
Men have it before their eyes,
handle it with their hands, yet know it not,
though they constantly tread it under their feet.

The Sophic Hydrolith

*G*ESTATION BEGINS WITH AN EMBRYONIC ALIVENESS that is made possible following *Mystical Union*. It is the beginning of tentative development and great surrender. This stage of your journey calls for you to slow down and go inside to learn about the *Divine Alchemy* of working with the *Divine Mother* in an embodied sense so that *She* becomes a palpable, felt-experience. *Divine Alchemy* is all about experiencing *Heaven on Earth* through *Her* and learning to bring spiritual qualities into all of your being. It is the part of the path where you feel the *Divine Mother's* love-light in all your experiences. It is both a revelation and a revolution because it changes everything.

During the gestating process, this soft touch of awakening is revealed in a multitude of deepening forms of awareness in your thoughts, emotions, ideas, intentions, dreams, wishes, pain, illness and all the other dimensions of being human. This gestational time is when you begin to work with your own process of perception and realize the mind that directs your thoughts becomes emotions and then actions. Working with your perceptions in an intentional way is a holy and transformative part of the sacred journey. To enter into this crucible, under the auspices of the *Divine Mother* is an incalculable blessing that melts you down and also transforms you back into your original form of high frequency light vibration.

This sacred process is a multidimensional experience. You simultaneously experience being in the womb of the *Divine Mother's* loving energy and carry inside of you the *Divine Mother's* loving energy. The enfoldment of you in *Her* love is what allows the unfolding in you to happen. It is part of *Her* mystery and provides the spiritual pilgrim to both reside in and hold a safe, consecrated place for this process of expansion and transformation to take place. It is the *Divine Mother's* gift to you in return for your willingness to continue to walk into the light of your own becoming.

During this embryonic gestation period, this enfolding and unfolding begins to take form. It is a time of surrendering to adjustment as well as expansion. How this happens is made manifest by your own pure intention and careful and loving caretaking of this precious and powerful gift. It is a time to take great care and to be very gentle with your self. Gentleness is one aspect of the *Divine Mother's* wisdom and something you can inculcate in your being over time, both towards yourself and others. Through gentleness, *Her* love and compassion becomes a light spark in every single cell and spiral of your DNA. *Divine Alchemy* is when your inner world is so transformed it shines forth as light into the world.

The *Divine Mother*, who croons a constant lullaby of love, light, and belonging, gently nurtures this sacred beginning of gestating. *She* sings in the deep silence of your being even in this very moment. This deep sacred space within you is a prayer in itself. This deep sacred space is secure and safe and completely created for divining the new. It is the crucible bubbling with possibilities where your light seeds are stored for their becoming. This sacred space holds the secret of beyond opposites and the secret of your awakening. Gestating energy holds the seeds of all your creative possibilities.

Gestation is about acknowledging, honoring, and nurturing your *Sacred Essence*. The word "sacred" means to belong to the *Divine*. The word "essence" means that which makes something what it is: the inward nature of anything. *Sacred Essence* is your holy nature and is the center point of every sacred circle expression. Sacred circle expressions include medicine wheels, mandalas, and labyrinths. Celebrated in dance, sculpture, painting, music, theatre, and sacred geometry, the centering point in each of these symbolic sacred circles is who you really are and how your uniqueness is a vital part of the cosmos. Finding and embracing your center is what the spiritual journey is all about. The centering point of *Sacred Essence* is where the experience of enfolding and unfolding occurs.

Hafiz says it poetically,

> *"One lives in the circle, so that the round knot*
> *in the Beloved's hair will become undone."*

By bringing your awareness gently to your center, you can begin to focus on your own *Sacred Essence*; your heart's distilled elixir. If this is a new way of being with yourself and others, then it is good for you to know that *Sacred Essence* includes everything in your own circle of life, including all you have experienced, thought, sensed, or imagined. It is the beginning of your unconscious mind becoming conscious. The brilliant psychotherapist, Carl Jung said, "Until you make the unconscious conscious, it will direct your life and you will call it fate."

You are moving beyond the realm of fate and into the realm of self-realization. It is here you begin to explore the hidden regions of the mind so that you can become freer and more self-determining through love and conscious expansion. Those thoughts and emotions that no longer serve you will be transformed and liberated, awarding you with new possibilities for your future and freedom.

What a profoundly beautiful way to express the circle of your life enfolding and unfolding, as a living, breathing *Divine* essence. How can anyone know this without embodying the *Divine Mother*? *She* is the holy, inward nature of virtually all phenomena and everything in the physical world. As *Her* beloved hair begins to unfold, it is symbolic of the inner unfolding within you of your understanding of your own sacred nature and the recognition of your own *Sacred Essence*.

It is time to see what the weather is like inside this gestating, embryonic sacred space. It is a place of the unborn, the expectant, the benign, and the inner temple's lotus throne. Your center speaks of stillness, silence, and quietude. Stay in this sacred space until you can hear the multitude of voices that comprise your being and let them emerge. Now is the time to let the light seeds activate. Call into being your inspirations, visions, and your own beauty through prayer and clear intent. Here is where the bounty of creativity resides, store housing mystical perception. While gestating, awareness begins to take notice of how and what you choose to take in and what you want to do with it. It is the time of possible and gentle transformation.

Mothering the Divine is an initiation in gentleness especially during gestation. The qualities of softness–sensitive tones, mild touch, smooth caress, snuggles, delight in being, and an open smile are all treasures of *Mothering*. This is a tranquil time, an expectant time. It is a time where longing becomes manifest. Your tenderness longs for expression, freedom, and a place to live in this world, for a special place of its own unique shining. Gentleness is underrated in our society but is so very crucial and important on the spiritual life path and fosters the enlightened activity of the *Divine Mother* through its innate life-enhancing and life-supporting energy.

It seems rare to find gentleness in modern life. We can find cool, slick, witty, sad, smart, violent, etc. but gentleness is a real treasure when you come across it in yourself and in others. Almost every day I have to remind myself to be gentle. We have to learn to cultivate and revere gentleness. If it were common we would not notice it so much.

Gentleness is a skillful method of pure perception. Through gentle energy you can radiate life-actualizing power that benefits all beings. I have never seen gentleness start a fight or a war or a conflict. I have never had the experience that gentleness makes a situation worse. I have never had it make my life crazier. The value of gentleness as a touchstone in one's life is to reduce stress and create a peaceful, relaxed attitude and manner. I never needed my hideout when someone was gentle with me. Self-acceptance, self-esteem, love, kindness, and compassion are all seeded in gentleness. Cultivating gentleness is a refining process, a skillful way to massage one's heart essence into blooming with sweetness. Gentleness allows you to relax and surrender. It is a way to deepen your surrendering until union is complete.

One reliable way to cultivate a gentle mind is to attune to your senses. John O'Donohue, the astounding Irish poet, explained that the senses are thresholds of the soul when he wrote,

> *"Your senses link you intimately with the Divine within*
> *you and around you. Attunement to the senses can limber*
> *up the stiffened belief and gentle the hardened outlook.*

*It can warm and heal the atrophied feelings that are
the barriers exiling us from ourselves and separating us
from each other. Then we are no longer in exile from the wonderful
harvest of Divinity that is always secretly gathering in us."*

Senses are your avenues of perception. According to Vajrayana
Buddhism, there are eight avenues of perception or consciousness.
In traditional mandalas, they are represented as an eight-petal lotus.
The first are the five senses: auditory, visual, olfactory, gustatory,
and tactile. The other three are conceptual consciousness, emotional
consciousness, and the seat of the mind or storehouse consciousness.
In this gestational period, it is beneficial to work with the five physical
avenues of perception in a gentle, loving, and direct way so you
begin to sense the *Divine Mother* in what you perceive. To work with
your consciousness, it is imperative that you understand what your
consciousness is. Examine it carefully in each of the avenues and
begin to get a full sense that your consciousness is much more than
your thoughts and emotions.

GENTLE HEARING: AUDITORY PERCEPTION

Gentle hearing frees your mind to be present with clarity and
non-judgment. Gentle hearing softly welcomes the other, whether
it is another person, an animal, a dream, or an idea. It is the freedom
of non-attachment to anything, anyone, or any idea. It is a present
state of listening that is pure and joyful. Within the energy of gentle
listening, you hear your own heartbeat, other's hearts beating, and
the heartbeat of *Earth Mother* herself. When we hear gently, we hear
the sounds of the inner voice, which reveals the holy inward nature of
sound.

You hear the way you are.

In great music there is as much space as there is sound. When
your heart beats, there is a sound and then silence, then sound, then
silence. Silence opens your mind to the vastness of space all around
you. When you are at the beach, the waves make a sound and then

there is silence, then sound, then silence. When you begin to hear in this way, you are attuned to your natural state of listening and gentleness is its inherent nature, the world's heartbeat.

I have learned so much about listening to the world around me from my husband, who has a keen sense of hearing. At the beach, he can distinguish the sound of a wave traveling over sand from the sound of a wave traveling over small pebbles. He has taught me to hear differently, because it is his passion and gift. Being a gentle soul, he hears from the tender regions of his heart and has offered this world to me. I am aware of sound in new ways all the time because of his wonderfully refined gift.

There are so many voices to hear. When you become quiet, the more clearly you hear them. The more you listen in silence, the deeper your hearing goes until you find you are once again connected to the world. Your heart beats and you hear the dimensions of song in a crystal, or in the *Devas* in your garden, or the longing of a child for attention, or in those across the sea that are hungry. You can hear other's thoughts when you listen gently, you can attune to them through your heart and offer them connection, communication, and blessings. You can hear another's need for love, another's impatience or anger, another's boredom with a tenderness of the *Mother. She* recognizes, sees, and makes the choice to interact or not. Have you ever heard that *God* was deaf? The result of gentle hearing is a refined sense of being in the world where everything slows down and you become fully present. When this happens, you are able to hear the *Sacred Essence* in the sound, which is the voice of the *Divine Mother.*

Silence is a paradox. The more I welcome in silence, the more I hear. I hear the noise and chatter of my own mind and the noise and chatter in another's. The more I welcome silence, the more my intimate heart-voice arises in song. The chatter begins to quiet and an ease of spaciousness spreads where joyful breath lives. I learn to hear in a way I have never heard before. Even in my dreams, the hearing is more intimate, the whispers more profound. It is where I can hear what the dream is really saying, in this silence. This silence is where I am able to hear the quiet voice of my heart, my longing, and my own tenderness, which whispers love from the *Divine Mother's* mind to my own.

When you hear gently, you are in tune with *Her*. There is no resistance to what you are hearing, what you are sensing is *Sacred Essence* through sound. Listening and hearing are indistinguishable. I produced a video for a fund-raising event where His Holiness the Dalai Lama was speaking and the director of the video was interviewing the artists on this project we were fundraising for. I observed the director and the way he listened to the artists. He was engaged fully and after several hours he looked at me and said how full he was. We spoke of the way he listens, with every bit of energy he can utilize to really hear others when they speak. His was an example of gentle, mindful listening.

To be able to listen gently, I call upon the beautiful, radiant *Bodhisattva, Kwan Yin* and the *Divine Mother Mary*. *Kwan Yin* is the *Goddess of Mercy and Compassion* and is a manifestation of the *Divine Mother*, much the same as the *Divine Mother Mary*. They have a very similar vibration and are both incredibly beautiful. Many feel they are the same field of loving, embracing energy. Many think of *Kwan Yin* as the counterpart of the *Divine Mother Mary*, as *She* is considered by many to be the Buddhist *Madonna*.

Kwan Yin is believed to observe the world and all the sounds of the world, in particular. *She* listens deeply and with compassion to the crying sounds of all beings, whether they are verbal or mental. *She* hears all who are crying for help, or as the Venerable Dhyani Ywahoo says, "Those beyond the horizon."

In *Her* hands, *Kwan Yin* holds a willow branch, a vase of water, or a lotus flower. The willow branch is used to heal people's illnesses or bring fulfillment to their requests. The water represents the dew of compassion and has the quality to remove suffering by purifying the defilements of your body, speech, and mind. The lotus is the symbol of consciousness. The mystic beauty of *Kwan Yin* teaches us to hear through the heart of compassion and love. When you are able to cultivate this kind of sensitive listening, it is very freeing. It frees you from judgment and bias and the *Divine Mother* delights in your accomplishments.

Gentle listening feeds your own sense of self worth. When

you hear yourself through gentleness, your critical voice begins to have less power over you and your critical voice begins to soften. The new possibilities of joyful experience begin to arise and you begin to hear the genuine voice of the *Divine Mother* who speaks with love, understanding, and creative thought. Whenever obstacles arise, I say *Kwan Yin*'s holy mantra to call on *Her* presence within me:

NAMO QUAN SHIH YIN PU SA. NAMO QUAN SHIH YIN PU SA.

I repeat it for a few mala (prayer beads) rounds and it literally transforms the energy. It is miraculous. There is an innate, *Sacred Essence* of compassion and kindness in *Kwan Yin*'s beautiful mantra that shifts perception and experience, as if waving a magic wand.

Actually, anyone can be like *Kwan Yin*. With your compassion, you can bring harmony into this world. It all begins with gentle listening and shifts the energy to sweeten the experience and your understanding. Somehow, the magic wand of speaking a *Sacred Essence* sound does that automatically. All holy mantras work in this way, as they are the sound forms of enlightened fields of energy. Begin listening gently to the new forms of consciousness arising within you right now.

GENTLE SIGHT: VISUAL PERCEPTION

The first sense most people think of is sight. Recently, I was in a retreat where we did a practice of opening and closing our eyes consciously as a way to understand our perception and awareness. Every time we open our eyes, it is an opportunity to see the world freshly. Try it. Hold a thought of gently seeing the world, bright and new in your heart. Close your eyes and contemplate this for a moment. Consider this as your motivation for seeing. Then open your eyes again with the motivation to see deeply into the *Sacred Essence* of everything.

Practicing the presence of the *Divine* in every moment brings the *Divine Mother* to life. The *Bible* says the meek shall inherit the *Earth* and this statement sings of gentleness. Looking deeply and intimately at something is to look gently. Deepening your vision is *Mothering the Divine.* You see through *Her* enlightened vision, through *Her* sacred view. Sacred view is to really see things as they are, not through your own filter. If you are afraid, you see things that scare you. If you are happy, the world is a joyful place. If you are always grasping for more, you see the world as only meant for what you want. If you see the world through control, it is limited and closed in. If you see through gentle sight, there is unlimited vision that is clear and able to absorb, intimately, what you see. The physical world begins to take on a new luminosity and you begin to see and perceive subtle forms and other dimensions.

When you see through gentleness, it brings you to the realization that everything you see is light, that you are light. This is enlightened vision. It is the way to see every moment, every perception as an opportunity to embody spiritual essence.

The gentle heart is the realm of the transcendent *Divine Mother Mary*, also known as the *Queen of Heaven. She* epitomizes loving kindness. I love the Byzantine icons that portray *Her. She* is called the *Virgin of Tenderness* and engenders gentle sight. It is said that just by gazing upon *Her* icon tenderness and loving-kindness are evoked in the viewer. In the icons of loving-kindness, the motherly caress of the *Mother* of *God* is indissolubly connected with loving sight.

One of the most celebrated icons of the Eastern Church is *Our Lady of Vladimir* or *Our Lady of Tenderness–the Lady Who Saved Russia.* The miraculous image is also known as *Eleousa,* the Greek word meaning, *Mother of Tenderness.* In this icon, the *Christ Child* nestles tenderly close to his *Mother* and gazes at *Her* while *Mother Mary* looks out at the people. The origin of this ancient icon can be traced back to 1125. For many, The *Lady Who Saves Russia* is honored as the unconquerable shield of the Russian people. It eventually became the sign of the Russian Orthodox Church. Today, there are thousands of representations of it exemplifying the power of *Her* gentle, compassionate sight.

If you choose to call on *Her* to assist you in gentle viewing, here is a simple prayer that was recently offered by Pope Francis in

Rome at Saint Peter's,

"Mother of the living Gospel, wellspring of happiness,
for God's little ones, pray for us. Amen. Alleluia."

Another very ancient supplication to the *Divine Mother Mary* is:

We turn to you for protection, holy Mother of God,
Listen to our prayers, and help us with our needs,
Save us from every danger, glorious and blessed Virgin.

The *Divine Mother* created the entire physical world through *Her* love and revealed the true essence of every being is love. It is here your gentle perception comes from, right smack dab in the middle of your heart, and it is the key to transfiguration, transformation, and enlightenment. When you see through the heart of love, the entire world is transformed into one of beauty and the *Divine Alchemy* of compassion arises spontaneously.

GENTLE OLFACTORY: SMELL

Smelling gently begins with the breath. Focus on the breath of air coming into your nostrils during your inhale and softly leaving when you exhale. This begins the process of smelling softly. The airflow becomes a caress of love.

A delightful friend works very creatively with flower essences and is a fragrance diva. *She* mixes the most sublime, exquisite, and illusive mixtures and I can never guess what they are. It is great fun. Another friend calls himself a sensorial archaeologist and travels all over the world in search of rare and exotic oils and essences for his healing balms and perfumes. Lotus flower oils, tea leaves, herbal spices, newly cut grass, ocean breezes, dirt, and tree barks all have their own smells. Nature walks are great for getting a whiff of all kinds of fragrant bouquets.

Aromas can call up memories and powerful responses, almost

instantaneously. A certain scent–food cooking, a loving presence, flowers blooming–can bring on a flood of recollections and can influence your mood. Because the olfactory bulb is part of the brain's limbic system, an area so closely associated with memory and feeling, it's sometimes called the "emotional brain."

Often you will forget an experience completely until you smell something that awakens your memory. Freshly sharpened pencils remind me of one of my grade school teachers who had me sharpen pencils. Chalk smells remind me of fifth grade. Cinnamon always reminds me of rain. Touch these memories softly, with love. The more you softly touch them the more gentleness there will be in your life. Smell is a memory maker, so why not make good ones? If a smell opens the memory of something unpleasant, it is especially mindful to touch it gently and then release it with love.

During some teachings on transference of consciousness at death, called *Phowa*, I learned that your sense of smell actually stays with you, in traces, for up to three days after you pass from the physical body. You can actually help guide a being to a higher realm, even at that point, through their sense of smell. In Vajrayana yogic practices smell is celebrated and harnessed towards attaining liberation and various incenses are used for sadhanas or group ceremonies. Some are used to call various *Beings* to join in the ceremony, others are used to announce the appearance of the *Deity*, and others are used as offerings to the mandala. It is such a glorious celebration of the sense of smell. It is said your sense of smell can carry you all the way to the *Pure Land*, which is a heavenly realm.

It is interesting how you can shift an experience through your sense of smell. When I am in an uncomfortable situation if I can find a smell that I can touch gently it eases my mind and body. You can harness this to making many spaces in your life breathe the breath of gentle smell. If you have trouble driving, spray your car interior with spritzers or smudge it with sage sticks; make your car an oasis. This can be applied to literally any area in the physical world that you want to soften and make holy. Sacred oils and diffusers work really well for transforming workplaces into more ideal, life-supportive environments.

In my home, I have three shrine areas and I make offerings daily to each of them. One of the offerings is incense. Incense infuses the air with a sacred quality because it shifts perception. This is very useful in healing. The smoke from the incense becomes clouds of offerings to the *Deities* in the mandala I am working with and helps to bring them into being. The smell becomes a sacred pathway.

You can remake and heal memories through a gentle and aware sense of smell. Smell can change your experience completely. According to research, when you study information in the presence of an odor, the vividness of that remembered information will become more intense when you smell that odor again. Fragrance can vivify your experience and enhance memory. This also works in sacred ceremony to anchor in the experience of transformation and healing in a felt-sense, which deepens and consecrates it.

GENTLE TASTE: GUSTATORY

Your quest of the gentle mind stream leads you now to taste; the same area of geography as speech, the tongue. Gentle taste is about nourishment on so many levels. It is about cultivating taste and about realizing the quality of the food you eat. It is about being grateful for food, water, and those who cultivate it, package it, ship it, buy it, prepare it, and most of all, share it with us. Gentle taste is about becoming intimate with what you take into yourself. Gentle taste is about considering the life force it contains. It comes from our *Divine Mother*, our *Mother Earth*. *She* is always offering you food, water, and air. In every bite, you taste the gifts from your *Mother*, the gift of love. Every time you taste something you have the opportunity to feel connection to what nourishes you.

I notice when I actively seek gentle taste I slow down automatically. I begin to remember the rituals of gathering around a meal that is as old as human existence. When you taste gently, you remember gratitude. Gratitude completes the circle of reciprocity and makes it a whole experience. A group of women I know get together to eat consciously and enjoy meals together. They begin by sharing their prayers and end by sharing their prayers. In between, they taste consciously and in silence. What a joy to remember what a rich tradition gathering for a meal can be!

Gentle taste also is receiving the *Divine Mother's* nurturing. What do you feed yourself? What do you eat everyday? Is it sweet, sour, tangy, spicy, rich, hot, salty, bland, bitter, cool, creamy, gooey, juicy, savory, bitter, sticky, gritty, hearty, lean, smooth, herbal, infused, smoky, tangy, watery, or zingy? I love the term "acquired taste." Tasting gently is an acquired taste wherein with every bite you enjoy your awareness of the *Divine Mother* feasting with you.

Once I had an experience of gentle taste with a beautiful, ripe, red strawberry. I felt the texture of the seeds and skin with my tongue and the liquid joy in the first bite. It was a mesmerizing experience. The *Divine Mother* opened my mind so I could feel the plant energy in the strawberry, feel the rain feeding it while it grew, feel it being picked and sent with others to the store, and the ride to our house. I tasted the sunlight and starlight it grew within. One gentle taste and the universe opened up to reveal itself. What a joy.

On the *Full Moon* I perform a feast offering to all the seen and unseen beings. In this ritual, you beautifully prepare and arrange varieties of foods and place them on the shrine as an offering to all those who are hungry and lost and dedicate the feast offering so all beings may have food. I take a few small bites and practice gentle taste. It is always a transformative experience. On a more hidden level, you are offering to all the obstructers of your spiritual practice so they are satisfied through enlightened taste and so they will now support you instead of hindering you.

Gentle Touch: Tactile Perception

Touch is a way of taking the intimate, gentle wisdom of all five senses into the world. The way you touch the world exhibits the quality of your gentle heart and connects you to the world and others.

How does the *Divine Mother* touch us? Through *Her* beauty, love, and *Her* beingness. When you touch another, do you sense *Her* presence? Can you imagine the quality of *Her* caress? Try touching as if *Her* holy hands were inside of yours because they are. They are your hands as light. Begin to touch the world with hands of light and see how it feels, and what it opens up to you.

Touching gently, you are intimate with the innermost region of the heart. The soft Ahhh of love is heard and embraced in these moments. Imagine if everyone touched the world gently at the same time. Can you sense the relief *Mother Earth* would feel? The relief we would all feel? It is my prayer that some day this will happen, an international day of touching gently.

When you touch gently, you begin each relationship with tenderness and openness. Touching a leaf softly, you feel the veined, indented texture and you can also hear its song. Touching a bumpy, etched stone, gently, you can hear its ancient voice telling its story. Holding and touching sandy sea foam speaks to you of endless spirals in your own being. I love holding dehydrated seaweed, grooved driftwood, and fluted shells. Each touch informs of loving connection and speaks of the beautiful blue Pacific Ocean I so love.

Gentle touch breathes with each motion. When you touch the downy cheek of a newborn child you can feel the innocence and say, "Hello, welcome to the world." You are breathing love into the child and helping *Her* feel safe. You are breathing and touching with the same love that the *Divine Mother* breathes and touches you. When you feel a soft breeze, it is the *Divine Mother* saying, "Hello, I love you." When you dip your hand in a pond or creek, *She* is greeting you. It is really fun to walk in nature with this awareness and to feel the *Divine*, invisible embrace all around you. When I meditate in the mornings, I feel the *Divine Mother* holding me and breathing with me and it is profound. In these moments, I understand the *Sacred Essence* of the *Divine Mother's* eternal embrace in the entire physical world.

Conscious touching is an enlightened action demonstrating your understanding of this interconnection. When you touch anything in the phenomenal world in a loving way, all alienation and separateness disappear and the understanding arises of your place in the web of life. Touching consciously through love absorbs you both in the giving and the receiving of love. You inhale love and you exhale love. What you are touching and what is touching you become absorbed in each other. You become one. You become its wisdom and it learns yours.

Touching the *Earth* is a yogic practice that helps to generate love, compassion, and peace. During this practice, you touch the *Earth* gently six times, every day. You touch the *Earth* through a prostration pose, which means to touch the *Earth* simultaneously with your forehead, two hands, and two legs. Prostrations are done so that the body and mind form a perfect and whole unit. You are bowing, offering, praying, and perceiving through this consciousness. It is quite beautiful and refreshing. It is an expressive, prayerful salute of love and gratitude to our *Mother Earth* and *She* hears it and feels it.

The Buddhist monk, poet, scholar, and Nobel Laureate, Thich Nhat Hanh, teaches about learning mindfulness in walking meditation where every step is a breath, a prayer, and a teaching. It is a very powerful way to learn to touch the *Earth* consciously, gently, and with reverence. If you live near a labyrinth, which are now in many Episcopal churches, you can learn to do mindful walking while experiencing the labyrinth. There is one near my home and it is one of my favorites. It is out in an open field next to a farm with dairy cows and I love walking it with them close by, near the wide-open sea. It makes me very happy.

GENTLE IDEAS: CONCEPTUAL CONSCIOUSNESS

This aspect of consciousness is about becoming more familiar with the concepts your mind lives with all the time. All human beings form ideas they feel will help them survive and stay happy. How you reason is a very important part of being a human being. How you reason, the ideas you live with, constitute what actions and forms you bring into your life. Thought creates form.

This sixth avenue of consciousness is the function that integrates and processes the various sensory data we have just been exploring. It helps us to form an overall picture or thought based on what our five senses are communicating to us. It is primarily with these six functions of life that we perform our daily activities. To tune into our thoughts gently means to touch them with non-judgment and a loving curiosity. In this early phase, that is all that the gestation period is about; just touch them gently and look at them softly, kindly. Begin to become aware of your mind's activity. The depth exploration of your thoughts will come later. For now, just welcome them in and say, "Hello, we are living together, let's see if we can live together in peace."

GENTLE RELATING: SELF-SENSE CONSCIOUSNESS

On this deeper level, the seventh avenue of consciousness is about your inner life and is largely independent of sensory input. The seventh consciousness is the basis for your individual identity and attachment to a self, distinct and separate from others. It is the emotional intelligence in your sense of right and wrong, your emotions around your morals.

According to the teachings of the *Buddha*, there are delusions in the seventh level of consciousness regarding the nature of the self. These delusions rise from the relationship between the seventh and eighth levels and form the part of the mind known as the ego consciousness.

To gently accept this part of you now is all that is required. To just recognize, "Oh, I usually feel and perceive myself as separate from the rest of creation. That is another paradox of perception!!!!!" Because you often feel alone, you perceive you are alone. This alone feeling is just a function of the mind that has stepped outside the wisdom of the heart that knows that you are *Divine*, connected, and a very vital part of the web of life. Here you begin to touch that part of your consciousness gently and tell yourself, there is another way, another understanding that is much more spacious, open, and connected. You begin to believe you are a vital and integrated part of the *Divine* matrix and not separate at all.

This part of my mind, the ego, I used to like to leave at home when going to sacred ceremonies because it is so bossy. Now I take this part of my mind with me and honor and love it for all it does for me. I introduce it over and over again to the truth so it can just relax. The *Divine Mother* loves to hold and embrace this part of you, your ego mind. This part of you is a piece of the gift of being a human being, an expression of the *Divine*, so for myself I do not try to destroy it like so many traditions teach. Instead, I try to get it to expand, expand, expand.

When you begin to tell this part of you that you are perfect, it might try to convince you otherwise. Like I said, the ego is bossy and wants control. Just sit with it gently and tell it again. Its voice is fierce sometimes, but with gentle perception, it can transform even its fear of death.

GENTLE SEAT OF THE MIND: STOREHOUSE CONSCIOUSNESS

This is the eighth level of consciousness, sometimes known as the karmic storehouse or the karmic river. This lies on a deeper plane than the consciousness of self and existence. Some teachers describe it as a kind of spiritual database in which wisdom and experience are stored and which remains even after the death of our physical body.

This part of you is what preserves the wisdom and experience through all the cycles of death and rebirth. Storehouse consciousness is where your karma resides. This consciousness is like a spiritual DNA, passed on through each reincarnation. It is the seat of the mind. Through it, the wisdom and learned experiences of all your lifetimes are available to you.

Every moment you are imprinting information on this spiritual DNA. To realize that, with gentleness, is crucial to understanding the call for pure motivation and to stay on the spiritual path at this point.

Karma is undeniable. The good news about karma is it can be changed through gaining merit, through spiritual practice, and through taming your mind, gentling it. The *Divine Mother* is a field of consciousness that can help you to change your karma. Karma in itself is not as literal as we often think it is. If you have something precious stolen from you, it does not mean in another life you stole from someone. Karma does not work like that. It is the intention and vibration of the action that accumulates and with the right causes and conditions, something occurs that matches the vibrational baggage you carry. In a simplistic way, you can think of it as a calling forth from the storehouse consciousness that which is required to help you wake up. When you understand there is a deep part of you that carries through in all your incarnations, there is even more motivation to wake up.

Everything you do relates to this part of your consciousness. To begin to gently explore this, just look at your life here and now. What is working, and what is not? Are you happy? Self-fulfilled? Connected? You can magnetize the conditions for joy if you are willing to give up the obstacles that stand in your way of being truly happy. The first way to touch this wisdom gently is to determine that everything in your life, at this very moment, is of your own creation. Just sit with this gently and call in the *Divine Mothers Kwan Yin* and *Mother Mary* to assist you in your understanding. There is no blame or shame; it is just a time to accept fully where you are right now. What would you choose to have recorded forever and what would you like erased?

The *Divine Mother* will hold you and comfort you as you explore this level of understanding. You can call on *Her* to help you unfold this mystery and provide a spiritual perspective on how to magnetize the spiritual qualities that will enhance your karmic patterns to becoming a fully realized human being.

GENTLE VOICE: SPEECH

Gentle, mild speech is another jeweled wisdom, as well as a quality of sound. It is not a sense but it is important to mention during this gestational time. I feel gentle hearing and speech are interlinked. When you remember one, you remember the other. The sounds you make and the words you speak create form. The *Bible* says, "In the beginning was the word." Words create forms. Your speech is one way you pour your inner self into your immediate environment. It requires vigilance and courage to be responsible for what you say and how you say it. This mirror of self is quite revealing.

Soft, gentle speech does not mean speaking in a whisper. It means speaking with loving tone and clear intention. This includes the inner voice as well as the outer voice.

Language is such a resource. I am fascinated by ancient and magical languages: Cuneiform, Hebrew, Arabic, Sanskrit, Tibetan, Chinese, Greek, Coptic, Runes, Latin, Enochian, Tarot, which originated from hieroglyphs and symbols. Many of these alphabets are sacred codes based in the ancient sciences of numbers and relationship. In many meditation practices there are mantras chanted. The accumulated mantra recitations are potent energy forms of the particular *Deity,* or field of energy, that the practitioners are calling forth within themselves. The mantra is the sound form of the *Deity* that is being evoked. The actual letterforms of the mantra are the shape and form of the energy channels in the body, the wisdom body.

People use language every day without considering meaning, without intention. Words fly out of our mouths at random or will, and often we do not really think about what we are saying and how we are saying it. What are you creating with your words? What world are you bringing into form? If you desire to live in a world of beauty, it is a good idea to consider deeply how you speak and to cultivate your speech with gentleness and kindness.

The language of the heart is beneficial to fostering and creating in our culture, in our world. The world needs this kind of speech so desperately. When you examine the voices that are the most dominant, they are not loving for the most part. Our media, press, and culture hosts a lot of voices and it is productive to notice their timbre and intent. If you spoke that way, what would you be truly saying? When you listen gently, how do these voices make you feel?

It is more fruitful to listen to Masters who have gone before. Their beauty and grace still lives on, transcending time. In Europe, we still find innumerable saints and poets, Gothic chants, alchemists, and environmentalists. Traveling south to the Holy Land, there are many ancient and contemporary layers of teachings from the *Bible* where weeping is heard and many languaged prayers and in Persia, you find the traditions of Rumi, Hafiz, and their beloved Attar. In India and the mountains of a remembered Tibet, there are holy ones chanting *Om* in its many forms. All across the world, ancient indigenous wisdoms chant and drum the great mystery from Australia, Africa, North and South America, Japan, and all across the Mongol Steppes. Island people throughout the great ocean regions of the world still remember the star songs and their guiding message of love. Somehow they remember how to listen and speak with gentleness, with spaciousness, with kindness, with clear intent, which is the voice of the *Divine Mother.*

RECAP

During this fragile time, it helps to know how to be tender. Newness requires it. May this trusting flourish, deepen, and gather and ripen within until you feel safe, secure, and joyful in your exploring and embracing.

May you gather to the sacred springs of your body that which is your way of being here, a blessed gift to the world. May you realize you are luminous, as your gestating seeds of wisdom grow brighter like sunlight, moonlight, and starlight; forming right now new tomorrows, new todays, and new yesterdays, ever so gently.

In this time of gestation, you are beginning to reflect on the unfolding inner landscape and what it reveals to you about yourself. There is an old saying, "You are what you eat." You are also what you feel, see, touch, think, and perceive. You already have everything you need to be gentle with yourself.

When a woman is nurturing new life by carrying a child, *Her* roundness grows and expands. Similarly, when you nurture the *Divine* within, the sacred spheres within you expand. They begin as tiny little seeds of light, like tiny seedlings in early spring with the possibility of new life maturing over time. It is a wise person who is aware of this and caretakes these parts of the self with gentle awareness, gentle sensing, and gentle care.

Gently, gently, you train your mind. Tenderly, you let old

thoughts and habits no longer useful, go. You release any outgrown patterns and seek the peace of a soft silence inside.

- What do you find then? You find the *Divine Mother* and *Her* universe made of love.

- What do you hear? The *Divine Mother's* sacred lullaby.

- What do you taste? The nectar of Love.

- What do you touch? You touch the sacred heart of the *Divine* center of your being.

- What do you realize? Total Enlightenment.

You perceive energy as a stream of light and you find *She* opens your heart to the immense treasures within you.

Moon Mother Goddess Luna

Attunement 5

FLOWER MOON

FIFTH MONTH OF THE LUNAR CALENDAR

*T*HIS NEXT TWENTY-EIGHT DAY CYCLE OF THE *Moon* is known as the fifth month, the month of May, which is traditionally called the *Flower Moon*. It is a perfect time for the gestational phase of your journey. May is when gardens are beginning to bloom and is the time of gentle appearances of new life beginning.

HOME FUN

Take a few moments every day to meditate on gentle breath, feeling the breath softly on your inhale and exhale.

Visualize yourself being held by *Mother Mary* or *Kwan Yin*, or both.

❧ Feel them holding you gently, lovingly and embracing you.

❧ Feel them breathing with you.

❧ This is your sacred essence, the *Divine Mother*, you as a holy being.

❧ When you feel comfortable, ask for their assistance with the new forms growing within you, and the strength and courage to be a gentle presence within your own life. You are creating your own garden within.

❧ Make a note in your journal of what new sacred life forms you are feeling at this time, what aligns with your sacred essence and what does not.

❧ Make a collage of the garden of spiritual delights you are creating through this *Divine Alchemy*.

❧ Create an image of your touchstone; gentleness, and add it to your mandala in whatever way pleases you.

❧ Dedicate all this to the benefit of all.

The Great Round Womb
Of Blessings

Chapter 6

THE GREAT ROUND WOMB OF BLESSINGS

A dark place of blessings this womb,
A magical bowl full of glowing seeds,
Embraced in a wet and fecund silence.

Shan Watters

I LIKE TO THINK OF THE DIVINE MOTHER'S *Great Womb* as a round, holy bundled environment full of a wet, nurturing elixir. It is a rich, fecund place broadcasting deep safety, silence, and spaciousness and, as such, is a perfect place to grow your awareness.

This *Great Round Womb of Blessings* is where you recognize that you are both *Divine* and human. Babies in the womb reside both in heaven and earth, part light, part physical. As they form their physical bodies the possibilities become limitless. The womb is a place of tender and safe nurturing with a silent communication of wonder, joyful expectation, and mystery. This place is a safe haven for the tender stages of new life that is waiting to be born, but still needing to be bundled in a holy way. Feeling safe and secure is essential during this sacred time. What is conceived but not yet born is still so fresh and new it partly resides in the realm of *Spirit*, not yet completely manifest in the physical world. Feeling safe is a welcoming bridge that allows incarnation to expand into becoming. It is here you let yourself be wrapped in a holy bundle that nurtures and protects you in mysterious ways, allowing your own unique magic to begin to grow.

If you are able to experience safety during your time in the womb, you will always feel welcome in its silence. If not you can cultivate this sense of safety as a spiritual aspirant. When you tune into *Her* deep silence, you shift into remembrance of both your humanness and *Divine* nature, simultaneously. Silence is the open seed of the *Divine* in all beings. The writer, Roger Barrie, says the eloquence of the deepest silence echoes from the eternal. Originating in the eternal and reverberating through the ripples of time and space, silence bursts forth in shimmering waves, forming light and color, shadow and dimension but it remains unchanged. Never affected by the slightest permutation of outer phenomena, silence forms the woof and warp of all things seen and unseen and yet, is accessible in any instant. To the mystic and spiritual seeker, silence is the ground. It is the core of reality because everything emanates from it. Why if this is true, don't we seek it more often? It is because the mind is so busy and easily distracted by outer-worldly phenomena. But silence is always there waiting for us.

The *Great Round Womb of Blessings* is the vessel of delicate change in creation's process. It is the place of generating and softly holding in silence while maturing in the light. It is where the wholeness of the *Great Mystery* abides and is available to nurture your creations with the *Divine Mother's* elixir of unconditional love. Every day you and *She* together, add the light of your increasing wisdom to your creations and it grows beyond your imagining in this sacred place of beauty just waiting for intentional direction.

You sense this womb place through your developing awareness and begin the process of manifesting. What do you want to bring to life? What hidden imaginings have you pushed aside, or kept locked in your heart? It is here in this womb that you now bring your dreams and aspirations into form. It is the time to plant the seeds of awareness you want to grow and birth in your life. This includes the prayers for your own goodness, expanded awareness, self-love, compassion, faith, trust, honesty, clear vision, empathy, loving kindness, patience, humility, joy, interconnection, forgiveness, happiness, understanding, health, and wisdom. It is a time of ripening the seeds you have been planting. It is the month of the *Strawberry Moon,* and *Her* power is in increasing holy potentials, qualities, aspirations, and visions.

You wonder at this new mystical life you are carrying, this new understanding of your innate holiness arising. How will it appear? How will you feel as it grows? How will it change our life? Many questions arise and you look back to what you know and where you have come from. You know if you are clear with your intention and gentle with yourself, all these musings will quiet down to join these miracles growing within. The vastness of this pristine space speaks in silence and this awareness arises from veiled seeds of wisdom longing to become fertile.

Bring in the *Divine Mother* and ask what is not a part of *Her*? You cannot name anything that is not part of *Her* because from *Her* all life arises. That flower over there, is an expression of *Her* beauty.

That wave is an expression of *Her* gift of life to you. That fire is an expression of *Her* spirit and yours. Heartbeat to heartbeat, you are *One*. You are vast, you are a part of it all and it is all a part of you. It is the *Divine Mother* manifesting within and without. It is *Her* womb and *Her* womb is the mandala of life. Is *Her* vastness not a part of you? Vastness expands your awareness. *Her* vastness is your vastness where anything becomes possible.

Angerona is the Roman *Goddess of Silence*. *She* is depicted wrapped within layers of veils and a finger always closes *Her* mouth. *She* represents the ancient, secret magical name of Rome, which was not spoken aloud by anyone because it was too powerful. Only the priests and priestesses could utter the sound of *Her* name. Interestingly, *She* is also the *Goddess* of the winter Solstice who helps the sun get through this darker period of time when day time is short and the night time is longer. *She* is less known and more obscure than most of the Roman *Deities*, but *She* is a subtle whisper in their multitude. *She* is almost invisible except *Her* presence is palpable when you tune into *Her* and *She* is full of many secrets that are revealed to you only in silence. When *She* speaks the universe answers in silence and in your own heart you must find the courage to go where *She* is calling you.

How do you learn to be silent so that you can reside in this vast, nurturing womb space? There are voices here that do not use words, so you have to learn to listen. How will you learn to listen to them? One way to listen to your own innate wisdom is to tune into your intuition; your inner knowing. Intuition is the voice of silent, hidden knowledge. You are always in a relationship with this hidden knowledge but often do not realize it because your mind is on other things. That is why the *Mother Goddess Angerona* is both present and elusive; it is the same as your own wisdom voice of intuition. It is both present and elusive as well.

Silence is commonly thought of as the absence of communication, but that is not so. All sound emanates from silence, which means silence is pregnant with potential. Silence is also regenerating and reviving, providing the busy mind a place to rest and an opportunity to hear deeply within itself where your own innate wisdom lives.

Learning to be silent takes graduated steps. Begin with ten minutes a day of sitting in silence and then increase your time as you are able. Find a quiet spot in your home or in nature and allow yourself to relax into it gradually, over time. Sometimes it is beneficial to do a day or weekend of silence in your home and invite members of your family to join in. Recently, I did this and everyone in my home was quiet, my husband and the cats and dog. We learned how much we communicated instinctively with each other and it was a wonderful experience for my husband and me. I was able to hear my own inner voices more deeply. It is interesting to note how deeply instinctive communication really is.

In Babylonia, the powerful and fecund *Mother Goddess Ishtar* was the most important cult *Goddess* in ancient times and embodied many aspects of the *Divine Mother. She* is the daughter of the *Moon Goddess* and has stars as part of *Her* raiment. Interestingly, *She* is also associated with the lion, the way *Durga* is in India, which denotes royalty and great power. For the Assyrian people, *She* was the ultimate *Mother Goddess. Her* womb opened to the entire sky and as such, *She* was known as an opener and sustainer of the womb of silence. Call upon *Ishtar* to assist you in finding your own deep silence where you can hear more deeply the silent sounds of your own wisdom voice. *Her* lion aspect will boost your own bravery and allow *Her* to help you open to the wisdom of the *Divine Mother's* womb, which we are enfolded in all the time. *Ishtar* is a beloved *Mother Goddess* and you can call upon *Her* to assist you to open up to *Her* mysteries when you want some womb time.

Intuition is something you can learn to trust. Intuition lives and is fed by the womb's silent voice. It is the direct perception of truth, without need of any verification. You know, when you know. Spiritual intuition is experience of the transcendent beyond any intellectual process. It is the inner knowing perception that one navigates through the heart with deep surrender. Through practice, we can learn to listen to our spiritual intuition rather than the everyday voice of the senses, the ego, and the normal way of perceiving.

My own journey with intuition has taken a lifetime to understand and accept. I was a very sensitive child, born in between two boys. I never really felt like I fit into my family and often wondered if they accidently gave me to the wrong people in the hospital. The only thing that made me know they hadn't was that I resembled family members, physically.

For as long as I can remember, back to when I was a little girl, I have been able to sense things and see things that were seemingly unnoticeable to others. This made my family and others uncomfortable. If I said I could "see" something, my brothers would make fun of me. If I said I could hear voices in the natural world–the trees, the stones, flowers, etc.–my mother would dismiss it all as child's silly nonsense. When I sensed someone was telling a lie or distorting a fact, they would say I was crazy.

My father was a Marine fighter pilot. When I was three years old, he was called up to fight in the Korean War. The day he was scheduled to ship out happened to be my cousin's birthday. I was all dressed up to go to the party. When it was time for my father to leave, I insisted on going to the base with my parents to say goodbye. I had a fit when they tried to talk me out of it. I just didn't want him to leave and cried and cried and begged him not to go until finally, they gave in. On the tarmac he took the ribbon out of my hair and put it in his jacket pocket. He kissed me and said goodbye and climbed into his plane.

Soon after that, I had a terrible vision. My father was in a burning plane that was about to crash. I screamed and ran to my Mom and told her what I had "seen." She stared at me and frowned telling me to go away and play. The next day, two uniformed officers came to our home to notify my mom that my father had been shot down in a skirmish over Korea exactly at the time I had my vision. He was presumed to be dead. My mother looked at me, came over and picked me up and threw me against the wall screaming that I was a little witch. It is the earliest psychic event I can recall.

After that I never trusted my mother or myself again. I learned to keep what I saw to myself, because in my child's mind, I was sure

I had killed my father. To complicate matters even more, after the news about my father, my mom became very ill and was hospitalized. I thought I had made her sick as well. My visions, hearing, and perceptions became very dangerous to me. I hid them from everyone. I believed they could hurt others. They terrified me. To this day, I am still cautious about sharing what I know and see, but I trust my intuition a lot more. It is a healing journey. The more I rely upon the *Divine Mother*, the more this all eases and the more I am healed.

Growing up in the fifties and sixties, all the powerful spiritual icons I knew of were male, but I kept seeing the angelic presence of *Mother Mary*. *She* became a great comfort to me and as I grew older, more manifestations of the *Divine Mother* would appear when I was in trouble, needed comfort, or perceived things that seemed invisible to others. There were many, many times in my rebellious youth that I did foolish and dangerous things, but I always felt protected by *Her*. I would hear a deep toning that I have come to realize was the sound of *Durga*, the beautiful Hindu *Mother Goddess*. Slowly and over my lifetime, I have come to understand that the entire creation of the physical world arises as an expression of the *Divine Mother*. Bit by bit, I learned to trust in *Her*.

After my father died, we went to live with my grandmother for a while. She was a tiny leprechaun of a woman, who actually left bits of food and milk out on the stoop for the *Little Ones*. It was through her I began to realize that there were other people who sometimes saw things that were invisible to most. It was a tentative beginning but she helped to reopen the world of magic within me.

Over the years as I grew up, it seemed the more I tried to squelch this tendency, the stronger it became. I began to hear what people were thinking and knew when something was going to happen. In the sixties, my reality expanded through the music and the social changes that were occurring. I purposely and consciously wanted to expand my awareness. Something in me began to understand the limitations of my old ways of thinking. I felt caged and I wanted out of the reality constraints I grew up with. It was a strong, motivating force that began to lead me on a lifetime of searching for spiritual truth.

These days, many, many people do not trust their intuition or choose to ignore and bury it. It is their way of ignoring the voice of the *Divine Mother* within. Their relationship to this inner knowing might not have resulted in the dramatic circumstances mine did, but it doesn't matter the degree. It is the habit of ignoring that you need to be aware of and heal.

Your inner knowing is the foundation of trust and real connection to the *Divine*. Intuition is the gestating form of having holy sight, holy knowing, and holy awareness. Spiritual intuition is a key to developing your awareness and expanding beyond what you know. When you sense into the relative world, when you utilize spiritual intuition you can expand beyond the visible world to higher states of awareness.

What is intuition? Intuition is the ability to acquire knowledge without inference or the use of reason. The word intuition comes from the Latin verb intueri, which is usually translated as, "To look inside or to contemplate beyond normal perception." Spiritual intuition is a state of awareness that is beyond condition; it is a hyper-perception.

> *"Intuitive realization is the king of sciences,*
> *it is the direct perception of truth...*
> *the imperishable enlightenment,*
> *attained through ways very easy to perform."*

Krishna (The Bhagavad Gita)

Intuitive realization, or spiritual intuition, is being one with your essence, or natural state. You can begin to develop this through quieting your mind and listening deeply in silence. Silence is so nurturing, as is solitude. Silence and solitude are both very beneficial at this stage because outer worldly distractions are a strong habit and pull us away from our inner sensing, which is an important part of intuition and a vital part of this stage of our journey. Harnessing what you have learned from becoming gentle through your sensing is extremely beneficial in developing a deeper level of intuitive realization because you begin to touch the inner realms through the surrendered energy of gentleness.

Intuitive realization is the *Divine Mother's* wisdom spring from which all the awakened senses arise. *Her* awakened senses include the psychic-intuitive senses or the higher subtle senses of clairsentience (clear sensing), clairaudience (clear hearing), clairvoyance (clear seeing), clairol faction (clear smelling), and clairgustant (clear tasting).

Many people have some amount of psychic awareness, naturally. Psychic awareness operates on a higher frequency band of energy than the normal everyday senses and full intuitive realization operates on a higher energy frequency than psychic awareness. To transform psychic awareness into the higher vibration of intuition requires empathy. Empathy is like compassion, but with a felt-sense awareness through the heart center. Empathy always involves others. Negative emotions such as jealousy, fear, anxiety, hate, and anger disturb the natural electrical frequencies of the heart rhythms, whereas positive emotions are supportive. To be coherent with the higher vibrations of intuitive realization you will need to learn how tame your mind and emotions so your natural empathy flows clear, pure, and resonant.

Empathy ranges from physical empathy where you register others' physical conditions; feeling empathy where you feel others' emotion; mental empathy where you can sense causes and conditions of others; relational empathy to determine others' needs; verbal empathy, or channeling; visual empathy or revelations; spiritual empathy, which utilizes many methods to help others; shamanic empathy to visit other realms; soul empathy, which involves world harmony; natural empathy, which reveals wisdom through the natural world; and force empathy, which harnesses various energetic forces to help others. Empathy is the innate capacity in the Mothering the *Divine* journey to share or recognize emotions and experiences of another sentient being.

In this sacred space of the *Divine Mother's* womb, you do not need to seek your intuition because it is innate. All that is required is that you listen. The actor, Alan Alda, once said, "You have to leave the city of your comfort and go into the wilderness of your intuition where you will discover something wonderful; yourself." Your intuition is the doorway to your own true nature and the space where you find it, is in the womb of silence.

This protected silence is reviving and expectant in this holy space of becoming. When you relax into this rich silence your mind becomes still and all the senses retreat. The avenues of consciousness that are higher in vibration than your normal sensing, may take over and begin to intuit the mystery of these mystical seeds within. Your inner knowing begins to recognize its wisdom.

His Holiness the Dalai Lama teaches that there are different levels of consciousness. The more rough or gross levels are very heavily dependent upon the physical or material sphere. Since one's own physical aggregate (the body) changes from birth to birth, so, too, do these gross levels of consciousness. The subtler the level of consciousness, the more independent of the physical sphere and hence the more likely it will remain from one life to the next.

In His Holiness' teaching it is clear that one's consciousness is always evolving from lifetime to lifetime. The deep, rich, life-force enhancing realm of the *Divine Mother's* womb is the perfect condition for this to happen. It is like a cocoon where you get to be held in a soft embrace while growing, daily. Sally Kempton says that every part of life is permeated with the love of the *Goddess* from our heart to the heart of the universe and until we find *Her*, we are always looking outside ourselves. Through this womb time of tuning into your intuition, you begin to tune into the love of the *Divine Mother* inside of you and feel *Her* presence. You are able to look within yourself safely, securely, and with *Her* assistance.

Another quality of this sacred womb is spaciousness itself. The vastness of this spaciousness you find yourself in, is like a spiritual vitamin. Spaciousness always makes a situation healthier, better, and more relaxed. This vastness is your wholeness, the entire circle of your being. You take this vitamin of awareness with gratitude and sit for a while breathing slowly into yourself, going deeper and deeper.

Try to imagine a limitless space. Then try to imagine a limitless, luminous space where anything is possible. This spacious expanse is the *Divine Mother's Great Womb of Blessings*. It is the consecrated space of all holy origin. It is the birthplace of your magical life. You just have to recognize it and call upon it. Look to the sky or to the open sea and then look inside. It is all there. It is who you are and you don't have it access it, just remember and feel it.

Your body is 78 percent water, your blood is composed of the same saline content as the ocean, and 99.99 percent of each atom in your body is space. If you took the entire amount of real physical matter of all human beings on this planet, it would condense down into the size of an average sugar cube. That is not much matter and a whole lot of space! Imagine all physical matter condensed to the size of a sugar cube! You are mostly space too, so this place of deep space is a place of refuge and a remembering of your own true nature; spaciousness.

There are many, many *Mother Goddess*es associated with the sky that are the *Mother*s of space, silence, intuition, and life. Aditi is one of my favorites. *She* is the powerful Vedic *Mother Goddess* who is not only the *Mother* of all the *Gods* and kings as well as all twelve zodiacal spirits from whose cosmic matrix the heavenly bodies were born. *She* is the *Mother* of space and silence. *Her* history is very ancient, revered, and remembered. *She* is a reliable form-holder for this aspect of space and silence and feels unlimited and vast as you tune into *Her*. While attuning, it is very helpful to chant *Her* mantra,

OM SRI DURGAYA NAMAH.

Another beautiful heavenly star *Goddess* from the Celtic tradition is *Arianrhod*, who is often identified as the *Goddess* of *Reincarnation*. She represents the *Mother* aspect of the *Triple Goddess* in Wales and *Her* palace was *Caer Arianrhod*, or what is now known as the secret center of one's spiritual being, which is your own true nature. *Arianrhod* is not only powerful, *She* is still very present today and completely available to assist you in accessing the deep space within yourself which is also your own spiritual center, which is your Christ-mind, your Buddha-mind, your enlightened nature. This idea is depicted in many sacred geometrical forms, especially traditional mandalas where the center point symbolizes this truth that every single sentient being carries this pure nature of mind within. In other words, the seed is inside you but it is up to you to uncover it.

Nut, the ancient Egyptian *Goddess of Space and the Sky*, is another of my favorites. *She* is depicted as a beautiful female figure arched over with *Her* hands touching the ground. *Her* dark blue body is full of gleaming stars and shining heavenly orbs, radiant and quite gorgeous. *Her* body spans the entire cosmos, exhibiting that *She* is the cosmos and all that resides in it has *Her* blessing. *She* is often shown with a delicately engraved pot on *Her* head when *She* is in a standing position. The idea of the *Mother Goddess* as a maternal womb is embedded in sacred history. Cauldrons, pots, receptacles, and ceremonial bowls are all symbols of the womb and the womb-vessel, which was revered and respected for its inherent fertile and life-giving power in traditions all around the world. The ceremonial bowls in *Nut's* Egyptian temples were called the *Shi*. These bowls were used in various kinds of rituals and held everything from water, herbs, blood, or any other sacred offering. The holy water fount in Christian churches today is also a symbol of the womb that holds the water that bestows blessings or grace. In the Christian tradition, the grace comes from *Jesus Christ* who came from the womb of *Mother Mary*. The womb is the original source of the blessing.

Like *Nut*, the beloved Hindu *Mother Goddess Bhuvaneshwari* is the *Goddess of Infinite Space; She Whose Body is the World. She* is both ancient and contemporary, celebrated still today throughout India. As you try to conceive infinite space, imagine it as *Her* body. Imagine further that every single thing in the physical world is part of this infinite space, including you. This is the truth that we all live in the body of the *Divine Mother Goddess* with *Her* constant blessing and enfoldment. *She* is the highest of beauties, the most beneficent and in this holy place, *She* pours into you the *Divine* nectar of *Her* unconditional love. It is like the amniotic fluid that human babies live in; a magical, blessed light-filled elixir from the *Divine Mother's* heart to the heart of the universe, to the heart of the world, to the heart of you. The nectar of *Her* love is what feeds all beings. This *Divine* nectar of the amniotic fluid is represented in African cosmology as the *Great*

Mother Water Goddess Yemaya. Yemaya represents both the change and constancy of the womb where *She* brings forth life, protects it, and changes it as necessary. All life begins with *Her*, including ideas, dreams, and wishes. *She* resides in the depths and that is where you can find *Her*.

A formal archetypal symbol for this round, rich wholeness inherent within us is the mandala, which is part of the great, round, circle traditions that exists in virtually every culture. The mandala is the *Divine Mother's* womb and is depicted as a circular design that contains concentric circles, geometric forms, and often *Deities*, all of which represent totality or wholeness. Traditionally found in Hinduism and Buddhism, when you delve into the intricately layered symbolism of traditional mandalas, they are about the center; your center. They are the representation of you in a complete, enlightened state of spacious luminosity.

Touching gently the ideal of your own wholeness through sacred art forms, is very powerful. I had the good fortune to be the Project Coordinator on the Shi-tro mandala for Universal Peace Project under the auspices of His Eminence Chagdud Tulku Rinpoche and Lama Gyatso Rinpoche. This five-year project involved building the first three-dimensional Tibetan mandala in the United States; a twelve foot by twelve foot ornate, traditional mandala. While the team of artists worked on the ornate traditional mandala, people would visit the studio site and ask questions. From this interchange, the idea arose in my mind to create a community outreach project available to anyone who utilized the sacred form of the mandala to teach the peace and nonviolence, which are inherent in the mandala's intricate teachings and symbology. From this we created a community arts program entitled, Tools for Peace. Tools for Peace was tested with over 12,000 students in the Los Angeles area and became a curriculum used by many schools in California to this day. Tools for Peace has expanded to having an app called Stop, Look and Listen that is now available to the public and over one million people are using it.

During this five-year project, I witnessed the power of the mandala as a meditational vehicle. This particular mandala was the representation of the sadhana practice of the *Tibetan Book of the*

Dead, where each part had a powerful and hidden meaning for devout practitioners to meditate upon. They say by just seeing the mandala in your lifetime, you will enlighten, just from that blessing alone. I began to understand through meditating with this beautiful creation that it was indeed possible to open your mind to all kinds of states of being to bring benefit to yourself and others.

Japanese mandalas of the *Womb World* are some of the earliest examples of mandalas in Buddhist Asia. In the center is Vairochana, known as the *Buddha of Infinite Light,* who plays an important role in the development of Esoteric Buddhism. The *Womb World* symbolizes the possibility of Buddhahood in the phenomenal world as perceived by the practitioner.

Another mandala that contains the symbol of the womb is the mandala of the *Two Realms* or the mandala of the *Two Divisions,* which contain the *Diamond Realm* and the *Womb Realm.* The *Diamond Realm* represents the unchanging cosmic principle of the *Buddha,* while the *Womb Realm* depicts the active, physical manifestation of the *Buddha* in the natural world. The two together represent the totality of the *Dharma* and form the root of the Tibetan Vajrayana teachings. Interestingly, in Vajrayana Buddhism the *Womb Realm* is the metaphysical space inhabited by the *Five Wisdom Kings* who are the third type of *Deity* after *Buddhas* and *Bodhisattvas.* In Vajrayana they are known as *Herukas.* The womb in all these mandalas is the *Great Divine Mother,* who is the *Mother* of all *Gods,* kings, enlightened beings, and you.

"There is a voice that doesn't use words, listen."

Rumi

This beautiful line is the perfect instruction here. Go into your womb time to explore the expansive silence and spaciousness and to taste the sweet elixir of the *Divine Mother's* unconditional love in complete safety. See what is reflected back to you through your inner knowing and ask what wants to emerge, to come forth, to be born now from deep within you. Call upon the *Strawberry Moon Mother* to help you ripen your spiritual intuition through the blessing of silence and spaciousness. This womb is a magical space where dreams begin to come true and to manifest in the physical world

Moon Mother Goddess Luna

Attunement 6

STRAWBERRY
MOON

SIXTH MONTH OF THE LUNAR CALENDAR

THE STRAWBERRY MOON CYCLE IS ALL ABOUT ripening through blessings. The seeds in the garden have been planted and it is time for them to ripen to their most glorious fullness. How does ripening happen? It is the same mystery that brings a fetus to full term. It is blessing of the *Divine Mother*, cloaked in mystery, silence and spaciousness. Spaciousness contains the unlimited potential that the *Mother's Great Womb* offers to all beings to grow and mature to their full ripeness, to get ready for birth.

HOME FUN

❧ Spend the *New Moon* days of this cycle in a regular practice of silence and spaciousness.

❧ Light a candle

❧ As the light of the *Moon* begins to grow, tune into the seeds of awareness arising within you. Carefully and with intention, write them down on a piece of paper and place them in a ceremonial bowl.

❧ Place your ceremonial bowl next to the candle.

❧ On the other side, place your mandala.

❧ You have created an altar to attend and focus on daily. You can add whatever other elements feel right to you, including pictures of the *Divine Mother*, flowers, offerings, quotes, and incense.

❧ Sit with your mandala and reflect upon the messages in it.

❧ When the *Moon* reaches *Her* fullest point, take the papers in the bowl and place them in a pan and burn them. Scatter the ashes in a garden or in the sea as an offering of goodness and interconnection so they will continue to grow inside the *Divine Mother*.

Birth Of The Divine Child

Chapter 7

Muhammad spoke to his friends about a newborn baby,
"This child may cry out in its helplessness,
But it does not want to go back to the darkness of the womb.

And so it is with your soul when it finally leaves the nest,
And flies out into the sky over the wide plain of a new life,
Your soul would not trade that freedom for the warmth of where it was.

Let loving lead your soul and make it a place to retire to,
A kind of monastery cave, a retreat for the deepest core of being.

Then build a road from there to God,
Let every action be in harmony with your soul,
And its soul-place,
But don't parade those doings down the street.

Keep quiet and secret with your soul-work,
Don't worry so much about your body,
God sewed that robe. Leave it as it is.
Be more deeply courageous.
Change your soul."

Ariduddin Attar

*O*NE COLD WINTER DAY IN 1996, I WAS IN retreat in Vermont at the *Sunray Peace Village* and I had a vision of the five *Dhyani Buddhas* coming down from the top of Hope Mountain, Odali Utugi, to assist in the birthing of the *Divine Child* within me. It was twenty degrees below zero, with the sun so bright the snowfields glowed with glittering light, and the sharpness of the air seemed to make everything vivid, including my senses. It was a moment of total clarity. Everything seemed possible. It was as if the streams of grace flowed uninhibited and I felt myself opening to the great love of being one with the cosmos. The five *Mother Goddesses*, the *Dhyani Buddhas,* celebrated, danced, and sang and the experience became ecstatic.

Divine Beings who assist in life's constant birthing are always available to us. If you look around, something or someone is always birthing. Every day at dawn the day is born as the heavens display this phenomena of birth. The cosmic *Mother* is always birthing new forms, new life, new awareness, and new opportunities. In a sense, every moment is a moment of birth for you, illustrated in this quote by Gabriel Garcia Marquez,

"She allowed herself to be swayed by her conviction that human beings are not born once and for all on the day their mothers give birth to them, but that life obliges them over and over again to give birth to themselves."

You are birthing yourself all the time and at this point of your journey you open yourself to recognize this. Birthing marks the beginning of the act of bringing forth, the point of origination. It is the time of making manifest in the physical world, to incarnate, to embody. It is when your intention materializes into the physical realms. The physical form, the body, is made new at birth but the soul is as ancient as the universes. Transformation is present in the birth process as a new life emerges, full of hidden potential. The writer, Normandi Ellis says we are like *Gods* in hiding. Humans have access to all manner of transformative potential, but it requires giving up any idea of the self as a fixed, definable identity. It means experiencing your essential self not as a thing, but as a process. There is no end of becoming. When you lose yourself you meld into the universe. You become the world around you. You enter the mystic state wherein you are inhabited by *Divine* presence. You are *Divine* presence.

The notion of *Divine* presence in birth is worldwide and timeless. Many ancient traditions have stories of magical and *Divine Birth*s. Dr. Marguerite Rigoglioso has researched extensively the traditions in antiquity of virgin births. In a recent lecture at Harvard University she unequivocally stated that the *Virgin-Mother* phenomena did not originate with Christianity. She lists many self-generative-essentially virginal-female creators who become *Virgin Mother Goddesses* in pre-Christian religions and mythology, dating back several thousands of years. These *Virgin Mother Goddesses* include C*hoas, Nyx and Gaia, Athena, Neith, Metis, Artemis, Hera, Demeter, Persephone, Kore,* and *Gnostic Sophia.*

The Egyptians were religiously sophisticated and their *Virgin Mother Goddess Neith* was the *Prime Mover* in the cosmos. *Neith* is portrayed in various forms, being an ancient and complex *Goddess*. *She* usually has a scepter or ankh symbolizing *She* is both the *Queen of Heaven* and a ruler of *Earth.* As a divinity of the *First Principle, Neith* was an autogenetic or self-begetting *Goddess* who, in the ultimate mystery, created *Herself* out of *Her* own being. Autogenetic or self-begetting, means creating oneself out of oneself or self-arising. An inspiration on a statue of *Utchat-Heru,* a high priest of *Neith,* says that, "*She* was the first to give birth to anything, and that *She* had done so when nothing else had been born." *She* had *Herself. Neith* was both autogenetic, or self-arising, and a 7,000 year old *Virgin Goddess*; creating *Herself* out of nothingness and then creating the universe.

In certain Christian traditions the birth of the *Virgin Mary* is seen, as is *Jesus Christ's* birth, as a miracle. According to the tradition of the Catholic Church, the *Virgin Mary's* parents, *St. Anne* and *St. Joachim,* were childless when an angel came to them and told them they would give birth to a daughter. During the conception of *Mary, She* was preserved from the stain of original sin, just as with the conception of *Jesus Christ.*

There are seven miracle births in the *Bible*: I*saac, Jacob* and *Esau*; the Shunammite woman's son; *Samson; Samuel; John the Baptist* and *Jesus*. Their *Mother*s were either barren, beyond child bearing age, had closed wombs, or in the case of *Jesus*, experienced immaculate conception.

In the Judaic tradition the *Second Book of Enoch* states that *Melchizedek* was born of a virgin, *Sofonim*. When he was born he was physically developed, clothed, speaking, and marked with the badge of priesthood.

The Sufi tradition teaches that in 1440 the poet Kabir was born of a *Virgin Mother*, a widow, through the palm of *Her* hand. Interestingly, he was sent down a river in a basket, as in the story of *Moses*.

In Hinduism the *Deity Krishna*, was known as both the agent of conception and also the offspring. Because of *His* sympathy for the *Earth* as the *Divine Vishnu* himself, *He* descended into the womb of *Devaki* and was born as *Her* son. Some Hindus believe that when the emanations of the supreme *Being* are pratyacsha (obvious to the sight), they become sacra (or embodied), like *Krishna. Krishna* was such an embodiment and usually bore a human form. In that mode of appearance, the *Deities* are generally born of a woman but without any carnal intercourse and the birth is a celebration without pain. In all magical birthing stories, the *Mother* is more of an intermediary between the cosmic realms and the human realm. This mystery is something profound to contemplate because it shows the potential of that journey from the *Divine* world to the *Earth* world and vice versa. It is a testament to the hidden capacities you have within you.

This is the time in your spiritual quest to birth the *Divine Child* that has been gestating within you. The *Divine Child* is everything you have begun to embrace about yourself on this spiritual journey. It is the time to bring into the world your awakening consciousness surrounded and held within the loving embrace of the *Divine Mother*. When this happens, you sense that you are having the simultaneous or multidimensional experience of both giving birth and being born. When you surrender to the *Divine Mother* through your willingness, you feel connected and become a part of the birthing as well as being birthed. There is no separation in the experience. The *Divine Mother* within you takes over and it becomes a flow.

How do you embrace *Divine Birth* for yourself? First you acknowledge that it exists and has throughout human history. Next you examine the lives of the beings that were born magically, all of whom became great benefactors to human kind and helped to accelerate and advance human consciousness. In coming into the world in a *Divine* and intentional manner, these beings inform all humans that they too can experience an intentional *Divine Birth* and live lives of meaning and magic. Ask for your own *Divine Birth* and prepare to experience it in the very best way that you can. Since you are already in a human body, it becomes your choice to do this symbolically and as many times as feels right to you. It is a consciousness you can embrace throughout your life. When you open your eyes in the morning, you are being birthed into a new day. When you awaken your consciousness every step becomes an emergence into the light. Consciousness is always expanding and birthing. It is the first step towards the empowering energetic of awakening.

The *Buddha* himself embodied the fruition of human potential, the attainment of infinite knowledge, wisdom, and compassion. Buddhist teachers say this led to the realization that human life is very precious. My teacher, His Eminence Chagdud Tulku Rinpoche, taught this to all his students saying that the human body is a peerless vehicle for attaining enlightenment and a human body is extremely rare and precious. Only those with incredibly good karma and vast stores of merit attain a human body. This teaching was taught over and over and it changed my attitude about so many things. Whenever I start to feel sorry for myself or bored or want to be idle, I think of this teaching and it spurs me into more positive states of mind and action. It also totally changed my relationship with my mother. She gave me life, and I honor and love her now because she gave me the gift of a human life. What a gift of love.

During a series of yearlong teachings called the *Bodhisattva Peace Training* given by Lama Shenpen Drolma, I witnessed this teaching transform the lives of several gang members. One experience, in particular, has always stayed with me. A young man from the Bronx really hated his mother. She was a hard-core junkie on the streets and sold herself to pay for drugs. She gave him up at birth and his grandmother raised him and he rarely saw his mother after that. He really despised his mother. Through this teaching, he was able to soften his view and emotions bit-by-bit and over time, eventually reached the realization that he loved his mother and was grateful to her for the gift of life. He vowed to find her and get her off the street. It was a profound and moving transformation to witness.

The *Buddha* himself had a magical birth. His *Mother, Queen Maya*, is exalted and his birth is celebrated as a cosmic event. *She* gave birth in a forest, in a sacred grove where all the other women of *Her* lineage gave birth under the watchful care of the grove's *Mother Goddess*. The *Goddess* created a celebratory environment by hanging jewels and flower garlands from the trees and all the lotuses blossomed in the ponds. When the *Buddha* sprang out of *Queen Maya's* right side, the *Earth* shook, celestial music was heard, and rainbows appeared in the sky. *Queen Maya* experienced no discomfort during *Her* pregnancy and the birth was painless.

The Buddhist scholar, Miranda Shaw, says that in a stream of visionary ecstasy the *Goddess* became the miracle that took place in *Queen Maya's* body, beginning with an outpouring of brilliant light. All the lights in the billion-world universe were eclipsed by *Queen Maya's* light. The lights emanated from all *Her* pores pervading everywhere and extinguishing all suffering and illuminating the universe. *Queen Maya's* womb attained cosmic proportions, universes streamed forth from *Her* body while everything in this universe was in turn visible in *Her* womb. All the worlds, lands, and *Buddhas* were visible in each of *Her* pores.

Teachings in the *Perfection of Wisdom* tradition elevates the concept of birth and Motherhood above even that of Buddhahood itself. This philosophy introduces this cosmic female who embodies the radiant wisdom that gives birth to *Buddhas*. The *Goddess* is *Prajnaparamita*, or *Perfect Wisdom*, and is known as the *Mother of all Buddhas*.

The entire edifice of *Prajnaparamita* philosophy is built upon the principle that the birth-giver is greater than the one who is born. One of the daily practices I do is *Red Tara* practice. *Red Tara* is one of the twenty-one aspects of the *Goddess Tara. She* is also known as the *Mother of all the Enlightened Ones. She* represents the same recognition that the *Mother* is greater than all the *Buddha*s because of *Her* capacity to birth them. In Tantric practices and philosophy it is stated that those who fail to honor women cannot attain liberation. I love this quote by Master Thich Nhat Hanh,

Dear Mother,
You have given birth to countless Buddhas,
saints, and enlightened beings. Shakyamuni Buddha is
a child of yours. Jesus Christ is the son of God, and yet he is
also the son of Man, a child of the Earth, your child.
Mother Mary is also a daughter of the Earth.
The Prophet Mohammed is also your child. Moses is your child.
So too are all the Bodhisattvas. You are also mother to eminent
thinkers and scientists who have made great discoveries,
investigating and understanding not only our own
solar system and Milky Way, but even the most distant galaxies.
It's through these talented children
that you are deepening your communication with the cosmos.
Knowing that you have given birth
to so many great beings, I know that you
aren't mere inert matter, but living spirit.
It's because you're endowed with the capacity of
awakening that all your children are too.
Each one of us carries within our self the seed of awakening,
the ability to live in harmony with our deepest wisdom—
the wisdom of inter being.

Sacred birth of the *Divine Child* begins in the womb of consciousness where you are birthed by the *Divine Mother's* love, through the agreement with *Mother Earth, Gaia*, who holds the pure elemental frequencies for all that takes a physical form on *Earth*. The *Divine Mother* and *Mother Earth* are expressions of the same being and their love is unconditional and limitless. When you are already in a human body, the act of *Divine Birth* is created through the harmonious sacred marriage of both the *Sacred Feminine* and the *Divine Masculine*. The *Divine Child* is the resulting energy. In yoga practice, this is traditionally when *Shakti* kundalini arises in the spine. Herein it is metaphoric as the time for the dominant masculine forces within each person are subdued and balanced with the *Divine Feminine* forces now arising and coming back into consciousness through the *Shakti* energy experienced in the body.

These energies are a trinity of active, passive and neutral principles–the *Divine* essence of the masculine, feminine and child energies are innate in each human being. The *Sacred Feminine* is known as passive in this regard only; *Her* energetic frequencies. This is why you have been working with gentleness, silence, spaciousness, and intuition. These are all *Sacred Feminine* qualities. It is time for them reemerge so that they can merge with the *Divine Masculine* and create a *Divine Child* of joy and balance within you. When this *Divine* trinity is balanced within you, you become whole and so does the land where you reside. This is because the land responds to human consciousness. Our *Mother Gaia* is calling forth the hearts of people to help bring balance and harmony once again. It is a reliable pathway to the attainment of enlightenment and virtually necessary for our survival. Human consciousness and the physical world impact each other and are interlinked.

What is the *Sacred Feminine*? The *Sacred Feminine* celebrates everything that supports and honors life. It is the celebration of the creative energy within. The *Sacred Feminine* recognizes the importance of cultivating right-relationship with all that lives on *Mother Earth* and honoring *Her* for all *Her* gifts of life to us. It is consciously being aware of interconnection, the web of life. It encourages you to celebrate your intuition and rest the intellect at times. It helps you to listen to others and meet then through the heart by being peaceful and loving. It means cultivating loving sight, ecstatic taste, soft touch, openhearted hearing while embracing your sensuality. When you are not able to reach this consciousness you can sit in silence until it arises in your heart. When you surrender and trust in the *Divine*, you become a fountain of life and are able to delve into your capacity for understanding and inner guidance. You become a nurturer. You bloom with life and creativity and the being side of your nature is fully awakened.

On the other hand, what is the *Divine Masculine*? The qualities of the *Divine Masculine* arise naturally out of the ground of being of the *Sacred Feminine*, which are both gifts from the *Divine Mother* and *Father*. They are different sides of the same coin. They only appear separate because you live in this human dimension of duality. The *Divine Masculine* is active intelligence through disciplined, aware, strong, stable activity. It speaks of directness, purpose and becoming a *Divine Guardian* through inspired action. A single-minded focus that enables you to accomplish what you set out to do is celebrated here. It is being protective and far seeing. It is to act with wisdom that benefits the children, seven generations from now. It is the enlightened practical aspect of your mind where heroes arise to help others. It is where being linear brings power and focus to an activity and where your enlightened intent is firm and powerful. It is the sun shining on the quiet moon-draped elusive *Feminine* qualities enhancing and acting upon their wisdom. It means to have the wisdom to recognize the ground of being is the *Divine Mother* wisdom energy.

The *Divine Child* is the perfect balancing of this cosmic harmonic and your inner knowing and intuition guides your enlightened action. This cosmic harmonic sings clearly when your spaciousness is allowed in every decision and action and your goodness pervades all that you see, hear, touch, and feel. The *Divine Child* recognizes and feels the interconnection of all life and considers and celebrates this in every action within the sphere of unconditional love. The state of unconditionally accepting, honoring, and respecting the profound, ancient, wise being that flows back and forth between the *Sacred Feminine* and the *Divine Masculine* emerges in the *Divine Child*. The two energies are so supportive, they become one and it is a celebration of *Divine Love*, the *Divine Child*. The essence of both the *Sacred Feminine* and the *Divine Masculine* is love.

PREPARATION FOR THE BIRTH OF THE DIVINE CHILD

The birth of the *Divine Child* is an initiation into pure consciousness. To prepare for this birth requires willingness, humility, and letting go of the old way of thinking of yourself. It requires being able to step into your new way of being through trusting that you are worthy. This recognition arises through your spiritual intuition and you experience it as a subtle shift of energy.

When you are ready, the light begins to circulate within. At this moment you feel the *Moon Mother*'s energy supporting you. You begin to imagine and visualize yourself as totally pure and radiant. A Chinese text entitled, The *Secret of the Golden Flower*, says that when light is made to move in a circle, all the energies of heaven and *Earth*, of the light and dark, are crystallized. That is seed-like thinking or purification of the energy, or purification of the idea. Over the course of time, with concentrated work, it will become a genuine light known as the spirit-fire. That is what you are seeking here. The spirit-fire of the *Divine Child*'s pure consciousness, totally balanced, innocent, and wise, all at the same time. Your expanding consciousness is a sign that the birth of the *Divine Child* is imminent.

When you are aware of a clear sense of the light within, it is time to prepare for your birthing ceremony by purifying yourself with a bath. If you have a window, open it to the *Moon Mother*'s light and let it inculcate your sacred space. A candle can also represent *Her* beautiful glow. In *Her* light, smudge your entire body with sage or incense. You can celebrate your ritual further by anointing your body with sacred oils, perhaps a calming, restorative oil such as lavender. Rose oil is also supportive of the *Sacred Feminine* energies. Then it is time to meditate upon your intention to perform the sacred ceremony of birthing your *Divine Child*. Ask the *Dolphin Moon Mother* to assist you in all aspects of your ceremony.

THE CEREMONIAL BIRTHING

When a baby is about to be born there are signs that it is time. The most dramatic sign is usually when the mother's water breaks.

In this symbolic and multidimensional birthing experience, the water breaking initially releases all emotions and blocks from the one birthing and the one giving birth. Both become anew and are washed with the blessing of the water releasing.

Water is the source of life. It is the only substance found in nature that can be solid, liquid, or gaseous in form. Water and water vapor exist in continuous movements, allowing them to interact with everything around them. Many ancient and contemporary indigenous peoples view water as a living entity and as such, make ceremonial blessings to it. On my shrines are water offerings and I do daily water practices, sending prayers to the element of water. My teacher, the beautiful, Venerable Dhyani Ywahoo, teaches a profound water practice where you offer prayers and appreciation to the water to help purify and balance it and send those blessings out to the entire world. The treasured work of Dr. Masura Emoto is well known, which proves the efficacy of imprinting water with positive energies such as prayer. The water actually responds according to the quality of the prayer or message. Water is responsive, records, and has memory. It is not surprising birth begins with water as a sacred signal to the universe saying, "Hey, we are ready over here and something wondrous is happening!"

Another powerful force in birthing is the *Moon Mother*, who also strongly relates to the element of water. This month's *Dolphin Moon Mother Cycle* is one especially supportive to birth. *Her* gravitational pull causes high tides. Since the human body is made up of 80 percent water, the pull is believed to speed along the childbirth process. Planning your birthing ceremony during the *Full Moon* is very auspicious and supportive, especially in this cycle. The *Dolphin Moon Mother* celebrates joy; dolphins are recognized and loved as beings of high frequency joy. They surround you to celebrate this wondrous event.

Once you have bathed and anointed yourself, light the candle on your *Divine Mother* shrine and smudge the entire space with sage or cedar to cleanse the energies. You can also use a sacred spray or a diffuser to cleanse the space. Fill the bowl on your shrine with pure water.

BIRTH OF THE DIVINE CHILD

Call in all the *Divine Mother* aspects you have been working with. So far in this journey you have met, and traveled with *Atalanta*, the *Moon Mother, Amounet*, the *Snow Moon Mother, Mother Earth*, the *Storm Moon Mother, Cardea, Lady Venus, Dakinis*, the *Crow Moon Mother, Kundalini Shakti*, the *Pink Moon Mother, Kwan Yin, Divine Mother Mary, Flower Moon Mother, Angerona, Ishtar, Aditia, Arianrhod, Nut, Bhuvaneshwari, Yemaya* and the *Strawberry Moon Mother*. Call them forth, asking them to form a sacred circle around you. Send out a prayer of gratitude and clearly state your intention, asking for their assistance and support in this ritual. Ask them to bless the water so that all may go smoothly, painlessly, and with great joy. Add whatever other celebratory elements you like: incense, flowers, crystals, statues, pictures, and/or butter lamps. Dedicate your ceremony for the benefit of all.

At this point, thirteen more aspects of the *Divine Mother* begin to appear, forming an inner circle around you. They are all birthing *Goddesses*. The Greek *Goddess Eileithyia*, the *Goddess* of *Childbirth* comes and raises *Her* arms to welcome the light into the center of the ceremony. *Her* ancient Roman counterpart, *Lucina*, brings to you the power of the lotus with *Her* and at *Her* command a lotus grove sprouts up surrounding the entire birthing circle, filling the air with fragrance. *Aiysyt*, a Siberian *Mother Goddess*, arrives suddenly with *Her* power to provide sustenance for the soul of the newborn energies, closely followed by three powerful Roman *Mother Goddesses* who descend around you: *Candelifer, Diana* and *Deverra*. They clearly invoke the light to be a pathway for the baby to enter the world from the darkness of the womb. The beautiful Nordic *Goddess Frigg* arrives with *Her* arms laden with pungent smelling herbs and sacred grasses that help to ease the entire process and bring comfort to you. In a flurry, *Hathor* arrives from Egypt coming especially to bless the newborn's destiny, and right behind *Her* is *Her* soul sister, *Isis*, who immediately stands right behind you to guide and support you. The radiant Mayan *Goddess* of *Birth and Lunar Cycles, Ixchel*, comes to enhance the *Moon Mother's* power in the space, which now becomes luminous. The Egyptian *Mother Goddess Nephthys* stands by the birthing *Mother's* head to assist you in all aspects of the birthing, and *Ngolimento* from Toga takes great care of the spirit of the *Divine Child* before and during the birthing process, making a sacred energetic pathway for the child to emerge into the light of this sacred circle. The sacred circle of thirteen *Divine Mother Goddesses* of birth is complete when *Nintur* from Sumeria arrives holding the symbolic midwife's pail of blessing water that is shining with the *Full Moon's* light for all present to see. *She* offers a brimming ladle to each being present, including you.

When you taste the water from *Nintur's* pail, the birthing of the *Divine Child* begins, for a *Divine Alchemy* has occurred. The water you taste becomes the blessing elixir from the *Divine Mother's* heart to yours and the *Divine Mother* inculcates your being with this golden nectar of unconditional love, nourishing and sustaining you. *She* becomes the witness of your magical birthing. *She* is holding you; *Her* arms surrounding you from behind. Sitting in *Her* embrace, you are confidant in allowing the birthing to open you into an unknown realm that is somehow held in a distant memory. This unknown world, or consciousness, has been deeply buried within you, but it is there none-the-less. It is a part of you. When you are birthing into this new consciousness, you are like a newborn descending from the womb. The darkness of the womb no longer can sustain you and you must be in the light, for you are light.

In a natural human birth, beauty unfolds in the simple allowance of letting things progress, as they need to. Allowing here is key. Allow the birth to proceed however it needs to. Each birth is individual and unique. It has its own rhythm and cadence and occurrences. It is the same in birthing consciousness. The birth unfolds as the *Divine Mother* and you determine. Lean into the *Goddesses* supporting you in this moment. Take your time. The opening is usually gradual but sometimes it is intense and immediate. The birthing here is the body, heart, and mind opening, and staying open to this new form of being in the world. It is a symbolic emergence into the state of the *Divine Child*, the *Child of Bliss*. It is a tender, ecstatic time. It is a time to enjoy and savor.

As you open more and more, a magical mist envelops the

birthing space and all the *Divine Mothers* and their birthing angels transport you to a celestial realm; the *Divine Birthing Temple*. This *Temple* is guarded and maintained by all the *Mother Deities* and their angels. Arcs of rainbow love-light embrace the entire *Temple*. The *Temple* is a wondrous and sacred place where beings from all dimensions come to experience the miracle of *Divine Birth*. As you approach, you might see some of them. Birthing angels greet you at the entrance and at first you smell the splendid rose fragrance of the *Temple* garden until you enter and see it is full of every flower on *Earth* and some you have never seen before, all laid out in huge curving patterns along the meandering pathways. Multi-dimensions are palpable here and cascading, octavating frequencies of bells, harps, and flutes softly caress you as the angelic birthing angels guide you down the path. The pathways are inlaid with mysterious live symbols and you can stop and enjoy them and the garden whenever you choose to. There is no hurry. All is perfect in *Divine* timing and sometimes the symbols give you a message. Perhaps there is a particular symbol that speaks to you. For example, a circle speaks of your wholeness, a square of stability, and a triangle of strength. Each symbol has meaning.

As you make your way down the living pathways, you experience magical rainbow fountains in all kinds of lyrical and fanciful shapes and sizes attended by myriads of birthing angels. In the center of the garden is a circular golden pavilion held aloft by crystal pillars reflecting golden light in all directions. Between the pillars are garlands of fragrant flowers festooned to meet over the center of the pavilion and hang down to support and hold a giant golden egg inlaid with jewels. It is breathtaking. You make your way to the center of the pavilion and the birthing angels assist you.

Directly below the golden egg is a round, golden enclosure that has a circle of jeweled offering bowls full of scented holy water and golden barley offerings. Thousands of candles form a mandala around the enclosure. The entire space is covered with a golden dome inlaid with precious jewels. It is the holy birthing chamber blessed by the *Divine Mother*. The entire space feels Grecian in its influence with its many graceful crystal columns, flower garlands, mandala, and center birthing space. Together they create a giant sacred geometrical form in perfect proportions. You make your way to the center at your own pace, enjoying the beauty and harmony surrounding and supporting you.

As you approach the enclosure, the birthing angels gather around you, ushering you into it. You settle in and get comfortable, enjoying the feeling of welcome. When you repeat your pure intention to be birthed into this new consciousness, above you the golden egg begins to open. The symbolic water breaks through as the egg opens and its light, soft spiraling showers anoint you with blessings, beginning the actual birth. This holy water flows around you, becoming a liquid blessing. Everything no longer needed is released as this new life is making its way into the world. Open your heart, rely on the *Mother Goddesses* surrounding you, and relax. The more you are able to open your heart the more you birth!

Now the *Divine Mother Sophia,* known as the source of wisdom and the keeper of knowledge appears. *She* was born of silence and *She* gave birth to both male and female who created all the elements of the material world. *She* pours a soma elixir of pure light over you, which transforms all the water into an ocean of siddhis or blessings. All present sing the blessing of the water song,

We love you water. We thank you water.
We respect you water. We are grateful.

The water rinses you, bathes you, soothes you, baptizes you and you are born anew. The *Divine Child* within has fully emerged and you explode with light and love. Your heart is completely, totally open. You are a spirit voyager floating on the blessing water, the ocean of siddhis, a soma elixir full of liquid light. The *Divine* doorway is open wide and held in the highest vibrations by all the *Divine Mother* witnesses and angels gathered here who are singing to you and beaming you with love rays. It is a time of celebration and victory. Another one remembers and awakens.

A warm, delicious glow is felt by all, as both the surrender and opening is complete. Your pure intention is accomplished. You have emerged through the grace of the *Divine Mother* as *Her Divine Child*. When you feel your heart has been filled to full capacity, you can rise from the water into the arms of your most beloved *Divine Mother*.

Imagine your self being received and held in the arms of the *Divine Mother Mary*, or *Kwan Yin*. Sit in meditation and feel this *Divine* blessing fill you and the *Divine Child* you are. You are loved, you are light, you are made anew. *Her* love is eternal, infinite, and unconditional. You are being celebrated, welcomed, and loved completely for you own uniqueness; you are a treasure. You bask in the warm, safe, and beloved energies, and the empowerment of you having birthed this *Divine* consciousness. Let this new consciousness completely fill every pore, every cell in your body. Use your breath to make the deepest soul imprint you can. Feel into your ancestral lineage and all the way down the line feel it healing. Feel the activation of your genetic blueprint to be full of light in every cell. Every memory, everything that has ever happened or will happen is now emerging with a high vibration in your activated consciousness. You are expanded. You have changed. When you change, the whole world changes.

When you feel your heart has been filled to capacity, you can quietly make your way down the garden pathway, accompanied by the *Divine Mother* and gradually make your way back to your home, your own sacred space, carrying this consciousness with you always. Make prayers of appreciation, you have arrived anew, blessed and fulfilled. You have emerged from the cocoon. Welcome home and Namaste.

NAMASTE

I honor the place in you in which the entire Universe dwells,
I honor the place in you that is full of Love, Integrity, Wisdom and Peace,
When you are in that place in you,
And I am in that place in me,
We are One.

Moon Mother Goddess Luna

Attunement 7

DOLPHIN MOON

SEVENTH MONTH OF THE LUNAR CALENDAR

DOLPHINS ARE RECOGNIZED AND LOVED AS symbols of high frequency joy. Many believe *Dolphins* are more intelligent than human beings, especially when it comes to love. As water-beings, *Dolphins* relish water both physically and mentally. *Dolphins* love to play. In fact much of their time is spent playing and they have a wise, innocent purity that touches people deeply. They are perfect teachers/companions for the newly birthed *Divine Child*.

In this twenty-eight day cycle of the *Dolphin Moon Mother* begin to tune into your own sense of play and wonder.

Home Fun

❧ Add some small toys to your mandala/altar space.

❧ During the *New Moon* imagine the world anew. Your senses are newborn and so what would they be like?

❧ During the twenty-eight day cycle of the *Dolphin Moon Mother* how does your new perception of the world around you change and grow?

❧ How does your being in the world in this new consciousness change your actions and relationships?

❧ Make a list of things you like to do to play.

❧ Take time every day to play.

❧ Journal what you do daily to play, to refer to in the future.

❧ InJoy!!!! You have brought something new to life!

Please visit: www.motheringthedivinewisdom.com

for a free guided meditation of the Birth of the Divine Child.

Infancy

Chapter 8

Carrying vitality and consciousness,
Embrace them as one,
Can you keep them from parting?
Concentrating energy,
Making it supple,
Can you be like an infant?

Purifying hidden perception,
Can you make it flawless?
As understanding reaches everywhere,
Can you be innocent?

Knowing the male, keep the female,
Be humble to the world,
Be humble to the world and eternal power never leaves,
Returning again to innocence.

Tao Te Ching

*I*NFANCY IS A TENDER TIME FULL OF SOFT sighs and lullabies. Your heart increasingly opens to the expansive consciousness you have chosen to birth, as well as to the arising of your innate *Mothering* instincts of nurturing and protection. This multi-faceted awareness continues until both are fully integrated. *Mothers* need to pause after birth to reorient and recover, so this is the time to go into the deep stillness of your being. There is a regenerative and restorative energy available in the richness of silence. Sit with the realization that both the *Divine Child* and the *Divine Mother* are aspects of your being that are longing to awaken the mystical childhood that is your birthright.

Now that you have allowed this glorious birthing to happen there is a delicious time of sweet greeting and getting to know your *Divine Child*. Wonderment arises from the pure, joyous realization of meeting this aspect of your own being, opening to it and letting it breathe with glorious, transcendent aliveness. This new way of being also evokes many tender questions. How do you open yourself more completely to love this radiant *Divine Child*?

After the wonderment often comes bewilderment, which is simply, wow, how do I live this new consciousness and who am I to think I can? This juncture in the *Mothering the Divine* process is a chosen revolution. You begin to reshape your mind and entire being with a holy blazing interconnection on multi-levels. Reintegrating of the playful, innocent, free, and delightfully alive qualities of the *Divine Child* combined with the *Divine Mother's* enormous love wisdom, is transformative and life changing. But it can also be bewildering because we can feel a profound resistance towards this tremendous high frequency energy.

It is vital to reflect here upon the fact that this path of awakened consciousness is your *Divine* heritage. Every single sentient being has the seed of *Buddha-mind*. Every single sentient being has the seed of *Christ-mind*. In an ultimate sense there is no difference, as awakened mind is awakened mind. This means all beings carry within them a sacred seed of holy awareness embodied by the *Divine Child*.

The *Divine Mother* guarantees this is all a tangible vision. You don't have to figure it all out, just learn to trust and it will unfold in the highest way of truth for you through your clear intent. It will arise naturally in this process as the *Divine Child* awakens in you.

Throughout time, there have been some incarnations that embodied this aspect of sacred totality of the *Divine Trinity* or union of the *Divine Mother, Divine Father*, and the *Divine Child*. The Hindu saint, *Sri Anandamayi Ma*, was a sainted being who had a *Divine* birth and came into this world with full realization. *She* carried this fully integrated living truth of the *Divine Child* and the *Divine Mother/ Father* consciousness all *Her* life as a beacon of possibility for others. Traveling extensively, *She* brought blessings to all those who found their way to *Her*. *She* was recognized as the living embodiment of many sacred Hindu Goddesses including *Manush Kali, Durga, Lakshmi, Goddess Minakshi, Devi Narmada, Lord Gauranga*, and many others. Many followers while in *Her* presence said they saw in *Her* the very face of *God*. *She* was elusive and yet fully present. It is said *Her* blessing was incalculable, powerful, and sublime. I call on *Her* presence whenever I am meditating upon this aspect of being and feeling into *Divine Child* energy, especially if something is in the way of my connecting with it. *Her* invoked presence helps sweep away any confounding thoughts of separation, especially when offerings are made to *Her* such as flowers, prayers, or incense.

What does your *Divine Child* need right now to thrive? Just as newborns need nurturing and care, this is the time to discover your innate nurturing nature. The word nurture can be traced back to the Latin word nutritus, meaning to nourish. To nourish is to nurture. To nurture the *Divine Child* is to nourish this innocent and vulnerable aspect within you with spiritual sustenance. You know how to nurture in this way. This knowing is direct evidence of the *Divine Mother* within you. All of the *Divine Mother's* you have met carry this wisdom of enlightened nurturing and you can call on them for help. Enlightened nurturing is a key element in the *Divine Mother's* realm. *She* sponsors life in all its forms. *She* not only gives life but enhances it as well. *She* is an enlightened nurturer because all of *Her* energy and realization goes to creating and supporting life.

Enlightened nurturing is the high frequency choices of love, forgiveness, joy, and equanimity. A perfect guide at this juncture is the powerful Hebrew *Great Mother Goddess Shekinah. Shekinah* is associated with the transformational qualities of the *Divine* and as such can assist you in transforming any old habits or patterns that might get in your way of living these qualities. The *Great Mother Goddess Shekinah* is also known as the *Queen of Heaven* and is a manifestation of *Divine Presence* that epitomizes love, forgiveness, joy and equanimity. *She* is the perfect ideal for transforming old worn out attitudes and habits into energy to harness your new way of being as the *Divine Child. She* especially assists with enlightened nurturing and protection while nurturing awakening.

Shekinah means "presence of God" and relates to the feminine aspect of the *Holy Trinity. She* carries the energy that sanctifies from within the dimension of the *Holy Spirit.* This aspect of the *Divine Mother* lives within all beings and can be accessed through prayer and prayerful intent. Call upon *Her* for advice, protection, and guidance and *She* will respond for *She* nurtures all through *Her* blessings and wisdom of enlightened nurturing.

Enlightened nurturing can become a spiritual practice, not only for yourself, but others and the world. Many great spiritual leaders such as Desmond Tutu, Mother Teresa, Mahatma Gandhi and His Holiness the Dalai Lama were and are great nurturing beings. *Jesus Christ* and the *Buddha* continually nurtured their followers with *Divine* wisdom and they both birthed a new consciousness for all people.

What do you want to nurture within yourself? What spiritual qualities? It is time to consider developing high vibrational habits that nurture your consciousness. Treat yourself like a delicate newborn child, with intense concentration and an abandoned willingness to change. Newborns are nurtured with pure water, *Mother's* milk, wholesome food, staying clean, being bundled, snuggles, softness, gentleness, sunlight, and love. Go back to basics and evaluate your living habits. Do you drink pure water, do you eat the most wholesome food, are you being gentle with yourself, loving, and enjoying the simple gifts of nature? Are all of your habits conducive to raising this high vibration being, the *Divine Child*, in a healthy way? How can you simplify your life to focus on this awakening? What do you need to do to support this evolving awareness in yourself?

Enlightened nurturing draws upon the intuitive capacities you have and pays attention to all the subtle information you receive. Recently, my husband and I attended Grandparent's Day at my grandson's school. We were greeted with refreshments and then led to a performance by the kindergarteners. As we went into the hall I had the strongest urge to find my grandson. I walked up and down the aisles to see if I could spot him. The urge kept growing and growing. When that didn't work, I sent my husband. When he didn't return I went to look again and found my husband and grandson holding each other. Our precious grandson had tears streaming down his face because he hadn't seen us and was afraid we weren't coming. I was so glad I listened deeply and acted upon my intuition. We hugged him and he went on to perform to the audience of over five hundred grandparents with great enthusiasm and confidence.

This incident describes a moment of clear intuition. It was not a thought that drove this action, like I should find him, or would like to see him. It was a deeper urge that I needed to find him right then, that he needed me right then. Tuning into your own *Divine Child* requires a deep attunement and belief in what you hear.

The question is, how do you distinguish between a thought, whether positive or negative, and your intuition? In my experience intuition feels stronger; its voice is clearer. Random thoughts evoke feelings; intuition evokes knowing.

I know people who use the term intuition as a flag for rationalizing what they want. It's easy enough to do, and I've fallen into a similar trap at times. But intuition is not that. It is a deeper energetic flow of knowledge. It leads you to a knowing that is not rooted in your reasoning ability. You do not enter another psychological state with intuition. Intuition is purer as it involves instant realization. Emotions lead us to other thoughts and actions, whereas intuition leads you into awareness. Intuition is closer to instinct or innate knowledge, and emotion is a product of thought. Intuition is a doorway to awareness. When you are aware your heart leads you and the heart and awareness work together as knowing.

At this point in my own personal journey when the awareness of the *Divine Child* within was evolving, I felt very vulnerable. I knew I was walking on a path that was different from the culture at large and it made me feel like I needed to stay very "bundled." Being bundled is a Native American expression that means to hold yourself reverently and in quiet while things percolate. The expression in itself infers some protection of one's sacred nature. *Medicine People* bundle their sacred medicines and medicine objects that they use in ceremonies. It keeps the energy pure. When I travel, I bundle my meditation support; crystals, mala, candles, sage, incense, pure water, and sacred texts and only take them out when I am doing ceremony.

In this new time of connecting with your *Divine Child*, it is important that you are bundled as well, taking this precious *Divine Child* out only when you are completely focused and present with it. Newborns love to be swaddled. Swaddle yourself energetically with the *Divine Mother's* love while this new consciousness percolates within you. The *Divine Child* deserves reverent tenderness and a deep quality of attention.

All people feel vulnerable at times, and just like a newborn it is beneficial to trust others to help you out. Newborns are born perfectly vulnerable and people love them even more for this tender capacity. Newborns reflect back to us our own vulnerability that is emerging as we experience this fresh and fragile awakening. Being vulnerable is a tremendous opportunity for transformation to happen. I was so different from others as a child, and yet ironically, it was only when I met my own *Divine Child* within that I began to understand my vulnerability for what it is. I felt vulnerable showing myself in my authenticity, my true self, even to myself!

Allowing yourself to be seen by connecting authentically and deeply with others is the key to being vulnerable. Connecting is primal for human beings. Brené Brown, a research professor at the University of Houston who studies vulnerability, says connection is why we are here, and that shame is what prevents our ability to be vulnerable; that shame is simply the fear of disconnection. Shame in my own life was a huge fear of being discovered as not really and truly worthy of giving and receiving love. The shame was tattooed on my heart and I thought it was permanent and real. It was my submerged excuse for hiding and running.

When I met the *Divine Mother* this belief began to tease apart and my shame was uncovered in its immensity; it was a huge paper tiger of illusion. Facing it was the hardest part, and it took time. When the *Divine Child* was born I had to deal with it, because the *Divine Child* is all about connection with clear and innocent vision.

Brené Brown said in a recent TED Talk, tenderness and vulnerability are the birthplace of joy, love, creativity, and belonging. The more afraid you are of something the more we make it certain and solid. You can see this as being very evident in our culture, especially in politics and religion.

When you hide, run, and shame yourself you do it to everyone because we are all connected. When you heal your shadow, everyone heals and it is an act of service. What makes you vulnerable also makes you beautiful. What makes you tender also makes you beautiful. Film, art, and music show us that all people are vulnerable at various times. These days, I sit with energy of vulnerability and use it to draw, paint, and explore the sensitive qualities of nature. Sometimes it shows up in intimate conversations with friends or my children. Sometimes it shows up when I am meeting new people or in an unfamiliar environment. Sometimes it shows up in my body when it does not feel strong and balanced.

The *Divine Child* embodies pure love, innocence and immeasurable joy. Joy is a great healer and overcomes discursive emotions because it is such a high vibration of aliveness. Sustaining this higher vibration takes some getting used to as everyday life functions on lower frequencies. This is why in the beginning it is helpful to keep the *Divine Child* awareness bundled. Let the ideas and beliefs that hold lower, shadow vibrations begin to emerge and recognize them for what they are. Allow them to come out and dissolve in the shimmering light of awareness. It requires a consistent willingness to be positive and bright. A radical commitment to living in joy requires the intention and development of new habits of alignment, which is entirely possible and doable if you are willing to release your lower functioning habits and make an honest assessment of your vibrational state of being. Assessing your vibrational state of being is as vitally important as releasing your shadow. Many people fluctuate between their lower and higher states of being, and choosing the higher state of being takes full attention and discipline. It takes courage to face yourself honestly. Take your time and let it all unfold naturally. Be tender with yourself, kind, and compassionate. This is a time of revealing yourself to yourself through the reflection of the *Divine Child*'s wisdom nature. The nurturing begins to flow in a circular direction into you, filling you with the *Divine Child*'s goodness. Then it circles again as you nurture the *Divine Child* within to grow as well.

One of my favorite classical myths is the ancient Norse story of *Odin* and the *Tree of Life, Yggdrasil*. In Norse mythology, *Yggdrasil* is an immense ash that connects to nine worlds. It is considered very holy and the *Gods* go there every day. The branches of *Yggdrasil* extend far into the heavens and the tree is supported by three enormous roots that go to other locations; one to the well of *Uroarbrunnr* in the heavens, one to the sacred spring of *Hvergelmir*, and the other to the well of *Mimisbrunner*. All kinds of creatures live in *Yggdrasil* including the wyrm or dragon, eagles, and four holy stags or deer. *Odin* goes to *Yggdrasil* and hangs himself as an offering of himself to himself. *Odin* is a seeker but in order to gain knowledge he has to sacrifice himself first. Only then can he resurrect himself with the new knowledge of his true nature. You are going through the same process as under the auspices of the *Divine Mother* you nurture the *Divine Child*, which is within you. In this way, you are offering yourself to yourself.

The myth of *Odin* represents the struggle of every human being to evolve his or her consciousness and gain true and glorious knowledge of themselves. It is essential to open to the mess that life is and take a look, accept it, and keep what works and release what doesn't. It is very helpful to maintain a strong, positive point of view through this process so you don't judge yourself or become discouraged. Replace any negative thoughts with positive ones and eventually you will see the results, and your *Divine Child* will rejoice and live and the radiant light of joy will naturally arise as you honor yourself.

The *Divine Child* embodies the transcendent state of consciousness known as non-dual awareness, rigpa or wisdom. As opposing energies dissolve into this natural state the *Divine Child* consciousness becomes more and more clear in its blessed marriage between the *Sacred Feminine* and *Divine Masculine*. In this way of being there is no separation for there is no inner and outer, no his or hers, no up or down. It is all *Oneness*, but with varying appearances and love is its frequency. An awareness of non-duality gives you a vaster perspective and a wonderful sense of freedom and brings a more stable happiness. This awareness arises with increasing force as you release resistance and judgment.

If you have ever had a sense that there is something deeper, or more meaningful, that lies beyond your everyday consciousness you have had an experience of touching non-duality. This is where the *Divine Child* lives. Non-duality is a life-enriching awareness. You are in touch with something larger than yourself that is known by many names: the more spacious self, the *Great Spirit, God, Buddha-mind,* or *Christ-mind*. It is the enlightened cosmic truth living within each being. Recognition of your non-dual nature is to realize your own holy and enlightened self. To experience non-duality is to experience freedom.

The *Lankavatar Sutra* in Tibetan Buddhism states, "Non-duality means that light and shade, long and short, black and white, can only be experienced in relation to each other; light is not independent of shade, not black or white. There are no opposites, only relationships." Bede Griffiths, the Benedictine monk and Hindu yogi, taught that adavaita (non-duality) does not mean "*One*" in the sense of eliminating all differences. The differences are present in the *One* in a mysterious way. They are not separated anymore, and yet they are there.

Babies carry this awareness when they are first born because they come from the realm of pure light. Light is awareness. This new awareness is a tender part of you that is like a tiny, newly sprouted blade of grass peeking out from the earth in early springtime. Any disturbing energy can impact it. Now is the time to take great care, just as you would with any newborn, with nurturing and protection.

The primary principle of *Mothering* is to do what is best for the child. Sit with this beautiful *Divine Child* you have just birthed and attune to the energies of light and basic goodness *She*/He carries. Learn to listen deeply to this superbly innocent *Divine Child* and surrender to the simplicity of knowing within you. It is a time to listen deeply to your heart and practice the yoga of listening called *Nada Yoga*. When you listen deeply, your heart and the heart of your *Divine Child* are *One*. The answers to many questions become apparent. Always add love to your listening. Listening with love is a *Divine* recipe for nurturing spiritual awareness. Listening with love opens you to peace and joy and being in the present moment. Listening with love moves you out of any crucial judgment and shifts you into a relaxed, open state.

At first, *Mothering* can feel like a big experiment. When you learn to listen deeply in tandem with the heart of the *Divine Child*, many mysteries unfold their hidden magic to you. Follow the impulses that your intuition and clear intent guide you to. Maybe you will become guided to better self-care by feeding yourself with nutritional music, aesthetic inspiration, or a specific herbal support in your diet. Maybe you will be led to walk in nature with your favorite pet, dance with a child, pray for others well-being, or visit an ill relative. This is a great time to sit under the new cycle of the *Moon*, the *Green Moon Mother*, which is all about heart awareness and growth. Listen to whatever guidance your intuition evokes. Whatever guidance you receive from your listening yoga take your *Divine Child* with you to experience it in a non-dual state. Remember this state of consciousness is vast and open. The more you hang out together the more you become *One*.

Follow the impulses of your newly birthed consciousness and

use your motivation to lead you into actions that nurture the *Divine Child* within. Birth, in a sense, is waking up. Now that you have chosen this, it is time to take a look at your inner/outer coherence, which speaks to a deep intimacy and relatedness. The German mystic, Thomas Huebl, says that deepening the understanding of yourself and your relationship with self leads the way to deepening relationships. Awakening is when the radius of self becomes bigger, which is the way to build global awareness through self-expansion. It is like a spiritual awareness Internet. You start with yourself and because we are all *One*, it reaches out to others in all kinds of fascinating ways.

But first things first. We are spiritual babies at this point, praying for the wisdom of the *Divine Mother* to grow within us as we love and nurture our *Divine Child*. Prayer and meditation are ideal ways to nurture this innate spiritual nature within you. The great yoga master, Parmahansa Yogananda who founded the *Self-Realization Fellowship* in 1920, gave the following prayer as an affirmation that can be used to nurture a spiritual attitude you can bring to daily life,

> *"As I radiate love and goodwill to others,*
> *I will open the channel for God's love to come to me.*
> *Divine love is the magnet that draws to me all good."*

Love and goodwill are seeds in every being, that when nourished and cared for, teach you how to become receptive to a greater consciousness. The awareness in you that is receptive to this greater consciousness is called *Rigpa* in the dzogchen practices of Tibetan Buddhism, which is your sacred nature or your basic goodness. It is non-dual consciousness, which is the delightful radiant nature of your *Divine Child*.

Babies are nourished with the goodness of their *Mothers* and *Fathers*. Ideally, both parents love and care for their newborn child. This is ultimately true when parenting this new consciousness as well. It requires complete balance and integration of the *Sacred Feminine* and *Divine Masculine* for the *Divine Child* to fully manifest. The *Divine Child* is the full integration of the *Sacred Feminine* and *Divine Masculine* and crosses over into a new state of *Oneness* that is beyond them both because it resides in a non-dual state of wisdom.

Andrew Harvey, mystic poet and writer, says that it is the experience of *Divine Childhood* that the *Mother* now wants to give the human race directly, so you can know your humble royalty, the splendor of the world you live in, and work to save the planet. The world will be saved only by and for *Divine Children* who have awakened in the *Mother* to the fullness of their and *Her* being, and have become living transmitters of *Her* sacred energy.

This *Divine Child* you are tending is a *Divine* transmitter of both the *Sacred Feminine* and the *Divine Masculine* frequencies and a frequency holder of non-dual wisdom. Tune in.

God is directly present in the person who has
the pure heart of a child,
and who laughs and cries and dances
and sings in Divine ecstasy....

Ramakrishna

Moon Mother Goddess Luna

Attunement 8

GREEN MOON

EIGHTH MONTH OF THE LUNAR CALENDAR

*T*HE GREEN MOON MOTHER CYCLE IS ALL about heart awareness and growth. In this cycle the *Green Moon Mother* is speaking to you about being heart centered within an alchemy of grace and surrender to the *Divine Child* within you.

HOME FUN

❧ Throughout this twenty-eight day cycle track your building relationship with your *Divine Child*.

❧ Begin in the dark of the *New Moon,* making prayers of

appreciation and welcoming in this awareness.

꙳ As the *Moon* appears and grows, allow your perceptions to also grow of your being the *Divine Child*.

꙳ Write down and add to you mandala the qualities you perceive are evolving.

꙳ What do you intuit the *Divine Child* needs at this time to thrive?

꙳ At the *Full Moon* time have a *Divine Child* celebration adding beauty to your shrine such as flowers, incense, or music.

꙳ Create a collage, story, song, poem, dance, or artwork to remind you of this celebratory time and add it to your mandala.

A Mystical Childhood

Chapter 9

A Mystical Childhood

Children smile,
Naked to the now.

To primal wonder and miracles,
Only do they bow.

Shan Watters

*I*N ANDREW HARVEY'S ILLUMINATING work, *The Return of the Mother*, he says that *God* has the nature of a child–and of all the images of spiritual mastery, that of a child is the most magical and mysterious, and the most difficult to grasp. It is the key of keys, the secret of secrets. After enlightenment, the *Buddha* entered into child-mind, the kingdom of primal wonder and innocence. The guru, Ramana Maharshi as well as Ramakrishna, tells us that the nature of *God* is child-like, and that the realized being is like a child at peace in the womb of the *Divine Mother*, knowing he or she is fed at every moment by the grace and the light of the *Divine Mother*.

Child-like, as I refer to it here, is not about regression or rebirthing. It is about a state of consciousness that comes through the spiritual path of awakening. Once you have done the hard work of an adult practitioner, you have arrived at the free state of being that is the total joy of living in a state of surrender within the *Divine Mother's* grace. Ramakrishna embodied this child-like, transcendent state. You embody this transcendent state when you begin to experience a reverently mystical childhood and allow the *Divine Child* to inhabit the *Garden*, innocently and with resounding joy, celebrating, playing, and living in ecstatic love.

The *Divine Mother* and the *Divine Father* reach their pinnacle in the *Divine Child* consciousness, which is indeed their fullest aspect. Without the *Divine Child* they would be conceived of only as the *Divine Masculine* and the *Sacred Feminine*. In the *Divine Child*, they are inexplicably linked even though in most human beings the *Divine Child* consciousness is hidden within them. The *Divine Child* and the *Divine Mother* are also completely inseparable because *She* is the *One* who nurtures, feeds, births, and sustains the *Divine Child*. How could the *Divine Mother* exist without the *Divine Child*? Traditionally, a woman is not considered a mother until she bears a child. Once her child is born, they are inseparable, just as the child is indivisible from the father as well.

For the *Divine Child* to thrive and continue growing in

your consciousness, the relationship with the *Divine Mother* must be secure and cherished. When you are completely devoted to the *Divine Mother*, the *Divine Child* emerges in the sweetness of the *Divine* light in your expanding heart and reveals an openness, innocence, purity, and abandoned delight previously unknown. At this point in your spiritual journey, the most helpful thing to focus on is the aspiration to meet everything that arises within the *Divine Mother's* love. This love is the cosmic glue in relationship with the *Divine Child* as well as all of creation. It sounds simple but it is a profoundly wonderful way to meet life. Imagine yourself as the *Divine Mother* and feel into *Her* limitless, compassionate, and fierce loving capacity. *Hers* is a radical loving energy that encompasses all of creation. When you meet this newly revealed consciousness of the *Divine Child* within the *Divine Mother's* limitless loving wisdom, it opens you up without restrictions to the endless capacity of love for self. *Divine* love is a great magnetizing energy that unlocks the energy centers in your physical, mental, emotional, spiritual, etheric, and astral bodies and moves them in its natural flowing grace. When this natural flowing grace brightens in intensity, it increases your life force. This glimmering energy is what you see in the aura of saints who are depicted with a halo of light around them. Holy people who become extremely loving with total abandonment of any limitations shine with bright auric fields of glorious radiance. Tuning into *Divine* love as fervently as you can will nourish and nurture your *Divine Child* through this magnificently illuminating life-giving flow. The miracle is, the *Divine Child* receives this loving flow and returns it back to you!

Loving flow is a *Divine* life-creative, life-giving, life-enriching, and life-restoring force and a spiritual truth. In the profound teachings in the *Gita*, this *Divine* flowing energy is called the three gunas: satvas, rajas and tomas. A whole science of how this natural flowing love energy works developed in Indian and Tibetan cultures. In Tibet, Lamas prefer to work with someone with intense emotions because it shows their capacity for feeling. Because of the profound methods in Vajrayana, they can help turn any discursive emotion into the powerful force of love. If a student is apathetic, the challenge is greater because the capacity to feel is less.

Feeling deeply is very supportive of developing life-creative, life-supportive, life-enriching, and life-restoring energies. Feeling deeply is key to the path of the *Divine Mother*. Regardless, the quality of the emotional energy arising within you can be worked with it. Most children feel things deeply. They love unconditionally, before they learn otherwise. If it is love you are feeling, you can increase the love force by amping it up to a radiant and powerful *Divine* love energy. If it is anger you are feeling, you can work with the opposite energy of love to help transform it until you recognize the true wisdom nature of anger is love. This is where duality begins to dissolve and the *Divine Child* begins to live and play through the *Sacred Marriage* of opposites. Whenever this *Sacred Marriage* happens in consciousness, your heart-mind invokes the *Divine Child*. In the *Bible*, there are many references to human beings as the children of *God*. A child of *God* is the *Divine Child*. The *Sacred Marriage* of opposites or non-duality is a beacon for the *Divine Child* to emerge in openness, innocence, purity, and abandoned mystical delight.

Children are naturally full of life-creative, life-supportive, life-enriching and life-restoring energy. These are the foundations of a mystical childhood. To deepen your understanding of this it is helpful to work with the *Divine Child Wheel of Becoming*. The *Wheel* is inspired by the traditional *Cherokee Medicine Wheel*, which is a circle with four quadrants or directions, which all have a specific meaning and various symbols. At the top of the *Divine Child Wheel of Becoming* is the *North* direction, which represents the unlimited possibility of life-creative habits and views. What does it mean to be life-creative?

Joseph Chilton Pearce's classic work on the *Magical Child* states that from birth the child has only one concern; to learn all that there is to learn about the world. *Earth* is the child's playground and nothing should interfere with a child's play. When raised this way, the *Magical Child* is a happy genius, capable of anything and equipped to fulfill his or her amazing potential. When children play, they are not doing so to get away from stress or retreat from their jobs or to relax as adults do. They play to discover and celebrate life with all the fresh inquisitiveness imaginable. Fresh inquisitiveness is being life-creative, which is what the *Divine Child* is all about. Being life-creative is one of four foundations of a mystical childhood. Life-creative energy is being in the present moment with an open mind brimming with delight. It is where creative freedom flows like a river connecting you to unlimited possibilities. When you are in this field of energy you are tapping into the creator aspect of your being and completely aligned with the *Divine Mother* within.

Each human being has access to this infinite *Divine* life-creative energy. When you tune into this *Divine* life-creative energy, you hold in your heart a great secret, an immeasurable resource of possibilities that is virtually limitless.

The word "create" comes from the Latin word *creare*, which means to make, to bring forth, produce, arise, or grow. The mystical force of the *Divine* life-creative energy potential is a vast ocean of energy that you live in. It rises in you spontaneously. It is also the realm of the *Divine Mother* and the birthright of the *Divine Child*. The *Divine Mother's* life-creative energy is made manifest everywhere you look. Every mountain, star, lover's face, poem, song, road, building, universe, human being, and tree is made from *Her* creative forces. The openness, innocence, purity, and abandoned delight of the *Divine Child* magnetize and magnify the *Divine* life-creative force.

The *Goddesses* of the *Divine* creative force are the *Nine Muses*. They come from ancient Greece and are known as *Calliope, Clio, Erato, Euterpe, Melpomene, Polyhymnia, Terpsichore, Thalia* and *Urania*. The *Muses* are free spirited and love song. They celebrate the lives of all the *Gods* and *Goddesses* through artistic expression. Their music is transcendent, and it is said the whole world was created through it. Their song of *Divine* life-creative energy sang you into existence. These mysterious songs of creation are the *Divine Child*'s bedtime lullabies and inspirational nursery rhymes told in whispered secrets from the *Divine Mother* to *Her* beloved *Child*.

As you make your way around to the next quadrant of the *Divine Child*'s *Wheel of Becoming*, you find yourself in the *East* direction, which is depicted as the sunrise of a stunning new day. Here the unlimited potential of the *North* direction is made manifest in the world as the light rises. This is where you explore *Divine* life-supportive energies that help you invest in yourself spiritually and re-create life choices and beingness through a new level of spiritual nurturing. This is an alchemical refining process aided by the soft rays of new light in the sunrise. This is where your own embodied *Divinity* gracefully begins to blossom through the *Divine Child*'s openness, innocence, purity and abandoned delight and you return to the very heart of your life.

Here, at sunrise, you move into mindfully living in a way that supports and respects all life in every imaginable configuration. Discernment about all aspects of your activities, attitudes, and emotions is called for. It is a delicate and necessary process. Look with fresh eyes at your life and life choices and create energies that are life-supportive rather than those that deplete yours or others life force. What is your heart's calling right now?

Beauty and creativity are *Divine* life-supportive energies that are expressed, moment-to-moment, through the abandoned delight of the *Divine Child*. Creativity and beauty are related to love and goodness. Plato said that love was born of beauty and from then on, the ability to love beauty has created all good things that exist for *Gods* and men. Beauty is a threshold into pure love. Surround yourself with beauty and it will support you living in a magnificent love. Create beauty and you create love. Everything you learned in the *North* is carried through to this direction now in the *East*. Reach into the invisible where the *Muses* sing and invoke them in your activities. It is said each person has a *Muse* sitting on their shoulder, whispering in their ear, guiding them. At this time see if you can hear and surrender to making your life even more beautiful. The *Muses* are inspirational for creating and are reliable guiding forces for inculcating whatever you are creating with beauty.

Children naturally create through song, dance, art, playacting, make-believe, stories, and role-playing. Children completely absorb themselves in play because it supports their true nature. They love to explore, to live in the moment, and to enjoy life. No one has to teach them to be that way; they are born that way and it is their true nature even before they learn to speak. If you look deeply within your heart, this aspect of the *Divine Child* is truly there within you, has always been there, and radiates life-supportive energy. Many bury this aspect of their being but through much surrender, you can come full circle back to it by releasing everything that is in its way, including discursive emotions and negative habits and attitudes. Positivity feeds the life supportive energy and will make it grow. Add beauty and creativity and you will be dancing on your way.

When you shine the light of the *Divine Child's* radiant love on almost any of your daily activities you can witness the inherent transcendent beauty within it. It is as if you are traveling upward on a huge spiral of consciousness and when you least expect it you make another turn and bam, there it is. Your heart becomes light, full of love, and you just want to celebrate the sun, the moon, the stars, the trees, the green hills, the flowers, the shimmering light on the ocean, and yourself. When the *Divine Child's* iridescent light shines within you, you become witness to another glistening realm within this one.

The *Divine Child's* radiating light within you is the *Divine-*life supportive energy of a new day. It is not so much creating a new life as it is surrendering to a new life view in everything you do while bringing alive the *Divine Child* within. Through this process, the quality of your life will change. You will most likely soften and become more relaxed and priorities may shift. It is well worth the discovery to find your *Divine Child* nature gloriously alive in your life. Learn to revere, esteem, and adore this *Magical Child*.

In the next quadrant of the *Divine Child's Wheel of Becoming* you move into the *South* direction where the *Wisdom Beings* reside in the full light of day. Here is where you discover life-enriching energies. Enrichment means to make fuller, more meaningful, or more rewarding, and to go back to the heart of your life. Moving into the heart of your life is the mission of the *Sacred Feminine*. And the heart of your life is where the *Divine Child* lives in wonder, enchantment, and magic. It is here you find your highest potential and a life map guiding you through the openness, innocence, purity, and abandoned delight of the *Divine Child*, which are the qualities of your *Divine* energetic make-up or vibrational intelligence.

The *South* is a good place to contemplate or increase your

spiritual practice to attain the *Divine Mother* and *Divine Child* consciousness. Many feel the need to engage with the sacred through spiritual practice because the veil of illusion is very strong. To penetrate it so you can perceive the *Divine Mother* and *Divine Child* requires a spiritual practice. Spiritual practice helps create the room within your life for the sacred and to touch it continually. Deepen your practice or if you don't have one, begin asking for your practice to be revealed to you, to meet your spiritual teacher, or to find a tradition you resonate with.

Prolific writer and spiritual teacher, Ravi Ravindra, says,

> *"As spiritual searchers we need to become freer and freer of the attachment to our own smallness in which we get occupied with me-me-me. Pondering on large ideas or standing in front of things which remind us of a vast scale can free us from acquisitiveness and competitiveness and from our likes and dislikes. If we sit with an increasing stillness of the body, and attune our mind to the sky or to the ocean or to the myriad stars at night, or any other indicators of vastness, the mind gradually stills and the heart is filled with quiet joy. Also recalling our own experiences in which we acted generously or with compassion for the simple delight of it without expectation of any gain can give us more confidence in the existence of a deeper goodness..."*

I love doing spiritual practice daily. It is my time to connect deeply with *Source*, the *Divine Child*, and myself. I cannot imagine a life without it. My friend and teacher, Lama Yeshe Wangmo, says that spiritual practice lowers the volume of negative thoughts and emotions and increases positivity. Doing spiritual practice is the life-enriching energy for every spiritual seeker who wants to be connected to a force or field greater than themselves. It is the way to make your life a living prayer where each moment becomes a reflection of holy connection. It is where openness arises and where innocence lives. It is a reliable way to find pure essence and if you do it with abandoned delight, you have realized the *Divine Child*. Spiritual practice realizes, or is, the direct experience of the *Divine* within.

There are all kinds of spiritual practices you can do from meditation, yoga, prayer, ritual, chanting, prostrating, kneeling, bowing, sacred dance, mass, ceremony, singing, fasting, tithing, initiations, and pilgrimage. Often, people do some kind of combination of these whether Buddhist, Christian, Muslim, Hindu, Jewish, Taoist, Native American, Zen, Pagan, or Druid.

The foundation of my practice is meditation. His Eminence Chagdud Tulku Rinpoche taught that the root of all difficulty and conflict lies in the mind; therefore, the solution to all difficulty and conflict lies in changing the mind. To do this, you practice meditation. Mind itself is beyond birth and death. It is not born; it does not age or die–it is a continuum. The ordinary mind, filled with positive and negative thoughts and emotions, constantly changes. It lacks freedom for it is continuously influenced by external phenomena. You sit. You meditate. You do practice to change the mind. And it works. It enriches you vastly, spiritually and energetically.

The next turn of the *Divine Child's Wheel of Becoming* lands you in the *West* direction, the place of transformation. This is where the life-restoring energies are revealed. The *West* is where the translucent transformation of releasing what is no longer needed occurs, giving you a sense of spacious vastness.

Have you ever noticed the abandoned delight children live with all the time? They can spend time creating something and with the same verve, destroy it and laugh and laugh. My grandson does this with his Legos®. He will spend an inordinate amount of time building a freeform structure, play with it and then, with a fierce yell, will jump on it and completely trash it. It is breathtaking. I catch myself with a little hitch in my breath, thinking, "No, really, you want to do that?" But it always cleans the ground, just like when you create a garden. First you need to remove any debris and then work the soil before you can plant anew. Sweeping away what is no longer needed so transformation can happen is the opportunity of the *West*. In the *West*, the light begins to soften towards sunset and the *Moon Mother* arises in the golden pink-tinged sky. In this ninth cycle of the *Moon Mother, She* appears as the *Harvest Moon Mother*, where everything that has been sown is gathered and sorted through.

This is the time for re-evaluation, releasing, and reviving through resting, remembering, and forgiving. In a way, you take apart your life to put it back together in a new way. Put the excess in the fire. Make a fire offering, a fire puja. Dis-assemble so you can stand naked in the now as the *Divine Child*. Strip yourself down to your essence of pure, *Divine* love.

The word love is the most commonly used word in the spiritual traditions in the world. Yet humans search for the profound meaning of it. It isn't that you don't know what love is, it is that you don't know how to always live in love. Living in love means it is the driving force of everything in your life including your thoughts, feelings, hopes, dreams, actions, creations, relationships, and yourself.

This essay on love by Thomas Merton, a Trappist monk, writer and mystic, is a favorite,

"Love sails me around the house. I walk two steps on the ground and four steps in the air. It is love. It is consolation. I don't care if it is consolation. I am not attached to consolation. I love God. Love carries me all around. I don't want to do anything but love.

And when the bell rings it is like pulling teeth to make myself shift because of that love, secret love, hidden love, obscure love, down inside me and outside me, where I don't care to talk about it. Anyway, I don't have the time or the energy to discuss such matters. I have only time for eternity, which is to say, for love, love, love.

Maybe Saint Teresa would like to have me snap out of it,
but it is pure. I tell you I am not attached to it (I hope)
and it is love, and it gives me soft punches all the time in
the center of my heart. Love is pushing me around the monastery,
love is kicking me all around, like a gong, I tell you.
Love is the only thing that makes it possible
for me to continue to tick."

Thomas Merton is talking here about the transcendent love of spirit that lives in the heart of the *Divine Child* who has emerged in his being after many travails and fierce challenges. This state of surrendered grace is not easily attained but it is supremely sublime when revealed through the stripping down of the ego that prevents its discovery.

When I come close to this, I reach for the writings of great philosophers or Master teachers to heart-fully inspire me, to help me tune in to and hold the energy of love. There are so many, one can lean into for inspiration and guidance. Many are included in the bibliography of this book as I used them for resources in its writing.

In his wonderful poem, Andrew Harvey says it another way,

First allow "reality" to leave, and the light to appear,
go out in the light, go out completely, and then reappear,
as the arrived-here light, the light-matter Mother,
giving birth to the child in eternity, in time,
the complete Divine human, the complete human Divine
become empty enough to receive the purest gift of the Divine,
its eternal childhood, its Krishna-ananda, its Kali-bliss,
the apple suddenly irradiated with immortality,
and then, the transcendentally innocent part of you,
purified, exposed, merges with,
the transcendental innocence of God.

So the wound of samsara closes and heals along that perfect scar,

Now, light and matter fold over into one dancing light matter,
Now, the world is lived, consciously as Divine play,
As a mad, amazing game played beyond all known rules,
By a perfectly loving, illumined child,
With a Mother who is also a child,
By a child in love with all other child-beings,
Serving them with an awakened heart.

Moon Mother Goddess Luna

Attunement 9

HARVEST MOON

NINTH MONTH OF THE LUNAR CALENDAR

*T*HE HARVEST MOON MOTHER IS ABOUT celebrating the fruits of your labor and reaping the benefits from them. In this part of the journey, it is time to do just that. Take a deep breath and allow yourself to be exactly where you are and reflect upon on how far you have come. You are becoming the *Divine Mother's* loving child in every sense. How beautiful. To support this we will create a *Wheel of Becoming*.

HOME FUN

❧ Tune into the *Muses*.

❧ Put a sign outside your door that says, *Muses Only, No Critics Allowed*.

- On a nice piece of paper draw a large circle.

- At the top write the *North*, to the right quarter write the *East* at the bottom write the *South*, and to the left quarter write the *West*.

- In the center write the *Divine Child Wheel of Becoming*.

- In the *North* write: Life creative energies

- In the *East* write: Life-supportive energies

- In the *South* write: Life-enriching energies

- In the *West* write: Life-restoring energies

- Throughout this twenty-eight day *Harvest Moon* cycle work on this *Wheel*, listing those energies in the directions that you are working with.

- Use whatever imagery you feel inspires the energies you are working with.

- On another piece of paper, as you make your way around the *Wheel*, list all those energies you are releasing.

- On the *Full Moon*, do a fire ceremony and burn the list you are releasing, offer a prayer for it to be so, and thank the *Muses* for their assistance.

- Place the *Wheel* on your altar next to your mandala.

- Use the *Wheel* in your meditations to inspire you and to act like a compass for you each day, offering thanks to the *Divine Mother*, the *Divine Child*, and the *Muses* for assisting and supporting you throughout your day.

Mother Earth:

Where You Live

Chapter 10

The Elders say nature has never stopped speaking to us,
We just stopped listening.

Little Grandmother Kiesha Crowther

Is it possible there is a certain kind of beauty
as large as the trees that survive the hundred-year fire,
Trees we can't comprehend even standing beside
with outstretched arms gauging their span.

A certain kind of beauty, so strong,
so deeply concealed in relationship,
A conversation so quiet the human world
can vanish into it.
A beauty moves in such a place like snowmelt
sieving through the fungal mats that underlie giant firs,
Tunneling under streams where cutthroat fry
live a meter deep in gravel,
Fluming downstream over rocks that have
a hold on place lasting longer than most nations.

A beauty that fills the space of the forest with music
that can erupt as varied thrush or warble,
A conversation, not an argument,
a beauty gathering such clarity it breaks
the mind's fearful hold.
Steeped in a more dense intelligibility,
within which the centuries and distances,
Answer each other and speak at last
with one and the same voice.

Alison Hawthorne Deming

GROWING IN DELIGHT AND WONDER AS THE *DIVINE Child,* you begin to connect more and more to the world. The *Sacred Marriage* consciousness you are developing is about to extend and expand into the realm of *Mother Nature* as you progress along the *Mothering the Divine Path.* In *Her* realm you can see and witness the *Sacred Marriage* of masculine and feminine all the time. Every day, the sun, the *Divine Masculine,* radiates as sunlight to touch and awaken the body of *Mother Earth.*

Western awareness promotes a dual consciousness. What does this mean? It means we feel separate from the rest of creation. We think of male and female as opposites. Let go of this notion and we begin to view male and female as complementary energies that brighten life. We shift that original dualistic charge from the consciousness of opposing energies to the consciousness that they are united in one, singular energy that only appears different. In their *Divine* nature they are not opposites, but are expressions of energy that when in balance create, support, enrich, and restore life. In this regard they are similar to the elements, each having their own energy signature. They affect and transform each other but in the pure state they are not oppositional. It is said the *Divine Masculine* is like a clear crystal and the *Sacred Feminine* is the radiating rainbow light from the crystal. They are not separate They cannot exist without each other, but they appear differently.

When you consciously begin to erase the boundaries between seemingly opposite forces, their true essence emerges and your understanding and realization of inter-being and interconnection arises. For example, in many tantric practices it's customary to visualize sun and moon discs of light in your heart, upon which rests a sacred seed syllable. The sunlight and moonlight are conjoined representing their inseparability. In third dimensional awareness, you experience these as male and female; the sunlight being the male and the moonlight being the female. In higher frequency awareness, you experience them as inseparable. They are One through the *Sacred Marriage* of opposites.

In all of *Mother Nature*'s tremendously beautiful display, the dance of the *Sacred Marriage* is taking place. You can witness it when the sun drenches a wet road and the moisture evaporates, traveling to another location through the atmosphere. You witness it as a log burns and the fire rises up to touch heaven with smoky fingers. You witness it when the sun energizes the magic in a seedpod so that it bursts open to spread its wealth. You witness it in the conception of all animals and humans. The *Sacred Marriage* is the *Divine* Mystery you are surrounded by and live in. It is exhibited abundantly in *Mother Nature*'s verdant and effulgent display, which is always welcoming the *Divine Masculine* to energize *Her* kingdoms. Your own *Mothering* nature does this as well so you can experience the *Sacred Marriage* and live in *Her* garden of delight. Each being has a deep longing for completion and *Oneness*, for it is your true nature. It is interesting to note that the very word nature has the meaning of, "that which is being born." *Mother Nature* is in a constant state of birthing life as the *Divine Masculine* activates and penetrates *Her* body and helps to bring *Her* creations to life.

You live on a magnificent planet that provides us with everything we need from *Her* own body. Our glorious planet is a living being, a deity named *Gaia* or *Gaea*. In Greek mythology, *Gaia* was the personification of the *Earth* and the primal Greek *Mother Goddess*, who created and gave birth to the *Earth*, the *Universe* and all its beings including all the *Gods*. *She* is a *Divine* manifestation of the *Great Mother*. Our very planet is a *Divine Mother Goddess*.

How does a being become a planet? Very great beings of light have the capacity of limitless generosity, endless creativity, and everlasting offering of life to multitudes of beings and life forms. The *Earth*, *Gaia*, is such a miracle of creation. There are many thousands of planets but we have yet to come across one that has evolved to be able to sustain life as richly our own *Great Divine Mother*, *Gaia*.

Gaia is a master teacher of interconnection and relationship. Known in Native American cultures as the *Web of Life*, or the *Sacred Hoop*, this awareness beautifully portrays the concept of relationship and interconnection unity. Interconnection is a mutual bond, that two-way connection that creates a perceptible unity.

Without relationship and interconnection, life would simply not exist on this teeming planet. Every organism, animal, human, plant, and ecosystem depends upon the *Web of Life* for survival. For example, every organism, animal, human, plant and ecosystem has a relationship with water and in a sense, water connects them all, as does the *Earth*, air, light, and space. Certainly within this system there are varying degrees or spheres of interconnectivity, but they exist everywhere in *Nature*. There would be no life here without water. Water connects all life together on our planet as it is the agent of interconnectivity. Interconnectivity refers to the state or quality of being connected together. The concept is widely used in various fields such as biology, network theory, ecology and spirituality. It can be further elaborated as all parts of a system, which interact with one another and cannot be considered or analyzed as being alone or freestanding.

The following is a famous quote by Chief Seattle, a Dkhw'Duw'Absh or Duwamish Chief about the *Web of Life*,

Humankind has not woven the Web of Life.
We are but one thread within it.
Whatever we do to the Web we do to ourselves.
All things are bound together.
All things connect.

Chief Seattle

People, animals, and all creatures are the *Divine Children* of *Gaia* born into *Her* natural paradise. The *Earth* is the realm of the *Divine Mother*. The light from the *Sun*, the *Divine Father*, enlivens and energizes life everywhere in *Her* realm demonstrating the *Sacred Marriage* displayed everywhere in *Nature*. When you understand this, it is natural to honor and respect all of life because *Nature* is a network of relationships that affects all of life. When someone does not honor and respect every life form, they are not honoring their *Divine Mother*.

Professor Robin Wall Kimmer of the State University of New York teaches that in the woods there is a constant stream of data; lessons on how you might live, stories of reciprocity, stories of connection. Species far older than humans show you daily how to live. Being indigenous to place means to live as if you drink the water and to live as if the land feeds you; to live as if the birds sing for you; to live as if your grandchildren will live here and as if your grandparents are buried here.

Wisdom lives in the land, the water, the air, the light and in space. The elements that comprise your body carry this ancient wisdom in every one of your cells. When you commune deeply with *Nature* this wisdom speaks to you, but you have to get very quiet to hear it. Native Elders say you can learn a lot by listening to water. It will tell you what you need to know, what has happened before, and what is on the way. I feel land, air, light, and space are also wisdom keepers that you can hear with clear intent and quietude.

A few years ago my husband and I made a life changing decision to downscale our lives and make the sacred pilgrimage from city to rural living. We live in a pine and oak forest by the sea. It has changed us both beyond description, most especially in our awareness of how the natural world feeds us. The *Earth* is our *Mother* and we are *Nature*. We are learning to abandon ourselves to *Her* beauty and grace by connecting deeply to the seasons, the rhythms of the weather and tides, observing wildlife and tide pools, listening to the wind, and enjoying the forest quiet on a starry night. We are freeing ourselves from the facades that used to entertain us when we lived in the dense city of Los Angeles where my husband worked in the film business, which was fun, demanding and directed both our lives. In this process of recalibration and learning, we are finding it is as important to let go as it is to embrace. We are also experiencing a dazzling joy and an astonishing peace arising. The deeper we connect, the more *Nature* sustains us.

In this world where we live, everything may appear distinct and separate but as my husband and I are discovering everything is interlinked and related. Various traditions, similar to the Native American teachings of the *Web of Life*, also tell us this. For example, like the Hindu and Buddhist teachings on *Indra's Net* or *Indra's Jewels*. *Indra's Net* is a metaphor used to illustrate the concepts of dependent origination and interpenetration in Buddhist philosophy. *Indra's Net* is used to describe the interconnectedness of the *Universe. Indra's Net* is the *Net of the Vedic God Indra* that hangs over his palace on Mt. Meru, the axis mundi of Hindu cosmology and Vajrayana teachings. *Indra's Net* has a multifaceted jewel at each vertex and each jewel is reflected in every other jewel.

The British born writer, speaker and philosopher, Alan Watts, said,

"Imagine a multidimensional spider's web
in the early morning covered with dew drops.
In each reflected dewdrop the reflections of
all the other dewdrops are reflected.
And so infinitum; that is the Buddhist conception
of the Universe as an image."

Some yogic practices teach this as a column of awareness represented by vertical threads that run through it as in a loom. The warp threads are cognitive nature and the woof (or weft) threads are the phenomenal world. This is a stunningly beautiful image through which to understand the interrelated reality of existence. The depiction of a cosmic loom appears in cultures, worldwide. In Greek mythology, the *Moirai* or *Fates*, controlled the *Mother* thread of life of every mortal from birth to death. Both the *Gods* and humans had to submit to them, indicating their power. The *Fate's* cosmic loom represented the inter-relationship of each *God* and human being to the *Universe* and all within it. The ancient Greek word moira means literally a portion of the whole. *Harmonia* is the Greek *Goddess of Harmony* and concord and is the *Deity* that presides over the cosmic harmony woven into the cosmic loom. It is from *Her* we receive the gift of harmonious energy.

The *Great Chain of Being* is another classic depiction of this concept, which was derived by Plato, Aristotle, Polotnius and Procleus. It hints at interconnection and interdependence but focuses mainly on a hierarchical structure. The apex of the structure is *God* and then in descending order, angelic beings, humanity, animals, plants and minerals. Though linked together the hierarchical arrangement denotes separation between forms. It is interesting to contemplate all the ramifications of this way of thinking and how they play out in the Western mind traditions through the centuries. This idea has an interesting history.

Jean Shinoda Bolen in *Urgent Message from Mother* says that in the mid-60s, James Lovelock, an atmospheric scientist and Lynn Marguils, a microbiologist, formulated *The Gaia Hypothesis*, which proposes the *Earth* is alive and functions much as our bodies do to maintain homeostasis. The *Gaia Hypothesis* was startling at that time because it proposed the idea that the *Earth* is a single living entity, that *She* is alive.

As you can imagine, although this might have been a fairly new idea within the community of Western scientists, it has been recognized by the ancients and indigenous people throughout time. This wisdom is emerging more and more in the hearts and minds of people and will help restore and revive the *Sacred Hoop of Relationship* that is so desperately needed at present.

It is interesting to consider that the *Earth* is a sentient being, as are you. Ask yourself, does your consciousness contribute to the *Earth*'s? According to the Venerable Dhyani Ywahoo, they are inseparable. Once I was returning from the *Peace Village* in Vermont and my flight was unbelievably turbulent. Several very disturbed young people were on the flight with me. When I mentioned this to Venerable at a later date, she stated that the conflicted nature of mind created the turbulence. It can work the same way with pacifying storms or drought or any other kind of imbalance. Through prayer and offering gratitude, the water can be purified and pollution ameliorated. This is not wishful thinking, for there is much scientific proof of this.

Recently in Japan at the site of the Fukushima nuclear disaster, Little Grandmother, Kiesha Crowther brought many bundles of crystals that had been programmed with prayers and high vibratory chants. These were to purify the land and water at the plant. The results of placing these crystals in highly contaminated water were scientifically proven to have caused the radiation to completely disappear. Subsequently, she climbed to a high mountain peak where the source of water came from that lay under the plant and placed crystals there to help sustain the frequency of purity when it reached the contaminated area of the nuclear plant. Water can be programmed to heal itself. We know this through the beautiful work of the late Dr. Masura Emoto who documented the various forms of water crystals influenced by differing energies, both negative and positive. The positive energies made the water crystals more vibrant and glowing and the negative energies damaged the water crystals significantly.

Environmentally these are extremely troubled times. When you understand and revere your place in the *Sacred Hoop* and understand your relationship to the sacred ground of *Mother Gaia,* you can assist in bringing back the stewardship of honoring, respecting, and offering to *Her* what will help to rebalance, harmonize, and heal. Human beings are suffering as much as *Mother Earth* from the lack of connection. It is a reciprocal relationship.

A reciprocal relationship means having a mutual, cooperative interchange of energy. *Nature* never allows a vacuum or imbalance to exist for very long and nothing in *Nature* exists in isolation. There is always an ongoing giving and receiving energy *She* is offering to all living beings. Reciprocity is the act of responding positively and respectfully to that giving and receiving energetic loop, which then creates a strong, enduring relationship with *Mother Gaia.* Reciprocity is inculcated in many indigenous ceremonies, teaching us to establish a new and respectful relationship with our *Divine Mother Gaia.*

Earth-based traditions by their very nature promote reciprocity. David Crawford, a modern *Druid,* teaches about reciprocity and sustainable living. He says that permaculture uses the natural growth cycles and patterns to create an environment that enriches and heals the land rather than destroying it as modern farming practices do. To create a reciprocal relationship with the *Earth,* the environment and with all the animals living in your area you need to observe *Nature*, the cycles of the seasons, interactions of animals with the environment, and weather patterns. Through being good stewards of the land and changing ways of farming and gardening, you create this reciprocal relationship with your planet and all living beings benefit.

The land itself is our *Mother's* blessing to help us love being in our own physical body. When you stand on different places on the sacred body of *Gaia* and you ask to speak to *Her*, you can hear *Her* voice. The land is hospitable, welcoming, and sheltering. Hearing this, it changes your own vibratory signature to one of belonging and joy. It is very important for human beings to realize that many realms exist in the land that you can intersect with when willing. When I walk on the land where I live, I can hear the gentle singing of the Chumash women as they ground corn and prepared fish for the fire. I can hear the giggles of their children and feel the gentle life they lived in their ageless time of dreaming here. They never exploited the land but revered *Her* through ceremony and loved *Her* completely. You can perceive it in your feet and heart as you touch the land here. I am convinced it is part of the reason people are so happy here, currently, and take such good care of and fiercely protect the local environment. The foundation for a sustaining happiness was set by the Chumash's wise example of right relationship and stewardship, and in some ways is because their *Elders* still maintain their ceremonial cycles. There has never been a disaster here or war or any major conflict. The *Earth* and the people gave to each other and received from each other; a holy, reciprocal relationship. The Chumash sang creation songs to birthing chants to *Her* and the *Earth* absorbed them here and nourished *Herself* from their beautiful hearts. The energy of this beauty is still embedded in the area.

Restoration, conservation, and protection of the *Earth's* natural ecosystems and all *Her* creatures are the great work of this time. It is an immediate calling and each of us can respond to it in our own way as well as in community. The *Divine Mother* is holding us, and gifting us all with the opportunity to purify, heal, restore, and revere our own *Mother Gaia*. *She* is calling this forth. For many years, much of my spiritual practice has been dedicated to *Earth* healing. For over thirty years I have worked with the crystal as a holy partner and have created a six-sided shrine room dedicated to this work. The whole room is an *Earth Healing Shrine* containing traditional Tibetan Treasure Vases, Crystals, Water Bowls, Candles, Hawaiian Red Salt Offerings, Cornmeal Offerings, Boron, Stones, Sacred Herbs, Golden Grid shrine cloth, Sacred Flames Drawings, and Guru Rinpoche, Vajrasattva, Red Tara Thangkas, statues and a miniature stupa. On the main *Shrine* are many crystal bowls filled with sacred soils from sacred sites all around the world including:

- Guru Rinpoche's Subduing Meditation Cave–Chimpu, Tibet
- Yeshe Tsogyal's Southern Meditation Cave–Chimpu, Tibet
- Tsogyal Latso, Yeshe Tsogyal's birthplace–self-arising lake
- Lamaling–His Holiness Dudjom Rinpoche's Home in Southern Kongpo
- El Santuario de Chimayo, New Mexico
- Temple of Apollo–Delphi, Greece
- Stonehenge Altar–Stone, England
- St. Baume Mary Magdelene's Cave–Altar, France
- Dorjie Drak–Summit of the Copper Colored Mountain
- Medicine Rock–Chimpu, Tibet
- Yarlung Sheldrak Cave–Guru Rinpoche's first meditation cave in Tibet
- Temple of Apollo–Corinth, Greece
- Acropolis Healing Temple, Greece
- Various sacred sites, Jerusalem
- Lourdes–Altar, France
- Various sacred sites, Bethlehem
- Asklephelon–Healing Temple/Acropolis, Greece
- Earthkeeper–Hindu Temple, Kauai
- Emain Macha, England
- Avebury (major ley line conjunction/St. Michael/ Mary),

England

- Peace Village–Sacred Arbor, Vermont
- Serpent Mounds, clay/cornmeal mix, Ohio
- Glastonbury Abbey, England
- St. Francis Meditation Cave–Assisi, Italy

Just outside the *Earth Healing Shrine* is a *Water Shrine*. Friends and I have collected sacred water from various sacred sites, rivers, and lakes around the world and made a master tincture that contains them all that is offered daily to both *Shrines.* These include water from the Ganges, Lourdes, Bethlehem, Mount Shasta, Hope Mountain, Glacier National Park, Tibet, Bali, Kauai, Bhutan, Stonehenge and others. Daily prayers and formal offerings are placed in the water and carried through the crystals, out into the atmosphere, into the ocean, back into the atmosphere to become rain. And so it goes, another reciprocal relationship. Many small crystals are energized on the *Earth Healing Shrine* that will be buried in locations around the *Earth* to energize healing, restoration, balance, and gratitude. Whenever I travel, I take water from the *Shrine* and offer it to various places on my journey with prayers for healing, balance and gratitude, to help sustain and enliven *Gaia's Golden Net.*

Human beings and everything else on our beautiful planet are defined by their interconnection. *Nature* in *Her* relationships is a vast study of patterns, both chaotic and well ordered. There is an organization to ecosystems where one delicate movement changes the entire design. *Nature* can seem random, but when you sit quietly and observe *Her* there is an incalculable complexity and sublime sophistication to *Her* that humans are just beginning to comprehend.

Our *Mother* did not decide to incarnate on a whim. *She* incarnated to host all the myriad life forms living on *Her* verdant body. What has been considered random phenomena in *Nature* is now considered symmetry or broken symmetry by physicists, which offers endless possibilities for *Her* birthing new forms. The concepts of time-reversal symmetry are fun to consider as well as the abstract symmetry that abounds in *Nature.* Living beings are, by definition, intelligent and constantly taking in matter and energy and transforming them into what is needed. This is such brilliance and gives life immeasurable opportunities for expression on this magnificent planet.

Because all living beings have this remarkable capacity and intelligence of innate transformation, considerable possible futures await expression and manifestation. Never has there been such an opportunity to know the *Mother Goddess* as you now have. *She* is emerging from a long sleep and revealing *Her* immense glory, which will also reveal the *Divine* wisdom of the truly *Divine Masculine* at this particular time. It is a wondrous time to be alive and to be born again into *Her* garden as *Her Divine Child*.

When I sit in *Nature*, my artistic side is drawn to *Her* designs: the wonder of a perfectly symmetrical leaf, the transcendence of a horizon, the breathtaking grace of a blazing setting sun, the delicate braided chevron in a snake's skin, the looming shadowed apparitions in a wild mountain canyon, or a delicate vine tendril mimicking a twirling DNA strand. Beauty flows through all of *Nature*'s designs to a breathtaking degree. I am continually in awe of *Her* creativity of expression. *She* is the most magnificent artist. The *Mother* of all artists! *She* continually gives us a sense of awe and wonder, which always leads to the energy of wisdom.

In particular, I have a deep devotion and adoration for trees. Johnny Appleseed (aka John Chapman) was my great, great, great Grandfather and he had a love affair with trees and conservation his whole life. He planted many, many apple trees and I understand, many other tree varieties as well. His ancestral voice speaks to me often in the forest home where I live. Trees have often been my solace, resting place, a safe place where I could unravel daily challenges and share hopes and dreams.

There is a master Sequoia tree outside the *Earth Healing Shrine* room that protects the *Shrine* while broadcasting and disseminating the healing energy through the forests' worldwide communication system. Trees are masters of reciprocal relationship. In every forest or tree grouping there is at least one *Master* tree that holds the *Mother*'s life force energy for the area, and shares it with all the other trees in their group, casting an energetic net over the area. When one of these trees is dying, arborists have found that they actually transfer their life force to other trees to benefit them. Trees are *Bodhisattvas*, often surrendering their life force to others when needed to sustain the younger trees in their forest.

Trees are intelligent. They offer shade, fuel, oxygen, fruit and nuts, beauty, strength and shelter, and home to innumerable beings: birds, insects, lizards, monkeys, squirrels and others. Trees are so integrated within human experience and life that tree worship abounds throughout time and culture. From ancient Norse and Celtic mythologies to Nigerian, Indian, and Mongolian cosmological thought, to ancient Shinto and the nineteen tribes of the Malaysian forest people, sacred groves were and still are considered living temples. These temples are a place of refuge and ritual cycles. Ceremonies are still performed by priests and priestesses who also serve as guardians of these sacred spaces. To this day in India, trees remain sacred and are often found in the heart of temples where they are venerated through multiple daily offerings of sacred substances, prayers, and spiritual practices. One of the most famous of these is the *Bodhi Tree* in Bodhgaya, under which the *Buddha* attained enlightenment. Trees are an ideal place for nature shrines dedicated to the *Divine Mother*. In Thailand, there is a Buddhist practice of venerating and wrapping *Master Trees* with silk to acknowledge and honor them and monks and nuns offer prayers and gratitude to them daily.

The *Tree* as a symbol of the cosmos is a celebrated image from the Scandinavian *Yggdrasil* to the Persian *Gaokerna Tree* to the *Eternal Banyon Tree*, or *Akshaya Vata* in India to the *Celtic Tree of Life*. The Celts were famous for their tree veneration. *Druidism* as well as Germanic paganism involved ceremonies and sacred practices in sacred groves, especially the oak. The word *Druid* is actually derived from the Celtic word oak.

The *Tree of Knowledge* connects heaven to *Earth* and the underworld and is a form of the world tree or cosmic tree and has been given deep and sacred meanings throughout the ages. The tree is used in Buddhism, Christianity, the Latter Day Saints Movement, Swedenborgianism, German, Celtic and Norse paganism, Hinduism, Islam and Judaism.

I write love letters to the trees on our land. Our grandchildren designated one of our old oaks as their wishing tree. They hang written or drawn wishes, ribbons, bits of cloth, toys and favorite shells they have found and make a wish. I was amazed to learn this is a time-honored tradition in Europe where wishing trees are sites of pilgrimages, circumambulation, prayers and wishing totems! These trees have become shrines, organically, and it is my intuition this is another emerging ancestral memory from both my grandchildren's Celtic forbearers and mine.

Many of the *Divine Mother's* great forests are still there for us to commune with and visit. One of the largest is Amazonia, which crosses nine countries in South America. You can still fly for hours across some parts of Amazonia without seeing any human trace. Amazonia is the biggest tropical forest in the world, bigger than all of Europe and half the size of the United States. It is the most species rich environment on *Earth* and is home to one-fifth of the world's plants and birds. Some of it, to this day, remains unexplored, but the forest is being cut down rapidly. It is imperative that we conserve what is left of this magnificent and unique ecosystem.

Other great forests of *Gaia*'s are the cloud forests of the lowland rainforest in Brazil, a waterlogged world of peat and moss, ferns, and lichens. They contrast deeply with the majestic Blue Cedar Forests of the Atlas in Morocco or the huge California Kelp Forests. These underwater Kelp Forests of seaweed were endangered but through stringent conservation efforts and the establishment of the marine sanctuary along the entire central coast of California, they are reviving. In all, this sanctuary is home to five hundred species of marine mammals, sea birds, fish, turtles, algae, and others.

One of the most well known forests is Sherwood Forest; legendary home to magical folk and bigger than life hero Robin Hood. The largest tree in the world finds its home in the Sequoia National Forest in California, General Sherman, towers two hundred seventy four feet high and its body mass is that of two blue whales. *Mother Nature* really was showing off when *She* created this giant whose head is in the clouds most of the time.

The expression *Mother Nature* is a common personification that illustrates the nurturing, life-giving, birthing, nourishing, and protective aspects of *Mother Earth* as the *Divine Mother. She* is your *Mother Nature* as well. There is no separation from *Her.* You are *Her.* Cultural theologian, Thomas Berry, said that, "the world is a communion of subjects, not objects." He also stated that the greatest and deepest tragedy in losing the splendor of the outer world is that you will always have an inner demand for it and without it, your integral spiritual development can never take place.

Sublime and holy energy is *Mother Nature's* currency and life force, which flows through all the *Divine Mother's* interconnections and networks, including through you. *Her* energy is contained within you because your body comes from *Her* elements. You can influence and impact *Her* entire network with your thoughts and actions because you have a reciprocal relationship with *Her,* as do all living beings.

According to Venerable Dhyani Ywahoo, "thought forms are collections of energies." Cultures give power to thought forms, which then become concretized over time and these thought forms become a way of life and form beliefs. Thought forms of separation give rise to inhibitors that prevent us from realizing our purpose. There are holy encodings in rays of light that speak of the delicacy of interpenetration and *Oneness.* These strands of light are like the cosmic loom of awareness. It is clear how mindful we must all be with what thoughts we weave into its fabric. In this time, the signs of this are becoming clearer and clearer as the veils between the worlds are thinning. Thought forms are becoming more and more powerful and emergent in the *Net.*

Yesterday, I was writing about the *Web of Life* and meditating during practice on the Greek *Goddess Arachne.* I opened my eyes to find a spider had literally dropped into my view from nowhere. I could not see a strand of web anywhere. It hovered right in front of my eyes. This vivid display of interconnection provided me with a clear sign that this information and teaching needs to be energized now so that all can remember. It was a vivid display of interconnection.

How do you make connection to *Mother Nature*? You invite *Gaia* into your life in a fresh and inquisitive way so you can create a reciprocal relationship with *Her* to enrich, sustain, and vivify your life and *Her*s. Venerating *Her* is to venerate and celebrate yourself. Doing daily *Nature* celebration practice is very healing and uplifting. Enjoy being physical in *Her* realm. It is *Her* gift to you, your human body that is so magnificently mysterious and vital, like *Her*.

Invite in life's creative genius, *Gaia*, and let *Her* teach you. Begin by working with your motivation to make it very clear you want to learn and listen to *Her* wisdom. Meditate on valuing *Gaia*, remembering all *She* does for you in so many ways. Send *Her* love and gratitude every day.

Find a special place in *Nature* that you love: the ocean, park, meadow, river, forest, garden, or a wonderful tree or rock; a place to commune with *Her* regularly. Breathe into the place, connecting with *Mother Nature, Mother Gaia*. As you relax into the place, feel the *Earth* as a being that is supporting you and holding you safely in the entire surrounding area. Contemplate the elements in your body and observe them in the world of *Nature* and how they arise in various forms. Express gratitude for them and for your own body, your own unique gift from your *Mother*.

Through each of your senses begin to connect more deeply and tenderly. Remember that the senses are avenues of consciousness. Attune to the delightful creative, life energy that is the *Divine Mother* that flows in and out of all beings in *Her* ongoing flow.

- Through this practice of gentle sensing, relax into what the *Divine Mother* has to share with you and in you.

- Look at the surrounding textures, colors, shapes, and shadows.

- Touch the area through this awareness.

- Taste the wind, the sunlight, and the fresh air.

- Smell the sweet, pungent flavors of *Her* breath force.

- Hear the sounds of the wind in the trees, the buzzing of insects, birdsong.

- Meditate on the *Mother Goddess* in your own body through all the sensations, thoughts, feelings and energies.

- Recognize *Gaia* as a wisdom being, a *Divine Mother Goddess*.

- *Her* presence evokes wonder, healing, curiosity, and truth.

To further bring *Mother Nature* into your life, if you live in a city or apartment, you can create a miniature terrarium garden. Herbal bouquets and wreaths are wonderful for infusing the air with *Nature's* rich aroma and pungent fragrances. Fresh flowers are always celebratory offerings and fresh herb pots enrich and enliven any kitchen.

You can also create a *Nature Shrine* with favorite stones, shells, feathers, seeds, driftwood, delicate herbal bundles, painted sticks, fall leaves, crystals, water, and cornmeal. All are wonderful offerings to surround pictures of your favorite *Divine Mother* images and *Mother Gaia* photos. You activate the *Shrine* by lighting a candle and offering a prayer of gratitude to *Mother Gaia* for *Her* generosity, strength, and stability in providing life to all *Her* children. Activate your home with the blessing of *Mother Nature*.

Remember to tune into and observe the *Lunar* cycles and how they move energy through your body. If you live near the ocean observe how the *Moon Mother* affects the tides. In this cycle of the *Moon Mother*, we will be celebrating what is known as the *Hunter's Moon*, which is when the deer are fat and ready for eating. However in our exploration, you will be hunting *Mother Gaia* in your own body. To heal the body of our *Mother Earth* it is mandatory that the healing of our attitudes and disconnection from our own bodies happens. Examine your feelings, attitudes, and beliefs about your body and clear away anything that needs transforming into love. Heal through *Her* and with *Her* and learn from *Her*.

Another superb and creative way to invite *Mother Nature* into your life is through gardening. I absolutely adore flowers. In their smell, beauty, and design they are perfect mandalas. Through gardening you also get deeply in touch with one of *Mother Nature's* great patterns, the seasons. This pattern of life and death is a magnificent display of our own journey here in physical form. Gardening also attunes you to the life-giving force of rain and its many forms. This alone is a master's degree in interconnection, if you fully tune in to it.

Visiting *Her* sacred places and making sacred offerings to *Her* is a powerful way to begin to work with *Her* ley lines and inner realms. *Her* ley lines are mystical and spiritual alignments of various power places. They are spiritual and mystical alignments of landforms. The entire *Earth* has ley lines, which are *Her* subtle body's communication system. You can trace your own ancestral lineage through *Her* ley lines when you are able to connect with them. You can tune in with your inner ear to what a place has to communicate with you and with your ancestors. Ley lines are communication lines, energy lines that can connect you to anywhere on the *Earth Mother*. I do this often when working with various sacred soils on the *Earth Shrine*. If a particular place needs more energy or clearing, the ley line communication system is very helpful to work with. I tune into the area and simply ask *Gaia* to reveal to me what is needed for healing and balance, and *She* answers through the subtle realms of the crystals. They are so helpful to work with the *Earth* because they communicate through *Her* subtle fields or energy bodies.

You can connect with ley lines energetically, the same way you connect with the *Earth*. I recommend you do offerings first, then you dance, sing, and perform ceremonies of devotion to *Her* on a regular basis. It is said some medicine people can travel up and down *Her* ley lines.

The very best way to invite *Mother Nature* into your life is to celebrate *Her* daily. Write *Her* love letters. Fall in love.

I am in love with this world...
I have climbed Her mountains,
Roamed Her forests,
Sailed Her waters,
Crossed Her deserts,
Felt the sting of frost,
The oppression of Her Heats,
The drench of Her rains,
The fury of Her winds,
And always have beauty and joy
Waited upon my comings and goings.

John Burroughs

Together, it is possible to clear all the rivers, the oceans, and all the waterways through prayer and spiritual practice. Making sacred offerings to the *Earth*, the air, the water, and to the land can help to rebalance *Her* ecosystems. Dancing upon *Her* in celebration and veneration is also a holy act of repairing the *Sacred Hoop*, and when you dedicate it to all beings it benefits every living being.

Nature has many hidden secrets still waiting to be discovered to celebrate and rejoice in. Your own constant and intelligent heart awareness is a worthy guide to establishing a positive reciprocal relationship with your *Divine Mother* that has incarnated as the *Great Goddess Mother Gaia*. Let nothing separate you from *Her* again. Let each person weed out the old, outdated, concretized beliefs that do not support *Oneness* and unity. Master Thich Nhat Hanh teaches that you can build a deep spiritual practice with *Her*, based, not on dogmas or beliefs in things you can't verify, but entirely on evidence. To say the *Earth* is a great being is not just an idea; each of you can see this for yourself. Each of you can see that the *Earth* has the qualities of endurance, stability, and inclusiveness. You can observe *Mother Earth* embracing everyone and everything without discriminating. When we say that *Mother Earth* has given birth to many great beings including Buddhas, Bodhisattvas, and saints we are not exaggerating. The *Buddha, Jesus Christ, Moses,* and *Mohammed* are all children of the *Earth.* When we say the *Earth* has created life, we know it's only possible because *She* contains the whole cosmos. Just as the *Earth* is not only the *Earth,* so too are you not only human. You have the *Earth* and the whole cosmos within you.

Every advance in your understanding of yourself, your nature, and your place in the cosmos, deepens your reverence and love. Humanity needs a spirituality that we can all practice together. Let us learn to love outside our boundaries. Loving our *Mother* is a practice we can all join in and do together. It is the work of this time. It is the most valuable work you can do for future generations, for your grandchildren and mine.

Therefore,
Let nothing hinder us,
Nothing separate us,
Nothing come between us,
Wherever we are,
In every place,
At every hour,
At every moment of the day,
Every day and continually
Let all of us...
Hold in our heart and love,
Honor, adore, serve,
Praise and bless,
Glorify and exalt,
Magnify and give thanks.

Saint Francis of Assisi

Moon Mother Goddess Luna

Attunement 10

TENTH MONTH OF THE LUNAR CALENDAR

*T*HIS CYCLE OF THE MOON IS KNOWN AS THE *Hunter Moon* and celebrates the relationship between the *Divine Mother Gaia* and *Her* sister the *Hunter Moon*. Here you are hunting, or seeking, their connection and how it affects you in myriad ways. Seeking the *Hunter Moon*'s magic here on *Earth* is a magical journey of mystery, and herein you recognize yourself as a shamanic apprentice uncovering secret mysteries within yourself, where both the *Hunter Moon Mother* and *Mother Gaia* whisper wisdom to you.

The *Hunter Moon* and *Mother Gaia* communicate in many ways and are significantly affected by each other's orbits. The *Moon Mother* makes life here on *Gaia* more livable by moderating our planet's wobble on its axis, leading to a relatively stable climate and creating a tidal rhythm that has guided humans for thousands of years. The *Moon Mother*'s phases and *Her* orbits have been a mystery to humans for millennia. In a reciprocal way, the *Moon Mother* would not exist without *Mother Gaia* as *Her* gravity keeps *Her* in orbit.

HOME FUN

- Just as the *Hunter Moon* and *Mother Gaia* are in a reciprocal relationship, so are you with them both.

- Contemplate how the *Hunter Moon*'s phases have affected you throughout this journey.

- Can you now feel *Her* more in your own body?

- Now begin to feel into the *Gaia*'s energy.

- Can you feel *Her* in your body?

- If you focus on gentle sensing, you can go deeper with this connection.

- Imagine yourself for a moment as a planet.

- How would you feel with the way things are now?

- What would you need to be restored to full health?

- Examine your feelings, attitudes, and beliefs about your body being the *Earth*.

- In your own body clear away anything that needs transforming into love, and dedicate it to the healing of our beautiful *Mother Gaia*.

The Fierce Mother

Chapter 11

Who can explain Your play Mother?
What do You take, what do you give back?
You give and take again.

For You dawn and dusk are the same,
Nothing can stop Your perfect freedom.
You give exactly what's deserved.

Ramprasad Sen

HE FIERCENESS OF A HOWLING WINTER, sleet covered lakes, and craggy mountain crests concealed in snow and ice, the charred and burnt landscape of a craggy chaparral punctuated with black sandstone cliffs and dry stream beds, the resplendent fall leaves decaying on the ground like a Monet painting. These are the works of the fierce aspect of the *Divine Mother's* constant expression of change. This is when the *Divine Mother* turns back into *Herself*, like the day turning into nighttime darkness or *Her* seasons turning with the continual cycle of birth and death. There is a constancy here that is irrefutable. Every year, the magnificent and dramatic display of the seasons illustrates this great mystery of birth and death in a continual rhythm of transformation. *She* annihilates and destroys with apparent abandon only to reform and vivify everything with pulsating new life once again. It is a magnificent and supreme display of *Her* essential power.

The concept of impermanence and the constancy of change can be disturbing at times, especially to the ego that strives so desperately to hold on to security, safety, and things as they are. However, interwoven in your concept of a fixed self is the agent of change. It is always there. This fierce aspect of the *Divine Mother*, in *Her* compassion, keeps the flow of constant change present in all of *Her* creation as it is a *Divine* revelation of truth.

This ferocious aspect of the *Divine Mother* dances on the ground of illusion, stomping away staid ideations and mind-created deceptions. This wrathful *Mother* is a seeker of hidden and obvious delusions in your mind, as *Her* great love is the powerful force that shatters all illusions. *She* eats them for breakfast, lunch, and dinner. *She* grinds them into nothingness and transmutes them to a higher form of consciousness of *Her* vast primordial wisdom. *She* is constantly recreating and reshaping the world.

Up until this point in your journey the *Divine Mother* has flooded your being with love light. Now, *Her* piercing, strident compassion illuminates all the hidden shadow lands and subtle ego striving in your mind to assist you in liberating them. The more scintillating, razor-sharp light *She* provides, the more depth is revealed of the thick darkness within that seeks liberation into its natural state of freedom.

The *Fierce Mother* has been celebrated in many cultures and traditions. Perhaps the most well known of these is *Throma Nagmo, Kali, Hecate,* and the *Black Madonna*. It is time to call on this powerful wisdom aspect of the *Divine Mother* to give you the strength and fortitude you need to keep going, accomplish your path, and to free everything within that does not support your true goodness. Through *Her* fierce grace you can learn to dance skillfully through all the changes appearing in your life.

Throma Nagmo is the Tibetan Goddess known as the *Wrathful Black Dakini. She* characterizes the innermost secret aspect of the *Dakini* principle, which is the feminine embodiment of wisdom. In *Her* cycle of teachings this commanding aspect of the *Divine Mother* provides you with the extremely powerful means to cut through the mind's dualistic clinging to reveal to you your inherent wisdom nature. Traditionally, the means is a powerful practice called *Chod*. The *Throma* practice of *Chod* removes obstacles, both to your short-term happiness and those hindering your ultimate enlightenment. It carries extraordinary healing power and through its methods, one can accumulate merit and wisdom in a vast and rapid way. However, merely making a connection to *Throma Nagmo* can bring you great blessing in and of itself.

Throma Nagmo is the fierce form of *Vajravarahi* and is the *Mother* wisdom of all the *Buddhas* and *Bodhisattvas* in a wrathful female form. *Her Chod* practice was founded by Machik Labdron (1050-1149), who was the Tibetan female saint considered to be *Her* emanation.

Her story is interesting. Foreseeing the difficulties of future times the enlightened Master, Guru Rinpoche, also known as Guru Padmasambhava, revealed this very rare teaching of the *Black Dakini* to his chief consort *Yeshe Tsogyal* (the patron saint of Tibet) who later concealed this as a terma, or hidden treasure teaching.

This particular treasure teaching was prophesied by Guru Rinpoche to be discovered at the appropriate time in the future by one of the reincarnations of either Guru Rinpoche himself, or one of his twenty-five disciples, which is exactly what happened. His Holiness Dudjom Lingpa (1835-1904) received the direct transmissions of the *Throma* cycle in a vision from Machig Labdron. He kept the practice secret for some time before teaching it, but later, at least thirteen of his disciples attained rainbow body through the practice of *Throma Nagmo*. His Holiness Dudjom Lingpa's reincarnation was His Holiness Dudjom Rinpoche, my innermost heart Lama. His Holiness Dudjom Rinpoche revealed many, many termas and these revealed practices were the ones that Guru Rinpoche hid for this very time in history when they would be most needed.

Throma Nagmo is known as the *Extremely Wrathful Black Mother. She* is visualized with a blue-black body, wearing a garland of severed heads and is surrounded by the powerful flames of transformation. *Her* delicate bone-carved lattice jewelry adorns *Her* dancing body as *She* dances upon a corpse. All of *Her* imagery is meant to be fierce and symbolizes the overcoming of the ego and attachment to the human body as your identity. All visualizations and practices are ultimately to assist you to enter into the state of non-duality or liberation, which *She* embodies and emanates. *Her* awesome splendor is ultimately merciful and loving. *Her* super secret aspect is one of complete bliss and peace, depicted in *Her* heart as the blue and white *Samantrabadra* and *Samantrabadri.*

In speaking to other *Throma* practitioners, all seem to have the same common experience that *Throma* arrives on your spiritual journey at exactly the perfect time. *She* is a great spiritual heroine that can assist in the difficulties in life.

My first experience with *Throma Nagmo* was in a healing ceremony conducted during an eight-day tantric ritual called a drubchen. Practitioners had been deeply practicing for seven days and nights and those attending the healing ceremony were invited in and told to lie down in the middle of the vibrating shrine room. The immense power of the healing energy was palpable the instant

I entered the smoky shrine room. Among incense clouds, the roar of kangling horns and a rhythmic drum staccato, the mantras opened to *Her* realm. The power was so great there was no choice but to lie down. I could not have sat up if I wanted to. As I lay there I experienced the *Goddess* presence reaching deeply into realms of my mind of which I was not conscious. The recesses of my mind and body that harbored anything that needed healing were shaken out. At first I was fearful of *Throma. Her* power is that great. And yet, *Her*s is an extremely helpful practice, especially for people suffering both mentally and physically. *Chod* practice is said to be like a precious jewel, which is able to realize all the aspirations of all beings. When things get challenging, I feel *Her* presence strongly in my heart ready to reveal the truth within the illusion.

Over the years, as my practice has strengthened my respect and openness to *Her* has increased immensely. The deeper you go into practice the more you build the confidence and faith to rely on *Her* and call on *Her* whenever things get really difficult. *She* always comes. *Her* bone shell necklace rattling, cymbals clanging, drums beating, and *Her* mantra comes alive to work *Her* own unique transformational magic. Sometimes life is challenging and there is no way around that. When things in your life seem really tough, it is time to call upon this aspect of the *Divine Mother* that has the strength and capacity to lead you out of darkness. Paradoxically, this is the dark *Mother Goddess Herself.* If you are inspired to evoke *Her*, chant *Her* mantra,

OM VAJRA KRODHI KALI BAM
HA RI NI SA HUNG PHAT

And pray sincerely for *Her* to assist and guide you.

You might ask yourself at this point, what does the symbolism of the wrathful *Mother Goddess* mean? A wrathful presentation of the *Mother Goddess* is an aspect of the *Divine Mother* that is otherwise peaceful and beautiful. The wrathful aspect represents the victorious annihilation of all negative karmas and human vices, just as a peaceful aspect is the representation of all positive karmas. The *Fierce Mother* pulls upon and displays *Her* power in such a way as to support and powerfully uplift the spiritual practitioner so that not only will you find the confidence to overcome any of these forces, but will be able to summon *Her* fierce will and power in the process. Ultimately, *She* leads you into enlightenment, while overcoming any of the countervailing forces standing in your way.

Her wrathful aspect is like a costume or valence for the benevolent *Divine Mother Goddess*. In *Her* fierce or wrathful aspect, *She* symbolizes the tremendous effort it takes to vanquish negative forces such as violence and more importantly, to actually transmute them into positive energies. In this sense, the wrathful aspect actually represents the manifestations of the karmic "fruits" in your life.

In Hindu cosmology, *Throma's* sister spirit is the wrathful aspect of the resplendent *Goddess Durga* known as *Kali*. *Kali* comes from kala, which means black, time, and death. *She* is the consort of *Shiva* who is known as *Kala*, or the eternal time, and therefore *Kali* is known as the *Goddess of Time, Change, Power and Destruction*. Interestingly, like *Throma Nagmo, Her* earliest incarnation was a figure of annihilation of evil forces. In tantric yoga many believe *Kali* to be the highest form of the *Goddess*, a *Mahadevi*. There is no doubt that *Kali* and *Throma* are related to each other, their aspects are so similar.

However, there are some differences too. In Hindu belief *Kali* is known and revered for *Her* dual nature as the *Gentle Mother* and as a *Fierce Warrior*. *She* is a destroyer and a creator simultaneously. *She* eradicates sin, ignorance, and decay and restores you to balance. *Her* body is also blue-black, depicted thus as a way into *Her* darkness that is full of love, hope, spaciousness, and bountiful possibilities.

Kali's love is so great *She* actually absorbs karma. The word karma literally means action, work, or deed. It refers to the principle of causality where your intention and actions influence your future. Good intentions and good actions contribute to future happiness while the opposite contains only suffering for an individual or group. *Kali's* ability to absorb karma is a very great belief and power. *She* literally brings karma into *Her* dark vastness and transmutes it. To some this might seem scary or like sorcery. It is not. In the West, the tendency of spiritual practitioners is to focus on the light, to ascend heavenward as an automatic spiritual motion. If you are able to relax into the *Fierce Divine Mother* and go into *Her* darkness, you realize it is in fact, your darkness as well. It contains a deep, mysterious wisdom you can draw upon that reaches both upward and downward into your own depths.

A great yogini, Aditi Devi, teaches that *Kali* is the actual darkness. The gift of the dark is union with *Her*, in all *Her* forms, in all manifest and un-manifest existence. All of this exists within you as well. Instead of turning away from the dark, the shadow, the scary, the wound, turn towards it knowing it is a fertile source of wisdom and teaching. Many Native American spiritual teachers tell us that within your deepest wounding is indeed your strongest medicine.

Kali practice is often done in total darkness. Spaciousness and simultaneous dual awareness arises from the dark. The inner world opens to you, including what is happening in your subtle bodies. Practicing with *Kali* is, for me, the same as practicing with *Throma*; they are conjoined in my heart. You can look deeply into your fears and blockages and rest in *Kali* or *Throma's* power to help you untie the knots of attachment to these fears and blockages.

Remember that *Kali* and *Throma* are both surrounded by a ferociously hot fire. Fire is the alchemical solution in transformation. In *Hermetic Wisdom*, whose studies include alchemy, astrology, and theurgy, all of nature is fully regenerated and renewed through the occult power of fire, or in other words through fire, nature is reborn whole. Fire is eternal and visible or invisible; it is always present within you. Fire wisdom is one of the subtle elements in your body that you can access at any time. Calling upon the *Fierce Divine Mother* gives you the power and courage to do this in a way that creates positive change as well as an alchemical transmutation. Traditionally, the subtle inner fire is considered the main agent of inner transformation, the one without which spiritual evolution would not be possible. In the energetic or subtle bodies, this fire can occur at all levels of being.

It is interesting to consider that no deities in any tradition I have encountered ever display peaceful, beautiful deities with fire. Transformation is always depicted as the fierce, unwavering, powerful, hot, and sharp energy required for powerful obstacles and deep habitual patterns in the human psyche to change. This transformative energy empowers you to become a spiritual hero or heroine in your own everyday life.

Control is confronted and released by *Her*. Prejudice, hatred, disdain, jealousy, agendas, boundaries, habitual patterns, and fear are all crushed on under *Her* feet and incinerated in *Her* fire. What happens when that occurs? A deeper sense of spaciousness and freedom opens to you and you experience a deep and abiding peace.

Since *Kali* carries time in *Her* wisdom nature, it is good to recognize the timing on your path. While it might be wise to take the time to work on issues as they arise, if there is too much going on you might need to take notes and wait a few days to address them in your practice. Feeling and memory are close allies so you can always remember that felt sense you had when the issue arose and review it. While it often loses its potency, over time, the release of the intensity helps you to feel better. The important thing is to not ignore or bury emotions. However, you do not always have to act on them. It is often preferable that you don't. Self-restraint can help you to utilize the fierceness needed to keep going on the spiritual path with integrity and good heart.

The world can be challenging, especially to dedicated spiritual aspirants who want to stay authentic in their practice. The *Fierce Divine Mother* invites you into *Her* darkness whenever you need time to reflect upon things and harness *Her* courage, strength, and persistence to keep going. *Her* darkness is also, in a sense, womb-like. *She* offers *Her* protection as long as you are willing to stand honestly in *Her* river of change. Blessings arise in the darkness and that is why so many yogis go into dark caves for extended periods of time or lifetimes, to meditate. The paradox of the darkness is that within its fecund silence and boundless space we can experience the brightest light.

Many mystics believe this time is the time of *Kali*. According to the *Vedas* the "age of vice" or the *Kali Yuga* is happening right now. It is the last of the four stages the world goes through as part of the cycle of yugas described in the Sanskrit scriptures, within the present *Mahayuga*. The *Kali Yuga* is associated with a *Demon Kali,* who is not to be confused with the *Goddess Kali*. The *Kali Yuga* is associated with strife, discord, quarrel, or contention. The *Goddess Kali* is associated with the fierce, strong, clear, and compassionate energy needed to cut through the negative *Kali Yuga* energy. It is important for people to know the distinction so there is no confusion with the *Fierce Divine Mother* aspect of the *Goddess*.

However, it is interesting to note the seeming similarities. Andrew Harvey writes,

"Are we not living in Kali's time? And isn't the agony the world writhes in also potentially, if we can confront, accept and use it fearless, an agony of birth? And where will we learn the kind of wild mystic courage we will need to help turn dying into birth if we have not embraced the dark as well as the light power of the Divine Mother?"

The dark *Mother Goddess* requires of you a wild and mystic courage to dance with *Her*. *She* is not as well known as some of *Her* other forms. *She* has often been regulated to the *Underworld* or *Her* teachings negated into discursive expressions because people do not understand *Her* or *Her* powers. While in this aspect the *Divine Mother* is a mystery of the realms of the *Underworld* or *Otherworld*. *She* can assist you in re-forming into wholeness and purity through your darkest, most difficult experiences on the ever-unfolding spiritual path.

A poem written by the sixteenth century Spanish poet and mystic, Saint John of the Cross, narrates the journey of the soul from its bodily home to its union with the *Divine*. The journey is called *The Dark Night* because darkness represents the hardships and difficulties the soul encounters in detaching from the world and reaching the light of union or *Oneness*. The main theme is that this growth of the soul is a painful experience that people endure as they seek to grow in spiritual maturity. The term "dark night of the soul" is commonly used today as an expression for a spiritual crisis such as doubt, disconnection, despair, disbelief, striving, and so on. When you experience a dark night, call on the fiercely powerful *Divine Mother* aspect to help you cut through any obstacles you encounter.

Sometimes these obstacles appear as a crossroads. When you come to a spiritual crossroads in your life, you meet up with *Hecate*. *Hecate* is a classic Greek *Triple Mother Goddess*, (embodying the *Maiden, Mother* and *Crone*). Traditionally associated with crossroads, *Moon*, magic, and as a ruler over the *Earth*, sky, and sea as a *Savoir Being, Hecate* is an aspect of the *Fierce Divine Mother* energy and is the guardian of *Her* mysteries. *She* meets you at the crossroads to offer alternative ways of being. *She* stands in the center of the crossroads, surrounded by whirlwinds that move off into the four directions. *She* offers choices and directions that can take you deeper into *Her* mysteries if you can open your heart-mind to *Her*. *She* is also all about change.

Many times when you arrive at a crossroads there is an intense emotion compelling you to go in a certain direction and to take action in a particular way that relates to that emotional thrust. *Hecate* appears at that time to open your mind to other possibilities. When you meet *Hecate* at the crossroads, it is beneficial to take a time out to really contemplate each pathway and what it means for your expanding wisdom.

Hecate is associated with the *Underworld*, which symbolizes many things including your own deep, subconscious mind. Motivation to go in certain directions is often buried in this part of your mind so it is wise to spend quiet time with yourself to determine what is good and true for you. You may be pulled initially to the path most familiar. Upon reflection, another way might be the wisest choice. Be patient and take your time at the crossroads and the way will be revealed. The multi-powered force of the *Fierce Divine Mother* shines forth when truth is humbly and sincerely sought.

The world of duality poses a daily challenge for the spiritual aspirant seeking to transform negativity into positivity. The *Fierce Mother* is a kind of mystical magician that can reveal to you the love in anger and hate, the love in fear and longing, and the terrible destructive delusions of the man-made world and human consciousness. The joyful nectar in *Her* wisdom nature is that of the *Divine Child* who transcends duality to embrace fully the radiant light of bliss. To the *Divine Child* the *Fierce Divine Mother* aspect is pure love and peace. This is real, pure tantric realization.

When you are ready to look deeply into hidden issues that have negatively impacted your life, it is time to call upon the tremendous strength and clarity of the *Fierce Divine Mother* aspect to help clear these tendencies and habits. Maybe you have a strong habit of blaming others and this habit has only brought you into judgment and negative interactions. Realizing this, the fierce, roaring energy of the *Divine Mother* can help to annihilate this habit into oblivion and transmute the energy to a higher purpose for all. Every time the habit appears, call upon *Her*. Maybe your obstacle appears as anger at someone you have had issues with your entire life and you want to release it into love. The *Fierce Divine Mother* can assist you in letting go of anger and transmuting it into love. If you can recognize the anger as an illusion, the illusion instantly loses its power over you and you attain liberation.

The *Fierce Divine Mother* appears during the *Frosty Moon* cycle to remind you that you can literally melt all concretized or frozen limitations within yourself and liberate them into the vast spacious freedom of peace.

This brings you to the realm of the *Black Madonna*, which is one of spaciousness, freedom, transformation and miracles. *She* reveals everything that is hidden deeply within you. The *Black Madonna* represents the same qualities of the *Fierce Mother* and *Her* dark visage is in part, both a symbol and reflection of depth and the incomprehensible *Void*. In Western imagery the *Black Madonna* does not appear to be fierce, but the resulting energies from *Her* transformative power results in the miracle of freedom. In this way, *Her* fierce aspect is more hidden than *Throma, Kali,* or *Hecate's,* as *Her Void* annihilates all form. Mathew Fox teaches that the darkness is what the mystics call, "The inside of things, the essence of things." This is where your *Divinity* lies; the true self. The darkness of the

Black Madonna is where your illusions are broken apart to get to this truth. In this way *She* is like *Throma Nagmo* and the *Goddess Kali*; the black womb of light out of which all phenomena arise and return. The darkness is the presence behind all things. The *Black Madonna* evokes the darkness as the *Great Mystery* itself. The *Mystery* is beyond all rational, knowable, or understandable concepts. The *Black Madonna* is the essence of the *Great Mystery* within the *Great Mystery*. *She* is the cosmic bridge into the enlightened state of *Oneness* to the whole self beyond any boundaries into limitless light.

The *Black Madonna* or *Black Virgin* is found in paintings and statues in Spain, Sicily, Switzerland, France, Poland, and Czechoslovakia as well as in Turkey, Africa, Asia, and South America. In these representations *She* has dark skin and is often surrounded by the starry night. Generally, these statues and paintings were created in the Byzantine style in the thirteenth and fourteenth centuries. Many believe *She* is derived from *Isis* who was a multifaceted *Great Mother Goddess* of ancient Egypt that made *Her* way to Greece and Rome over time.

The *Black Madonna* honors the lower chakras, which are vital for spiritual seekers to embrace because most have the tendency to only reach upward and not downward deep into themselves and the *Earth*. This deep experiencing of density and darkness is the pathway into connecting viscerally in your human form, as well as spiritually to your *Mother Gaia*. Andrew Harvey says, "The *Black Madonna* is the *Queen of Nature*, the blesser and agent of all rich, fertile transformation in external and internal nature, in the outside world and in the psyche." To love embodying a human body is essential to the process of the *Sacred Marriage* that embraces both the *Divine Masculine* and the *Divine Feminine*. The *Black Madonna* assists in this process by deepening your understanding of the lower chakras and how they connect in *Holy Communion* with the upper ones. The physical meets the transcendent, becoming a union of opposites in the *Sacred Marriage*.

The *Black Madonna* welcomes you home when you leave your human form at the end of life and you become part of *Her* wholeness. *She* does not represent death. *She* is the *Great Expanse* beyond death.

In this sense, *She* is the *Divine Sister* of our own precious *Mother Gaia*. They both carry the full energy of wholeness that is being called forth as *Oneness* at this time. This calling forth is an exceptionally mystical and exciting invitation to everyone. Right now, this opportunity for *Oneness* is being broadcast through all of the forms of *Nature*, especially the elemental frequencies both planetary and individual energies of *Earth*, water, fire, air, and sacred sound/space. All around the world we are witnessing the annihilation of old forms and the reforming of new and exciting ways of being and living. We are witnessing the vibrant transformative legacy of the *Fierce Divine Mother Goddess*.

Her love is never dangerous but it will transform you for *She* is the *Goddess of Change*. Love itself is an alchemical fire with a fierce and powerful energy that can transform virtually any discursive emotion, energy, or force. Surrender to *Her* fierce love and let your world fall apart into *Her* heart of total bliss, peace, and freedom.

Moon Mother Goddess Luna

Attunement 11

FROSTY MOON

ELEVENTH MONTH OF THE LUNAR CALENDAR

HE FIERCE DIVINE MOTHER APPEARS during the *Frosty Moon* cycle to remind you that you can melt the icy, concretized limitations and concepts of yourself that you carry.

HOME FUN

✥ Make a list of the limiting views you have of yourself.

✥ Decide which of these you would like to liberate in this *Moon* cycle.

✥ Meditate and state your intention.

- Call upon whatever aspect of the *Fierce Divine Mother* you resonate with, and ask for *Her* assistance.

- Be patient and do this every day.

- Journal what insights you are given through meditating with the *Fierce Divine Mother*.

- Notice the process of liberating old outworn beliefs, and the many layers that appear.

- Make notes of these insights and changes in your mandala.

- Celebrate your courage.

- Make prayers of dedication and gratitude to the *Fierce Mother Goddess*.

Mother Goddess As The Compassionate World

Chapter 12

"If we have no peace,
it is because we have forgotten that we belong to each other."

Mother Teresa of Calcutta

*N*OW YOU FIND THAT THE FIERCE MOTHER has swept away your coveted illusions–everything inauthentic, emotional, mental blockages, and just plain resistance. *She* has cleared your pathway for an expanded awareness to arise. *She* has accomplished the necessary annihilation of the small self in order to revive your true, passionately loving self. This is an ongoing, repetitive process that occurs until you reach your full transcendent *Enlightenment*. To accomplish this alchemical process, a very real and symbolic death has transpired through the *Fierce Mother's* transformative power and you suddenly find yourself reborn anew into the *Divine Mother's Compassionate World*.

The *Mother Goddess*, as the *Compassionate World*, teaches you how to expand the consciousness of your own innate goodness through loving-kindness. The *Divine Mother Goddess* honors you with the incalculable blessing of rebirth into a vibrating new world perceived and experienced through *Her* glorious and exhilarating *Divine Grace*. When your heart is consciously attuned to the luminous cathedral of *Her* heart, you experience both the internal and external world in a radically different way. This holy awareness is a sacred gem that is witnessed and experienced by you as radiant peace in a multitude of ways, through *Her* unconditional love and compassionate care.

The cathedral of the *Divine Mother's Heart* is a wish-fulfilling jewel, the most rare treasure imaginable. There are many facets to this radiant gem of wisdom, including the enlightened energies of harmony, kindness, empathy, happiness, gratitude, nurturing, forgiveness, unconditional love, joy, peace, grace, ease, and mindfulness. *Her* heart is a mystical portal, a pulsating gem of wisdom available to you whenever you are willing to accept the *Divine Mother's* invitation and attune to *Her* great mysteries.

A good way to begin to attune to the *Divine Mother's* magnificent mystery of a *Compassionate World* is through mindfulness. Mindfulness is experienced, moment-by-moment through non-judgmental awareness coupled with the mental focus that helps you to achieve emotional awareness and balance. Gentle and simple breathing techniques let you attend to the state of your mind with a soft sense of physical presence. Mindfulness becomes the gateway for accepting exactly where you and others are in any given moment. As this occurs you can begin to relax and open further to the mysteries of the gem of the *Divine Mother's Heart*, which contains the illuminating treasure of *Her Compassionate World*.

In the very center of this gem of wisdom, the *Divine Mother* holds for you the resplendent treasure of *Divine* self-love. According to Paramahansa Yogananda, the greatest love you can experience is in communion with *God* in meditation. He teaches that the love within you between your *Soul* and *Spirit* is the perfect love, the love you are truly seeking. Millions of thrills pass through your heart. If you meditate deeply, a love will overcome you such as no human tongue can describe, and you will know *Divine* love. Within *Divine* love is the immeasurable capacity for *Divine* self-love.

This wise and compassionate Hindu master teaches that the world as a whole has forgotten the real meaning of love; only a few know the true meaning of it. Yogananda also said that, "Just as oil is present in every part of the olive, so love permeates every part of creation." In the universal sense, love is the *Divine* power of attraction in creation that harmonizes, unites, and binds together. Those who live in tune with the attractive force of love achieve harmony with nature and all beings and are attracted to blissful reunion with *Spirit*.

When your consciousness is immersed in *Divine* love there are no boundaries or sense of separation. The *Divine* inculcates your entire consciousness and opens your heart completely. This cannot happen until you include yourself and totally wrap yourself in *Divine* love. The *Divine Mother* loves you unconditionally and you are *Her*. *She* is a living presence in every complex, unique human being, glorious flower, animal, action, or thought. *Her Divine* love permeates all of creation. When you lean into this immeasurable loving force it will open your heart to yourself within all of creation. The *Divine Mother's Compassionate World* could not exist without *Her* being an active presence in virtually everything in the physical world. *Her* love is the cosmic glue that holds it all together including you and your body. If you don't love yourself how can you feel *Her* love anywhere much less everywhere? *Divine* self-love is pure radiant beauty.

I once attended a week long meditation retreat with a great Tibetan master, His Holiness Sakya Trizen. His lineage descends from the *Gods of the Realm of Clear Light*, whose family is known as the *Celestial Race*. Currently His Holiness is the forty-first Sakya Trizen and is the head of the Sakya Order of Tibetan Buddhism. He was instructing us on a particular mandala offering. It was a very detailed and precise teaching and everything he said was translated into English from Tibetan. My mind began to wander during the translation at one point and I was thinking of all the things on my "to do list." All of a sudden I felt this thwack on my head and heard the words, "Love yourself." It was so clear I actually thought at first that someone had whacked me on the head and uttered those words. I was shocked. I looked around the crowded shrine room to see who had done it. I quickly observed that all the practitioners around me were very intently listening to His Holiness. Needless to say I was a little flummoxed and during the break I asked our resident Lama Gyatso Rinpoche what had happened. He laughed and laughed which confused me even more. Finally he said that it was the *Deity* getting my attention and that, that specific practice would bring me great benefit. He added I should be particularly diligent in those teachings. Since then my offering practices have really deepened and grown and my understanding of the message continues to unfold.

But back then I felt like the explanation was incomplete. I sat with it for a few weeks and went back and asked Lama Gyatso if loving yourself was considered to be an important aspect of the tantric tradition. I had never heard that taught so directly before. He looked at me curiously and said, "Of course it is. If you don't love yourself you will never liberate because it is the self that liberates and it takes a great deal of love to accomplish that." Over time, and with a great deal of practice, I have come to understand that total liberation is the most surrendered act of *Divine* self-love you can achieve.

Divine self-love is the ignition switch of the heart-fire of *Spirit*. *Divine* self-love is an ever-expanding truth of consciousness. It is a key to the *Sacred Marriage*. *Divine* self-love is the essence of who you are. It is the purest, creative energy in the universe and is available to love yourself completely, no matter what, is a *Divine* act. Everything that appears in your life is an opportunity to grow your self-love, to learn from each and every experience.

Divine self-love is not narcissism. It is about caring about yourself and taking responsibility for yourself and every single thing in your life. It is the instinct or aspiration to promote your own well-being and self-regard as a child of the *Divine Marriage*. While there are many ways you already love yourself, there are many more ways you can care for your well-being. Those are the areas to reflect upon. What is it that prevents you or blocks you in those situations? Loving yourself means to have full radical acceptance of who you are right now and to understand the *Divine Mother* is already there ahead of you, holding you in *Her* vast field of unconditional love. You are already *Her* beloved. To feel yourself held in this grace, you can call upon the glorious *Divine Mother Mary* who holds you within *Her* luminous loving embrace, always. *Her* loving energy is a palpable and limitless field. *Her* miracle of *Divine* love is arising in many hearts and minds during this present time. Call on *Her* to ease your way and gently usher you into your *Divine* self-loving awareness that will change all of your perceptions. Your perceptions will grow to become founded in love. They will become completely pure.

Once you accept this gem of wisdom into your heart begin to engender self-appreciation from a *Divine* view of evolutionary consciousness, which is vast and eternal. Do you recognize your growth and learning from situations in the past? Do you understand where you can still grow and learn without judging yourself? Do you experience yourself in a new way? Do the mistakes you feel you made in your life begin to appear as *Divine* lessons?

You are here to grow spiritually. Everything you have experienced is a part of the *Divine* plan for your soul's evolution that you have created and is the movement of the *Divine Mother* within you. When you view your life from this perspective it helps you to have a larger, vaster sense of your experiences.

The great Indian sage, mystic, philosopher, and spiritual leader, Sri Aurobindo, wrote a small, beautiful, and concise work entitled, *The Mother*. I love this quote,

> *"There are many planes of the Mother's creation,*
> *many steps of the Divine Shakti. At the summit of*
> *this manifestation of which we are a part there are*
> *worlds of infinite existence, consciousness, force and bliss over*
> *which the Mother stands as the unveiled eternal Power.*
> *All beings there live and move in an ineffable completeness*
> *and unalterable Oneness because She carries them*
> *safe in Her arms forever...But here where we dwell*
> *are the worlds of Ignorance, worlds of mind and life and*
> *body separated in consciousness from their source,*
> *of which this earth is a significant centre and its evolution*
> *a crucial process. This too with all its obscurity and struggle*
> *and imperfection is upheld by the Universal Mother;*
> *this too is impelled and guided to its secret aim*
> *by the MahaShakti."*

MahaShakti is the *Supreme Divine Mother. Her* secret aim that Aurobindo refers to is the cosmic realm of *Oneness* that all aspirants aspire to attain through *Her* powerful and ineffable loving force and *Her* miracle of eternal beauty that lives in each being as self-love. In this sense, self-love and *Divine* love are the same; *Divine* self-love.

Divine self-love means to recognize yourself as a distinct expression and to honor your own uniqueness by celebrating, expressing, and living it. You have your own gifts that are your particular offerings to the world and everyone contributes to the whole. Nothing is separate. There is no part of you *She* does not love as *She* made all your parts possible. This unifying energy is healing and powerful to experience and to carry within you. Take whatever time you need to taste this sweetness. It becomes a blessed relief from any suffering, this sweet, golden transformative elixir of *Divine* self-love.

The next part of your journey is to tenderly and gently nurture this new self in whatever ways your inner wisdom reveals. Release any conflicting tendencies about loving yourself every time they arise, one at a time. Offer them up to the *Divine Mother* for *Her* to transform into a more positive energy for you and others. Doing this continually in a loving and empowering way will catapult you into a higher frequency of being that is in harmony with cosmic truth. This higher frequency makes it much easier to stay attuned and aligned with the immeasurable radiating force of pure *Divine* love.

When you feel you need a lot of energy to move something that feels solid or stuck, call upon the *Goddess Tara*. *Tara* is a great *Goddesses* and has twenty-one aspects. *She* is so powerful! *She* is known as the *Sweet Savioress* and is the embodiment of wisdom. *She* is beloved around the world in various forms and is believed to be millions of years old. The ancient *Druids* called *Her* their *Mother Goddess* and *She* is also the *Mother Goddess* of the Tibetans. *Tara* in Sanskrit means *Star*. *Tara* is known as the *Mother of all the Enlightened Ones*, or *Buddhas*, so you know *Her* power is radically transformative and reliable. *She* is also known as a fierce protectoress. You visualize *Tara* with an effulgent light body, saturated with rich color, sparkling with radiant jewels and surrounded by an orb of rainbow light. When you call on *Her* you can chant *Her* basic mantra,

Om Tare Tuttare Ture Soha

Red Tara is the aspect of *Tara* known as the *Goddess* that is an *Open Door to Bliss and Awareness*. *She* is a brilliant ruby red, which signifies the desire that all beings find liberation. *She* wears a crown of gems and wears jeweled ornaments and silken garments. *She* is radiant, smiling, and quite beautiful. Half of *Her* hair is gathered at the crown of *Her* head and half flows down *Her* back. *She* has three eyes. The mantra for the *Red Tara* practice I do daily is for magnetizing all good things and is,

Om Tare Tam Soha

I love this practice as the association of the magnetizing

quality of the red aspect of *Tara* is also that of compassion and love.

You have already met the *Goddess Kwan Yin* and this is the perfect juncture to delve more deeply into *Her* wisdom. *Kwan Yin* is the beautiful manifestation of the *Divine Mother* who serves all beings with the infinite grace of *Her* full, radiating, universal, and infinite compassion.

Kwan Yin was born a princess. When *She* was born the *Earth* trembled and fragrant blossoms sprang up in the winter snow. Even as a young child, *Kwan Yin*'s purity and kindness were evident. *Kwan Yin*'s parents, the King and Queen, were disappointed to have yet another daughter, even one such as *Kwan Yin*. When *She* grew older they tried to marry *Her* off to a wealthy man, but *She* refused and begged to be allowed to become a nun instead. Eventually, *Her* enraged father agreed, instructing the nuns to discourage *Her* from being a nun by making *Her* life extremely difficult. In spite of the terrible hardships *She* suffered, miracles kept happening around *Her*, which enraged *Her* father even more. He actually sent someone to kill *Her* but the huntsman could not go through with it when he saw *Her* kindness and virtue and instead, knelt and offered to become *Her* servant.

Finally, the clouds came down from the hillsides and carried *Her* to safety to a nearby island where *She* continued *Her* studies, out of *Her* father's reach, safely and in peace. *She* eventually sacrificed *Herself* to save *Her* father's life when he became dangerously ill. Through that act of selfless love and compassion, *She* ascended to the pure realms to become the *Goddess Kwan Yin* in the sky, manifesting a thousand arms and eyes of pure compassion and love.

The *Divine Mother's Compassionate World* is the realm of enlightened beings such as *Mother Mary, Kwan Yin*, and *Tara*. All of these great beings are *Divine Mothers* who actualized compassion for all beings. Their gift of compassion to you is so powerful it can transform any negative karma you have accrued. Compassion is a get out of jail card, the jail of suffering. His Eminence Chagdud Tulku Rinpoche taught that one instance of genuine compassion can purify karma accumulated over aeons! In his book,

A Change of Heart, he illustrates this with the story of the beginning of the *Buddha's* path to enlightenment. "It started when the *Buddha* was in a hell realm, as an ordinary being yoked to another, pulling a cart. Beaten mercilessly by guards because they had become too weak to move the cart, the future *Buddha* thought he might as well try to pull it alone and let his partner rest. When he told the guards, they replied, 'No one can protect another from his karma.' With that, they set upon the future *Buddha* so ferociously that he died and was reborn in another realm. Had it not been for that moment of compassion, he might have remained in hell until his karma had been purified through sheer suffering. Compassion is the universal solvent that dissolves the stain of negative karma from this and lifetimes past."

What is compassion? Compassion is the deep aspiration you create that all other beings be completely free from suffering which includes sympathy and understanding of their suffering. Empathy is the ability to identify with or understand another's situation or feelings. Many people believe empathy is compassion. Empathy helps you to embrace a compassionate view because it helps you to become closer to another. The closer you get to another person the more unbearable any suffering they experience is to you and it leads you to the profound spiritual quality of compassion. Compassion is vaster and more encompassing than empathy because it holds sacred action in its depth of relieving others of the suffering you can feel so profoundly and intensely in others.

His Holiness the Dalai Lama is the best teacher I have ever found for learning about compassion. He is considered the emanation of the great *Buddha of Compassion, Avalokitesvara (Chen Rezig)*. His extensive teachings on compassion are profound and magnificently intricate and precise. He speaks of empathy and compassion as founded initially upon closeness. He says that closeness is not a physical proximity, nor need it be an emotional one. It is a feeling of responsibility of concern for another person. In order to develop such closeness, you must reflect upon the virtues of cherishing the well-being of others. You must come to see how this brings you an inner happiness and peace of mind.

Compassion is the soft-heartedness you feel when you gaze upon an innocent and vulnerable child and want to help her. It is the sympathy you feel when you see a hungry or confused homeless mother with her children on the street and offer them something. Compassion is the kindness generated when you help another being in whatever way you can. It is the clemency you offer to someone who is critical of you. Compassion is the humanness you share with all other human beings. Compassion is the energy of belonging you feel when your heart is inculcated with the softness of the *Divine Mother's* unconditional love, which embraces all beings and is their very essence and sees beyond any negativity and illusion

You can practice compassion anywhere and in all kinds of situations. It is a riveting truth that by engendering compassion in your own life you can ameliorate your own future suffering! Compassion is the key to spiritual evolvement in your very own life. Compassion is essential for human evolvement and survival.

How do you begin to realize this kind of compassionate reality that is the *Heart* of the *Divine Mother*? Being kind to yourself is to celebrate the *Divine Mother's* gift of life in an honoring and mindful way in every moment. It sounds simple, but is it? Imagining and engendering a *Compassionate World* must begin within.

People do so much violence to themselves through their thoughts. Harsh self-thinking is debilitating. If, as you read, this you feel yes, but I did this or I did that and how can I be compassionate to myself over that? Begin by calling in the *Divine Mother* to assist you and bathe in *Her* light of unconditional love for you. In this field of awareness, a door gently opens to the possibility for you to generate self-compassion. You can rely on *Tara* as a very beneficial healing force in your life. See *Her* in *Her* fullness of twenty-one aspects that are all working to assist you in transforming whatever needs to be transformed.

Divine self-compassion is a healing field of energy that evaporates the tremendous past and transforms it into faultless memories of growth and expansion. *Divine* self-compassion is to realize you are *Divine* and have the capacity to end your own suffering, no matter what. It took many years for me to practice this and understand the power of it. Once in a teaching with His Holiness the Dalai Lama, I witnessed him actually weeping when He realized the depth of self-loathing people have here in the West. The energy of his deep abiding compassion somehow mysteriously and magnificently began to open the closed doorway in my heart to *Divine* self-compassion and acceptance, which has led to a real sense of freedom from suffering. All of us have a life story with some good parts and some not so good parts. The negative qualities, aspects, or memories will find acceptance in *Divine* self-compassion. Those hidden and stuck energies you are holding onto through your own tender heartedness will enter the flames. This is the alchemical transformational quality of the *Divine Mother's Heart*-fire that burns within. The alchemy of self-forgiveness and *Divine* self-love are the cosmic fuel for realizing *Divine* self-compassion.

How do you awaken this aspect of the *Divine Mother* within you? First, recognize the energy of compassion when it moves through the world around you. Compassion is the grace of kindness, mercy, and tenderness that is evoked when you call upon the *Divine Mother Mary*. Compassion is the strength of purpose to change suffering that arises from *Tara*'s power and skill. Compassion is the heart-mind of *Kwan Yin*.

Understanding the suffering of others is the foundation of generating compassion. There is nothing that tends to be more powerful or effective than focusing on your own suffering first. In modern culture we seek pleasure, entertainment, or anything else that can distract us from our own suffering. It is not that you want to dwell on your own suffering, but you recognize it, accept it honestly, and embrace it lovingly as a means to generate self-love and self-kindness. *Divine* self-compassion means to go even further, and to embrace yourself as a *Divine* being who does not need to suffer anymore. You are here in a human experience, which is an incredible opportunity for your *Soul*'s learning and growth. To embrace your life as a learning and spiritual evolutionary process is to begin to pierce through the mirage of illusion and to perceive the truth of who you really are. Realizing that you do not need to suffer anymore is profoundly freeing. It does not mean that things don't happen to you;

it is that you learn to work with your mind so they do not appear to you in the same way. The first step is to look deeply at suffering.

How do you begin to even look at your own suffering? The first step is to acknowledge you do suffer and you are worthy of *Divine* self-compassion, no matter what. You set the intention that instead of judging yourself for any discursive or negative tendencies you have or any negative situations you have created, you develop the understanding that the lessons that arose from them illuminates your awareness. Some of these lessons serve as major movements in your *Soul*'s evolution and some are minor ones. The important thing is to soften your heart towards yourself and forgive any judgment you have. Gently and softly look at any situation again through the eyes of your heart and compassionate understanding. You will see it through a new and wiser perspective. To be able to generate *Divine* self-compassion, it is imperative you contemplate self-kindness.

Gently, gently, gently begin to unwrap the memories of your suffering. Free any victim mentality you have into the understanding that all that has occurred in your life is for your own spiritual growth. You are the dreamer, the one who has created the dream you are experiencing. This begins to transform your view into a pure view of experience where your mind is unclouded by dualistic perception. Pure perception is a liberating experience that eases the heart into trust and beauty. The appearances in your life might remain unchanged but when your perception of their meaning and existence alters, they begin to be less real and have less power. *Divine* self-compassion is a practice of sacred beauty where you experience yourself as a radiant, *Divine* being full of beauty and goodness. It is to experience yourself through the eyes of the *Divine Mother*.

I grew up in a family with lots of secrets. One of these was to hide our true feelings and thoughts as a means of supporting my narcissistic mother's behaviors. Members of narcissistic families are usually disconnected emotionally from each other and from themselves. This disconnection can often cause deep splits in one's personality. Sometimes the split off portions begin to imagine other realities and when this happens, serious problems can arise. In my own case, I began to perceive other realities that I thought I had made up. In truth, they were different realms that I had actually attuned to.

It has taken a lifetime to come to terms with this. Through the practice of *Divine* self-compassion I began to let go of the fear of being strange and weird. When I relaxed, the realization arose that "my imaginings" were actual realities that I, as a sensitive child, had tuned into and visited. All kinds of nature and angelic beings turned up to befriend and support me through the difficult time of my childhood. Now that I have learned *Divine* self-compassion, they are appearing once again. You really never know where *Divine* self-compassion will lead you.

In exploring *Divine* self-compassion I have found that trees can be very helpful and supportive. Go to the forest to learn to root yourself in the *Compassionate World of the Goddess*. Trees are teachers. They stand tall in selfless service and are rooted deeply in their authentic beingness. See if you can find a *Mother* tree and sit with *Her*, feeling the wisdom in *Her* earthen womb reaching out through *Her* limbs and branches. This womb realm is a familiar place from your deep womb time earlier on in this journey. Going into this deep, dark, verdant space to create anew is very supportive. It is the place of quiet nurturing within you that is the *Compassionate World* of the *Divine Mother*. As you embrace your own suffering, let its wisdom unfold in your heart. Your heart already knows the reason for the suffering. It is not a mystery but a part of the mystery–the mystery of becoming. In the unfolding of its teaching the suffering will transform into a gift of growth and becoming.

It is essential here to not be trapped in a linear point of view. If you find yourself walking a straight and narrow path of right and wrong in your thinking, step off of it and explore all the nuances of the shadows, forms, lush undergrowth, and hidden magic here. A narrow path is too constricting for this consciousness. Let yourself expand with the forest's consciousness where alignment with the *Great Mother's* heart jewel is prevalent. It is the place where judgments fall away into love and the understanding of nuances and subtlety. Listen carefully with your ear to the ground so you do not miss anything.

If the forest does not speak to you, maybe a flower garden will. Flowers are unique expressions of beauty far removed from the duality of right and wrong. They just are who they are in each of their unique expressions of beauty. They don't judge each other or compete. They just open to the light, each in their own way. This is the way of *Divine* self-compassion where you let the tremendous past dissolve. Enfolded in the *Divine Mother's* resplendent gem of wisdom, you become fully present to your own shining and transcendent beauty. A single facet of this gem of wisdom is the vibration of harmony. About five miles down the road from where I live, is the tiny town of Harmony. Eighteen people live there in perfect harmony. What do I mean by perfect harmony? Perfect harmony is being one hundred percent congruent. This means your inner and outer worlds are in perfect alignment, singing a clear, pure song of beauty inward and outward. This happens when your beliefs and actions are perfectly aligned in a tune of surrendered grace. This is not a political or emotional treasure it is a spiritual treasure that can be expanded upon exponentially through *Divine* self-love and *Divine* self-compassion.

Divine self-love is when you connect with the Infinite Source at the very core of your being. *Divine* self-compassion is the ultimate embodiment of spiritual and emotional maturity. It is through *Divine* self-compassion that a person achieves the highest peak and deepest reach in his or her search to becoming a *Bodhisattva* whose whole reality is total and powerfully intense compassion for all beings. Transforming your world into a peaceful and loving place is the great work of our time to engender a peaceful world.

The great saint Mother Teresa of Calcutta had the pure perception to manifest the *Divine Mother's Compassionate World*. There is a story that one day while walking in the streets of Calcutta *She* happened upon a leper who had no feet or hands. His body oozed sores and he was not long to live. Mother Teresa, passing by in a hurry, stopped *Her* procession to sit down with the leper and hold him lovingly in *Her* arms. *She* caressed and kissed him and he cried out to *Her*, "Oh no, mother, you will become diseased like I am," and tears fell from his eyes. Mother Teresa looked at him and smiled and said, "Oh no, you are a perfect and precious being of love to me." *She* saw only the truth of him as he really was.

Can you imagine what it would be like to live in the *Divine Mother's Compassionate World*? Imagine the world as a place where every single person experienced deep compassion for every other being. Imagine a world where everyone's well being was cherished–where every being was so loved and taken care of that the concepts of separation would evaporate. There would be no war, no hunger, and no pollution. It would be a peaceful and pure realm of bliss and spiritual connection where all would manifest compassion for anyone's suffering. Imagine the entire world focused on your suffering and praying to ameliorate it all in an instant. Can you imagine the immense healing power of every single being on Earth praying for you to be free of all of your suffering? Can you imagine the unified field of consciousness that would be revealed? Can you imagine the field of love and compassion that would envelop all life? It would be astounding.

This immense healing power is what the *Moon Mother*, the *Blue Moon*, is all about in *Her* twelfth cycle. This healing power is a spiraling force in the *Divine Mother's Heart* that *Her* sister *Luna*, the *Moon Mother* carries and is there for anyone to harness and manifest at this time.

Deep feelings will arise in this part of your journey. You may be challenged by the magnitude of your emotions, especially as we have become so skilled in avoiding our feelings. But they are a key component of awakening consciousness. How deeply you allow yourself to feel is an indicator of how expanded your consciousness is. This is another paradox because while emotions are always changing and are not always totally reliable, they are nonetheless a key to developing spiritual insight and qualities. *Divine* self-love and *Divine* self-compassion begin in your experience of feeling and evolve into a state of consciousness that grows beyond conceptual thinking. Let yourself go deeply into your feelings at this juncture to remove any weeds from your garden of compassion. Compassion carries in its wisdom the awareness of the interdependence of all things. When you create a field of energy of *Divine* self-love and *Divine* self-compassion, you are healing the entire world through the wisdom heart of the *Divine Mother* and assisting the spiritual evolution of our planet to realize *Her Compassionate World*. You are helping to celebrate *Her*. Mathew Fox teaches that "Celebration is a part of compassion," and as Meister Eckhart says, "What happens to another, be it joy or sorrow, happens to me."

Celebration is the exercise of our common joy. Compassion is the best of what is available to our human species and the best of what we are capable.

"Love and compassion are necessities, not luxuries.
Without them humanity cannot survive"

His Holiness the Dalai Lama

Moon Mother Goddess Luna

Attunement 12

BLUE MOON

TWELFTH MONTH OF THE LUNAR CALENDAR

HIS TWELFTH CYCLE OF THE MOON MOTHER, the *Blue Moon*, contains an enormous healing power that is the essence of *Divine* self-love and *Divine* self-compassion. Blue is the color of the *Divine* healing ray.

You live in a loving, compassionate universe. Your true nature is illuminated by light. Now let us see how you can realize this more deeply.

HOME FUN

❧ Pray to the *Blue Moon Mother Goddess* to transform old habitual ways of being with yourself that you have become aware of in this part of your sacred journey.

- A common suffering today is the lack of loving being in a human body. Here is a way to begin to transform this prevalent source of suffering.

- Ask, what would happen if you loved your body?

- What would happen if you no longer carried body fear or denial or dislike?

- What would happen if you let yourself really feel your body with no fear?

- How would it feel if every sensation were a touch of the love of the *Goddess*?

- Imagine loving all physical phenomena.

- Write down every day in this cycle any negative feelings you have about your body.

- Write about your own suffering.

- Imagine yourself as a *Divine Being* filled with only love for yourself.

- On the *Full Moon* write down what lessons of *Spiritual* growth your suffering has brought you.

- Release it all to the *Blue Moon Mother* as a *Full Moon* ritual and generate compassion for yourself and all beings.

- Dedicate this as an offering to benefit all beings.

Mothering The Divine:
Claiming Your Wisdom

Chapter 13

The Tao is called the Great Mother;
empty yet inexhaustible,
it gives birth to infinite worlds.
When you recognize the children and find the Mother,
you will be free of sorrow.

Tao Te Ching

The walking dream comes to life,
and lives Her vision through me,
Emerging from the chrysalis,
She sets Her heart free.

Mother of the seeds of change,
Who nurture them as they grow,
You planted a dream in my heart
to illuminate all that I know.

You taught me how to give away,
My fear of becoming the dream,
Showing me how to walk my truth,
reclaiming self-love and esteem.

As I become all that I am,
then together we shall fly,
The spirit of transformation,
reflected in Condor's eye.

Jamie Sams

*M*OTHERING THE DIVINE IS ABOUT nurturing and becoming a wise being, an elder and master of wisdom. You transform and transmute your sense of self to embrace the *Divine Mother* as a real being within you that is vitally alive and luminously vibrant. Now is the time to shape your intention to bring forth your own inner radiating *Divine Mother* wisdom and to *Mother* your own immensely *Divine* presence. As you integrate and make manifest all of the lessons and spiritual teachings you have received you will evolve into a *Wisdom Being* and discover that you are on this path because the *Divine Mother* invited you here.

Transformation is not always easy. Transformation on the spiritual path can appear as confusion and pain. It can appear as separateness. The power to become a wise being is fired by change, which in my own experience came down to total surrender. Transforming yourself from an ordinary being to becoming a realized *Divine Child* changes everything. It has to. You have to give up old habits, ways of thinking, identities, anger, confusion, prejudices, notions, beliefs, the need to be right, and yes the big one, the ego. It is about being disillusioned with your teacher, guru, mentors, friends, and yourself. It is here the *Fierce Mother* usually shows up to break you apart even more in *Her* infinite compassion. During this intense process it is important to learn how to relax and rely on the *Divine Mother's* all-encompassing love and wisdom–all so much larger than you ever conceived. *Her* love and immensity gives you the courage, trust, and fortitude to keep going, no matter what, even when you want to give up and go eat donuts. Remembering that the *Mother Goddess* is directing the changes makes it easier to comprehend and embrace them.

Mothering the Divine is a transformative journey to becoming an elder of wisdom that has nothing to do with age. It has to do with your level of awareness and enlightened action. It is about claiming your mastership of spiritual principles that embody the sacred energies of the *Divine Mother*. In traditional indigenous cultures the elders are the people who live their spiritual teachings in a way that inspires others. The term *Grandmother* or *Grandfather* is one of ultimate respect. These wise elders hold the tried and true traditional lineage teachings for all their people and perform ceremonies and healing rituals for their community and all their relations. It is important to recognize that elders have grown into the wholeness of a bigger vision of life and often become wisdom mentors and a healing presence to others. It does not happen overnight. Most elders are older in years because it often takes a lifetime to transmute and transform into becoming a wise human being.

What is wisdom? Wisdom is having the ability to think and act using spiritual knowledge, experience, understanding, common sense, and insight. Wisdom is regarded as a spiritual virtue. Wisdom has its own singing vibration that others can sense because it is the heart's highest spiritual intelligence and presence. This implies a possession of insight and spiritual knowledge that can be applied to any given circumstance that might arise in your life or in other's lives. Your heart's intelligence carries the understanding of people, objects, events, and situations and the willingness as well as the ability to apply spiritual perception, discernment, and action in keeping with what is the most beneficial course of action for all. It means you have learned to control your emotional reactions so that rather than just reacting to a given situation you can choose your thoughts and action. In short, wisdom is the deep and mature innate nature of your heart's intelligence and perception.

Mothering the Divine is the expression of spiritual wisdom that brings soul texture and awareness to your life and to the life of others. *Wisdom Beings* bring a deeply loving, illuminating, and kind presence to the world. When you learn to live as a holy being, you demonstrate that you have the courage to spiritually evolve by staying on your spiritual path. You are no longer drawn into the play of limiting illusions that trap so many. Living a holy life is a process that changes you from an individual self to an expansive, spacious, infinite, and universal member of the cosmos: a *Divine Child* at play in the multitudes of heaven.

As your spiritual awareness increases, all your parts come into coherency with your heart's innate wisdom. Your way of being in the world radiates this mastership. A *Wisdom Being* has self-knowledge and experience that *She* utilizes to benefit others. Dusting away ignorance, the wise person uncovers *Her* own true nature, which is kind and loving. The heart of the *Divine Mother* expresses pure and unconditional love in a limitless flow. Everyone has their own unique journey to find this ever-flowing fountain of love within. The journey to this fountain is chosen by each of us and for most, it takes many lifetimes to find. My choice and creation was to go through an extremely painful childhood and rebellious youth in order to mature spiritually in this lifetime. This pathway of learning took me to many places and up twisting roads seemingly going nowhere, but ultimately lead me to the pathway of surrendering into love.

This world is a dream and you manifest your own dream creations through your karma and will. Within your dream creations, you have the choice to embrace your spiritual self in a beautifully unique and sovereign way. You are a unique expression of the *Divine Mother* and as such, fit into the totality of *Her* wholeness as a vital and expressively distinctive thread. Each thread of creation, every single being, is essential for the whole to be expressed fully as the *Great Mystery*. Each of us has their special, reserved place in the *Divine* pageantry of *Oneness*.

It is your choice how you vibrate. Vibrating as a *Wisdom Being* lifts the energy of the entire web of creation. Each *Mother Goddess* you have met on this journey does this and has chosen to be present in an enlightened and holy way in the world even though many are veiled and hidden. *Mothering the Divine* is so sweet because it evokes an intuitive sense of the universes being held in *Her* loving and nurturing embrace. This is the great treasure you discover on your way. It gives you a sense of fullness and limitless creative possibilities that are mirrored within your own soul. *Wisdom Beings* know how to work with the creative force of the *Divine Mother* to co-create a world of beauty through intention. As I have already said, intention is the way to consciously determine your experience; not the presenting phenomena, but your experience of it. How does this really work? If you set your intention to be more loving and compassionate you will live in the *Divine Mother's Compassionate World*. By stating that intention throughout your day and adhering to it diligently, it will transform experiences and outworn habits until you actually experience the loving intention as a reality. Try it for a week. Every day state this as your intention. When you brush your teeth, wash your face, eat your meals, meditate, interact with others, work, walk, and play, constantly state this as your intention. In this way your experience including those activities I've just mentioned, will begin to transform. You will be *Mothering the Divine* in every moment.

Next expand your intention to include all other beings. Try this for a week. State your intention to be more loving and compassionate, and this will cause the entire world to become a more loving and compassionate place for every single being, unequivocally. State this throughout your day and you will be amazed by what happens. Your perspective, experiences, and heart will all change. With this clear intent you will be co-creating a new world of love and compassion with the *Divine Mother* energy as you also strengthen your mastership. This mastership is how you vibrate at a higher frequency in every single moment.

If you want to be more aware and expanded then make that your clear intention. Make it vaster and include every single being in your intention. I intend to be more expanded and aware in every moment and this will expand and lift the consciousness of every single being as well. This is the way of the *Mothering the Divine* to become a being of wisdom. Your intention is the steering wheel of all your experiences, so it is vital to work with it continually throughout your day.

When I began doing this in a very real and active way my life totally changed. I no longer felt alone, confused, or isolated. I began to feel myself as a part of the vast web of life and increasingly joyful all the time. It made me realize that we all posses the power to create our own reality. Working with the intention to experience life from a higher vibrational viewpoint, the presenting phenomena will begin to metamorphose into spiritual opportunities for growth. It is magical. Even if the outer experience does not change the inner experience transforms itself. The *Divine Mother's* veiled mysteries have great power and are so embedded in our lives most people don't perceive *Her*.

Now is when the wisdom of the enlightened qualities reflected in all the *Divine Mother's* you have met so far begins to be realized within you. Every *Mother Goddess* you have met on this journey is a fully realized *Wisdom Being*. All of them are here to nurture your own shimmering beauty and innate wisdom. Which of these *Divine* Beauties most authentically represents you now? Which ones would you like to embrace more fully in order to live your own unique holy life?

Life is a spiraling journey and through this particular turn of your life's spiral you begin to recognize and embody the pure expression of your own energy signature as the wise being you truly are. It is now you recognize that all your experiences are doorways, which have had *Her* behind them. These doorways are there to teach you to grow spiritually. At this time, you are entering the thirteenth phase of the *Moon Goddess Luna's* cycle, the *Violet Moon*. The *Violet Moon* is all about transformation. Each *Divine Mother* along the way has been speaking to you in diverse expressions. It is now time for you to consciously choose and embrace those energies that you wish to claim for yourself right now, as a way of embracing your own transformation.

The first stage of this becoming is to create a ceremony where you establish a council of *Divine Mothers* who gather to continually support and guide you as you make your way into embracing the wise elder within you. Ceremonies are a wonderful way to both celebrate the *Divine Mother* and to consecrate your own unique passage into becoming a wise being of *Her* wisdom. They are a way to honor this spiritual milestone in your life.

As long as human beings have walked upon the earth they have created ceremonies to sanctify their lives. Ceremonies and plant medicine connect people more deeply to the world around them, to their ancestors, and to the *Divine*. *Mothering the Divine* in a sense, is a constant celebration ceremony of the *Divine Mother* in *Her* vast, *Maha*, or great aspects.

Ceremonies are a bridge between the mundane and spirit worlds. Ceremony will assist you as you come into alignment and resonance with the *Divine Mother* energy within you and without you, throughout time and space. It is a wonderful, integrative way to invoke the spiritual presence and blessing of the *Divine Mother*.

Wisdom elders prepare and perform ceremonies for their community. You can create them too in an authentic and expressive way that tells the story of where you are right now. This can be a very expansive time because once you do this it helps you to realize the strong foundation you have created on this journey so far.

Focus on what is calling you now in your wisdom heart-mind. It is time to move beyond who you have been and to step into a shifting internal landscape. Get quiet to do this so you can be sure you are stepping forward with clear intentionality. It is helpful to go into silence and look deeply at what you need to manifest your wisdom. Spend a little time looking at your life. What have you transformed? How you have grown? Contemplate how your story has changed and where you would like it to grow into more fullness.

CREATING YOUR SACRED CEREMONY

INTENTION & FOCUS

Performing a sacred ceremony unleashes enormous power so you want to make sure your intention is pure and clear. When performing a sacred ceremony you are focusing yourself in such a way that your thoughts, emotions, energy, and intentions harness cosmic energy. When you perform a sacred ceremony you are opening a channel for manifestation utilizing cosmic energy to come into the physical world. It is vital that your purpose is clear. The clearer you are the more potent your ability to attract and manifest what you want to call forth. There are all kinds of ceremonies and this one is to celebrate and initiate your self into being a *Wisdom Being* that *Mother*s the *Divine* every day.

PLANNING YOUR CEREMONY

SACRED SPACE

Choose where you would like to perform your ceremony. It

can be by your personal altar in your home or outside in nature in a quiet and secluded space you enjoy and feels special to you.

Taking a sage stick, place it in an abalone shell (or another large shell or metal bowl) and light the sage. Starting at the floor carry the shell/sage upwards in a clockwise spiraling motion all around the space to energetically clean it. Going from the floor or ground upward helps to lift the energy to a higher vibration, heavenward. Say a prayer, mantra, or sing a sacred song as you do this.

If you have chosen a space in nature, it is beneficial to circle the area with rocks and then to place the smoking sage/abalone shell in the middle of the circle to energize the center. Once this area is set, sprinkle a little cornmeal around the outside of the sacred space and inside of the circle as an offering to the local protectors, stating what you are doing and asking for their blessing. If you have chosen to perform your ceremony inside your home place some cornmeal on your altar in a small bowl and invite the local protectors into your space with the same clear intention of them supporting your ceremony.

Timing

Timing is important to consider and for some, the *Full Moon* is the most potent time for magnetizing. For others the *New Moon* seems appropriate to begin something new. You decide.

The Altar

Your altar inside your home, and/or the altar inside the sacred space you have created are similar. Creating an altar to the *Divine Mother* is a way of honoring *Her* in your own unique and creative way. In your home you can use a dresser top or shelf, or actually construct a formal altar. Any space you can dedicate to the altar is good as long as it is flat. A raised altar off the floor is best. Cover it with a beautiful cloth and place a candle in the center of it. Place water bowls and other offering bowls with cornmeal, salt, and/or sacred earth. It is wonderful to add elements that bring in the elemental frequencies;

you already have water and fire. Adding a feather for air, a stone for the earth, and an open shell for space, completes your elemental offerings. Add images of the *Divine Mother* that you particularly love and any other symbolic images that represent *Her* qualities. Place flowers on your altar as an offering of beauty to the *Divine Mother*. Place a bowl of flower petals next to where you will sit.

Bless your altar with prayers and smudge it. This is a spiritually creative time for you so enjoy this process. Place a crystal in front of the candle to record and enhance the energies. Place a bowl of rose scented oil/water in front of your seating area. Rose oil is the fragrance of the *Divine* Feminine and will assist you.

Cover the altar with a cloth until you are ready to perform your ceremony. Place a blanket and pillow where you will seat yourself whether outside or inside. You will also need several pieces of paper and a pen for your ceremony. If you have a bell place it by your seat. Place some matches and a metal bowl or container beside your seating area.

Preparing Yourself

Once you have prepared your sacred space bathe and clothe yourself in celebratory garments and anoint yourself. I use lavender and frankincense because I love the energies and smell. Put flowers in your hair and make yourself feel beautiful. You might want to spritz or smudge your aura to make sure you are really pristinely clean. You can smudge yourself by taking a lit sage stick or sweet grass braid and placing it in a shell or metal bowl. Breathe in the smoke, asking for its blessing. Then you move the wand or braid up to the level of your heart and let the smoke cleanse your heart area using your free hand to move the smoke towards you. You then go to your feet and work your way up your entire body until you feel cleansed and blessed by the smoke. If you are allergic to smoke or prefer mist, use a sacred oil/water spray mixture and spray the entire area around your body, starting at your crown and working your way around your body. All the while you are focusing on your intention for the ceremony. After smudging, anoint yourself with sacred oils, which help to clear stagnant energy from your field and to reset it to a higher frequency. Mantras and prayers also raise your energy vibration. Meditating upon your intention and getting very quiet will open you to receive an acknowledgment from your heart of when the time is ready for the ceremony to begin.

Performing the Ceremony

- Step mindfully into your sacred space.

- Sit for a few moments feeling into the energy of the beautiful sacred space you have created for your ceremony so that you resonate with it.

- Remember this ceremony is one of appreciation and celebration.

- Light the candle and state an opening prayer of appreciation for the *Divine Mother*, and invoke *Her* presence.

- Sit with the flame for a few moments tuning into the sacred fire.

- Say prayers to express your gratitude to all the beings and elementals that are supporting your ceremony and clearly state your intention.

- Write it down.

Traditional wisdom elders open the sacred ceremony by standing, facing, and calling upon the archetypes of the four directions beginning in the North, East, South and West, the *Mother* Earth and Father Sun. Here is a beautiful prayer for opening your sacred space from the Shaman Healer, Alberto Villoldo.

To the winds of the North
Hummingbird, Grandmothers and Grandfathers,
Ancient Ones
come and warm your hands by our fires,

Whisper to us in the wind,
We honor you who have come before us,
And you who will come after us, our children's children.

To the winds of the East,
Great eagle, condor,
Come to us from the place of the rising Sun,
Keep us under your wing,
Show us the mountains we only dare to dream of,
Teach us to fly wing to wing with the Great Spirit.

We've gathered for the healing of all your children
The Stone People, The Plant People,
The four-legged, the two-legged the creepy crawlers,
The finned, the furred, and the winged ones,
All our relations.

Father Sun, Grandmother Moon, to the Star Nation's
Great Spirit, you who are known by a thousand names,
And you who are the unnameable One,
Thank you for bringing us together
And allowing us to sing the Song of Life

If you prefer something from the Celtic mystical tradition here is a Celtic prayer to open your sacred space, adapted by the wonderful dream teacher and scholar, Robert Moss. Begin by facing the East, South, West, North, Inner Earth, and Sky. Then place your hands on your heart, singing this chant in a tune you wish.

Spirit of the Wind, carry me,
Spirit of the Wind, carry me home,
Spirit of the Wind, carry me home to my soul.

Spirit of the Fire, carry me,

Spirit of the Fire, carry me home,
Spirit of the Fire, carry me home to my soul.

Spirit of the Sea, carry me,
Spirit of the Sea, carry me home,
Spirit of the Sea, carry me home to my soul.

Spirit of the Earth, carry me,
Spirit of the Earth, carry me home,
Spirit of the Earth, carry me home to my soul.

Spirit of the Deep, carry me,
Spirit of the Deep, carry me home,
Spirit of the Deep, carry me home to my soul.

Spirit of the Sky, carry me,
Spirit of the Sky, carry me home,
Spirit of the Sky, carry me home to my soul.

Spirit of the Heart, carry me,
Spirit of the Heart, carry me home,
Spirit of the Heart, carry me home to my soul.

ESTABLISHING YOUR WISDOM COUNCIL

After opening your sacred space spend a few moments to review the following list of the *Divine Mother's* you have met here. You can also add any others you might prefer to have on your *Council.*

DIVINE MOTHERS

⇒ *Moon Mother Goddess Luna and Her Thirteen Manifestations*

⇒ *Atalanta, Ancient Greek Goddess of Running*

⇒ *Amounet, Ancient Egyptian Goddess of the Mystery and Air and Hidden Forces*

⇒ *Cardea, Ancient Roman Goddess of the Threshold*

⇒ *Lady Venus, Ancient Roman Goddess of Love & Beauty*

⇒ *Shakti Kundalini, Hindu Goddess of the Holy Fire*

⇒ *Kwan Yin, Asian Goddess of Mercy and Compassion*

⇒ *Mother Mary, Christian Mother Goddess; Queen of Heaven*

⇒ *Angerona, Ancient Roman Goddess of Silence*

⇒ *Ishtar, Ancient Babylonian Goddess of Silence*

⇒ *Aditi, Vedic Goddess of Space and Silence*

⇒ *Arianrhod, Ancient Celtic Goddess of Reincarnation*

⇒ *Nut, Ancient Egyptian Goddess of Space and Sky*

⇒ *Bhuvaneshwari, Hindu Goddess of Infinite Space*

⇒ *Yemeya, African Water Goddess*

⇒ *Neith, Virgin Egyptian Mother Goddess*

⇒ *Gaia, Ancient Greek Mother Earth Goddess*

⇒ *Eilethyia, Greek Goddess of Childbirth*

⇒ *Lucina, Ancient Roman Goddess of Childbirth*

⇒ *Aiysyt, Siberian Mother Goddess*

⇒ *Candelifer, Ancient Roman Mother Goddess*

⇒ *Diana, Ancient Roman Mother Goddess*

⇒ *Deverra, Roman Mother Goddess*

⇒ *Frigg, Nordic Mother Goddess*

⇒ *Hathor, Ancient Egyptian Supreme Mother Goddess*

⇒ *Isis, Ancient Egyptian Mother Goddess*

- *Ixchel, Mayan birth Goddess*

- *Nephthys, Egyptian Mother Goddess*

- *Ngolimento, Togan Mother Goddess*

- *Nintur, Ancient Sumerian Mother Goddess*

- *Sophia, Byzantine Mother Goddess of Holy Wisdom*

- *Shekinah, Hebrew Mother Goddess Womb of Creation*

- *The Muses, Nine Divine Creativity Goddesses*

- *Throma Nagmo, Tibetan Wrathful Goddess*

- *Kali, Hindu Wrathful Mother Goddess*

- *Hecate, Ancient Roman Mother of the Crossroads*

- *Black Madonna, European Fierce Mother Goddess*

- *Tara, Twenty-One Aspects; Tibetan Mother Goddess of Liberation*

Invite these powerful *Divine Mothers* to always be there as a supportive energy for your holy life in all its aspects. Offer a heart-felt prayer that their wisdom will continually arise in your being and in that of all beings.

When this deep prayerful connection feels complete draw a simple circle and pick out thirteen of the *Divine Mothers* that speak to you most clearly and intimately to be your Wisdom Council. Follow your instinct and intuition.

Invoke the *Divine Mother* and the *Mother Goddesses* you have chosen to be in your ceremony with you. Sit with them for a while until you can sense their presence. When this is completed, state your intention and take refuge in your Wisdom Council. Visualize them surrounding you and sending you blessings.

❧ Next offer a prayer of purification. To do this state anything that you would like to transform so that you can *Mother* the *Divine* in your life. Write the things you want to release down on piece of paper. Burn the paper in the metal bowl and bury the ashes in the earth. Ask the Earth *Mother* to use these ashes for something else that brings benefit, such as fertilizing a tree or a flowering bush.

❧ Then offer yourself as a vehicle for receiving and embodying the *Divine Mother* in your life. Offer your attention, goodness, actions, energy, commitment, light, awareness, heart, and whatever else you feel is right to offer at this time. You can also offer beauty from the physical world to the *Divine Mother*. Light incense, ring the bell, make food offerings, offer up prayers. Scatter rose petals around you to make of yourself an offering.

❧ After making offerings, sit for a while and feel the transformation and embodiment of your intention and aspiration prayers arising in you and the *Divine* Goddess energy inculcating your being. See the *Divine Mother* Council sending light to your heart, imbuing your being with love, joy, and spiritual wisdom.

❧ With transformational awareness, step into yourself now as a *Wisdom Being*, accepting with gratitude this new way of life. The light force of the *Divine Mother* shines *Her* radiant beauty on you, and through you. From this moment forward you embody *Her* more fully. *Her* love expresses itself through you in every moment as *Her* wisdom unfolds in your awareness like a beautiful lotus flower opening to the sun through your adoration. Ask *Her* to reveal in you *Her* bliss and goodness.

❧ Ask that *Her* fullness ripens in you the true radiance of *Her* beauty through revelation and perfect *Oneness*. You have become *Her*.

❧ Sit for a few moments in silence to hear the specific message *She* has for you at this time.

Closing and Dedication

When you feel complete, offer a closing prayer that every moment gets you closer to the truth and light that you are, that every experience becomes a spiritual lesson for *Her* wisdom to ignite more love and understanding within you. Dedicate your ceremony to the benefit of all beings in all worlds and that the wisdom of the *Divine Mother* be revealed in every single being.

This ceremony may become a regular ritual for you every *New Moon* and/or *Full Moon*. A regular ritual becomes imbued with more and more power and efficacy over time. The purpose of the ritual is to continue to evoke the *Divine Mother* presence within and around you for the benefit of all. The more you do this the more real and actualized *Her* energy becomes within you. Ritual is a regular calling forth of the *Divine Mother* to assist you and to reveal *Herself* to you every day. All sacred rituals start out as a ceremony and echo the celebratory quality of the original ceremony.

This ritual will continually create an open, direct, and embodied experience of the *Divine Mother* to and within you.

Conclusion

You have completed a tremendous journey, a complete turn of the spiral of your life. You have committed to having a spiritual life and you can take this journey or parts of it over and over if you wish. As you go on from here, your spiritual life will likely evoke more subtle forms of the arising mystery. Some of these forms might include touching two worlds simultaneously. You may bring forth wisdom from other dimensions of the invisible realms. You might discover the dreamer within you. Signs and synchronicities will begin to be revealed in very real ways. Some make the way to time travel here, and others sit with illuminated visions that can help others. Visitations from other realms often occur and animal helpers appear as guides. This can be a magical and inspiring time as you open to your more expanded sense of self and touch the universe in rapture and wonder, with the eyes and open heart of a child.

The veils of different dimensions are becoming clearer at this time. You begin to perceive life in more than one awareness and time simultaneously. This is known as multidimensional experiencing. It can take many forms and various individuals have varying capacities for it. Even more have various beliefs about this as a possibility. If your view of the world is very fixed you might have to take a leap of faith to embrace this phenomena.

Human beings perceive through their senses and awareness. Many people feel that what you see is what you get. The truth is there is much more to life than this. Paul Lenda, a writer for *Waking Times*, says that the illusion of a stable dense reality that we call the third dimension can distort our very understanding of what we are, how we are, and why we are. We often times put too much trust in our basic senses without seeing if there is more that meets the eye. The new physics validates many understandings of life, the universe, and reality as a whole that were experienced by the sages, the mystics, and the mediators, of ages past. One of the most incredible validations is the reality of multidimensionality.

Multidimensional experience is now an acceptable part of human experience and physicists have known for a long time of the existence of a multidimensional universe. Some people manifest multidimensionality in out of their body experiences, such as in dreams when you travel outside your body while asleep.

Multidimensional experiences can also occur in various time zones. You can be present in more than one time zone simultaneously. Many books and films have used this as a theme and it makes for interesting stories. Sometimes experiences knock you on the head so hard you just can't ignore them and you have to believe multidimensional experiences are possible and actually quite enjoyable and expansive.

No matter what arises on your path remember that the basic principles of spiritual growth remain the same. The *Divine Mother* is always there to inform and guide you into deeper understanding of *Her* profound mysteries. Whenever you choose to stop running and hiding and consciously step into *Her* world of nurturing and love you are *Mothering the Divine*. Whenever you feel magic in your life you are witnessing *Mystical Union* with *Her*. When space and silence becomes your way of life you are deep within *Her* womb of incalculable blessings getting ready to birth another aspect of the *Divine Child*. When you care deeply and nurture, love, and protect, as a way of being you are *Mothering the Divine*. When you are in total joy and resonance with the world around you and love every step you take on *Mother* Earth, you are *Mothering the Divine*. Sometimes challenges will bring you to your knees and you will recognize the *Fierce Mother's* ultimate blessing guiding you until, surrendering, you enter *Her Compassionate World*. All through your experience you are *Mothering the Divine* because it is your true nature.

As this journey comes to a close, for now I send love, deep respect, and gratitude to you. At the conclusion of any sacred time together my teachers have shown the wisdom of always giving thanks and of making a dedication. Gratitude is its own wisdom and dedication seals the goodness for all time so it never dissipates or disappears but goes on for infinity.

May this time together benefit all beings in this and in all worlds and remember...

Spread love everywhere you go,
Let no one ever come to you without leaving happier.

Saint Mother Teresa of Calcutta

Moon Mother Goddess Luna

Attunement 13

VIOLET MOON

THIRTEENTH MONTH OF THE LUNAR CALENDAR

THE VIOLET MOON CYCLE IS ABOUT THE success and completion of the transformation cycle. The *Violet* ray is a ray of light that reflects the quality and relationship that exists between spirit and matter. This is the ceremonial ray; a ray of rhythm and ritual. It speaks to you of being fearless, confident, loving, compassionate and empowered, of being able to *Mother the Divine* in *Her* full majesty.

HOME FUN

❧ ~Sit with this feeling of empowerment.

❧ ~Know the Divine Mother is active and alive within you.

❧ ~Reflect upon how this will enhance your life and the lives of others.

❧ ~Give yourself a gift of celebration.

❧ ~See you in the light!!!!!!

May the *Divine Mother's Wisdom* ripen in every being.

Index

Frosty Moon 250, 253

G

Gaia 156, 160, 161, 216, 217, 220, 221, 222, 224, 227, 229, 230, 231, 232, 235, 236, 251, 252, 292
Gentleness 108, 110
gestation 25, 107, 110, 122, 126
Green Moon 185, 189
Gyatso Rinpoche, Lama 146

H

Harmonia 219
Harvest Moon 203, 207, 208
Harvey, Andrew 187, 195, 204, 248, 251
Hathor 165, 292
Hecate 242, 249, 250, 293
Hera 156
Hunter Moon 235, 236
Hypothesis, The Gaia 220

I

Indra 219
Indra's Net 219
intention 11, 53, 66, 67, 70, 71, 72, 73, 74, 75, 76, 77, 79, 81, 82, 87, 88, 89, 93, 108, 123, 125, 136, 150, 155, 163, 165, 168, 183, 245, 253, 269, 281, 283, 284, 286, 287, 288, 289, 293, 294
Ishtar 138, 165, 292
Isis 165, 251, 292
Ixchel 165, 293

J

Jesus Christ 145, 156, 160, 179, 233
Johnny Appleseed 225

K

Kali 91, 178, 204, 242, 245, 246, 247, 248, 250, 251, 293
Kimmer, Professor Robin Wall 218
Krishnamurti 23
Kundalini 91, 97, 165, 292
Kwan Yin 113, 114, 124, 129, 165, 169, 265, 268, 292

L

Lady Venus 73, 74, 75, 76, 77, 79, 82, 165, 292

T

Tantric 26, 68, 92, 93, 160
Tara 26, 160, 223, 264, 265, 267, 268, 293
Terpsichore 198
Thalia 198
Thich Nhat Hanh 23, 121, 160, 232
Throma Nagmo 242, 243, 245, 251, 293
Tibetan Book of the Dead 146
Tree of Life. See Yggdrasil

U

Upanishad, The 40
Urania 198

V

Vajrayana 50, 93, 111, 117, 147, 196, 219
Venus 73, 74, 75, 76, 77, 79, 82, 165, 292
Violet Moon 285, 299
Virgin Mary. See Mother Mary

W

Water Shrine 224
Watts, Alan 219
web of life 120, 122, 161, 284
Web of Life. See Sacred Hoop
Wheel of Becoming 197, 198, 200, 202, 207, 208
Wisdom Being(s) 281, 282, 283, 285, 286, 294
Wrathful Black Dakini. See Throma Nagmo

Y

Yemaya 146, 165
Yeshe Tsogyal 23, 223, 242
Yggdrasil 183, 226
Ywahoo, Venerable Dhyani 50, 164, 220, 228

Bibliography

APPROACHING THE PRIMORDIAL DARK GODDESS THROUGH THE
SONG OF HER HUNDRED NAMES ADITI DEVI
  Hohm Press
  Chino Valley, Arizona 2014

AWAKENING SHAKTI: THE TRANSFORMATIVE POWER OF THE
GODDESSES OF YOGA
  Sally Kempton
  Sounds True
  Boulder, Colorado 2013

CHANGE OF HEART: THE BODHISATTVA PEACE TRAINING OF
CHAGDUD TULKU
  Compiled and edited by Lama Shenpen Drolma
  Padma Publishing
  Junction City, California 2003

DANCE OF THE FOUR WINDS: SECRETS OF THE INCA MEDICINE
WHEEL
  Alberto Villoldo & Erik Jendresen
  Destiny Books
  Rochester Vermont 1990

ENDURING GRACE: LIVING PORTRAITS OF SEVEN WOMEN MYSTICS
  Carol Lee Flinders
  Harper Collins
  New York, New York

GODDESS: A CELEBRATION IN ART AND LITERATURE
Jalaja Bonheim
Steward, Tabori and Chang/ Abrams
New York, New York 1997

GRACE AND MERCY IN HER WILD HAIR: SELECTED POEMS TO THE
MOTHER GODDESS
Ramprasad Sen
Translated by Leonard Nathan and Clinton Seely

MOTHER TERESA: A COMPLETE AUTHORIZED BIOGRAPHY
Kathryn Spink
Harper
San Francisco, California 1997

MYTHS OF GREECE AND ROME
Thomas Bullfinch
Penguin Books
New York, New York 1979

PARABOLA: MYTH, TRADITION AND THE SEARCH FOR MEANING
ECSTASY
Kali Who Swallowed the Universe
Ma Jaya Sati Bhagavati
VXXIII Number 2, May 1998
Denville, New Jersey

PARABOLA: MYTH, TRADITION AND THE SEARCH FOR MEANING
THE CALL
Winding the Golden String
Bede Griffiths
VXIX No 1 Spring 1994
Denville, New Jersey

PARABOLA: MYTH, TRADITION AND THE SEARCH FOR MEANING
The Threshold
Crossing into the Invisible
Laura Simms
V 25 No. 1 2000
Denville, New Jersey

PARABOLA: MYTH TRADITION AND THE SEARCH FOR MEANING
SUFFERING
Five Full Minutes
Robert Chodo Campbell
V 36 No 1 Spring 2011
Denville, New Jersey

QUEEN OF THE NIGHT: REDISCOVERING THE CELTIC MOON
GODDESS
By Sharynne MacLeod NicMhacha
Weiser Books
York Beach, ME. 2005

THE GREAT MOTHER
Erich Neumann
Translated by Ralph Manheim
Princeton, Bollingen
Princeton University Press
Princeton, New Jersey 1963

THE MOTHER
Sri Aurobindo Lotus Press
Pudicherry, India 1907/1995

THE MYTH OF THE GODDESS: EVOLUTION OF AN IMAGE
Anne Baring & Jules Cashford
Arkana, Penguin Books
London, England 1991

THE SECOND COMING OF CHRIST: THE RESURRECTION OF THE CHRIST WITHIN YOU
  Parmahansa Yogananda
  Self Realization Fellowship
  Los Angeles, California 1994

THE SUBTLE BODY: AN ENCYCLOPEDIA OF YOUR ENERGETIC ANATOMY
  Cyndi Dale
  Sounds True
  Boulder, Colorado 2009

THE 13 ORIGINAL CLAN MOTHERS
  Jamie Sams
  Harper
  San Francisco 1993

THE WORDS OF MY PERFECT TEACHER
  Patrul Rinpoche
  Shambhalla Press
  Boston, Massachusetts 1998

RETURN OF THE MOTHER
  Andrew Harvey
  Tarcher/Putnam
  New York, New York 1995

SELF COMPASSION: THE PROVEN POWER OF BEING KIND TO YOURSELF
  Kristin Neff, Ph.D.
  Morrow/ Harper Collins
  New York, New York 2011

SHAKTI MANTRAS: TAPPING INTO THE GREAT GODDESS ENERGY WITHIN
  Thomas Ashley-Farrand
  Ballantine Books
  New York, New York 2003

SHAKTI: REALM OF THE DIVINE MOTHER
  Vanamali
  Inner Tradition
  Rochester, Vermont 2006

SON OF MAN: THE MYSTICAL PATH TO CHRIST
  Andrew Harvey
  Tarcher/Putnam
  New York, New York 1998

To learn more, please visit:
www.motheringthedivinewisdom.com

Made in the USA
Lexington, KY
30 November 2016